Social and Economic Studies within the Framework of Emerging Global Developments, Volume -1

Muhammed Veysel Kaya (ed.)

Social and Economic Studies within the Framework of Emerging Global Developments, Volume -1

PETER LANG

Bibliographic Information published by the Deutsche Nationalbibliothek
The Deutsche Nationalbibliothek lists this publication in the Deutsche Nationalbibliografie; detailed bibliographic data is available online at http://dnb.d-nb.de.

Library of Congress Cataloging-in-Publication Data
A CIP catalog record for this book has been applied for at the Library of Congress.

Cover illustration:
© gorodenkoff

ISBN 978-3-631-88113-2 (Print)
E-ISBN 978-3-631-88350-1 (E-PDF)
E-ISBN 978-3-631-88351-8 (E-PUB)
10.3726/b19907

Peter Lang – Berlin · Bruxelles · Lausanne · New York · Oxford

This publication has been peer reviewed.

www.peterlang.com

Prof. Dr. M. Veysel Kaya

Foreword

This first volume of "Social & Economic Studies within the Framework of Emerging Global Developments" includes empirical and theoretical original chapters written by researchers from different countries and universities. The target audience of this book is researchers, students and academics interested in social and economic studies.

Challoumis indicates the theoretical background of the theory of the cycle of money, hinged on the Keynesian and Neoclassical concepts. *Viera*, *Flores* and *Fontoura* examine network analysis to characterise the countries' trade in value added at the world level in the twenty-first century, by using the more recent time point present in the World Input Output Database (WIOD). *Panetta* and *Leo* examines how M-Payments have made the financial system more permeable to new players, highlighting the financial system changes brought on by mobile devices and applications. *Chodnicka-Jaworska* analyses European sanctions impact on the Energy Sector Stock Prices during the Ukrainian War. *Tseng* and *D'Andrea* examine three case studies, Peloton, Reddit and Twitter, during the COVID-19 pandemic and illustrate how these digital services and platforms facilitated forms of social capital despite being solely online. *Aytekin* analyses the relationship between economic growth and health services in Türkiye for the 1967–2019 period. *Trifu* examines home environment of a firm/entity that is the relationships between the main elements of the human factor of production, the entrepreneurs/owners and the workers/employees. *Zulfuoglu* analyses the relationship between indirect taxes in the Turkish Tax System and the inflation rate. *Jaworski* analyses the impact of the beginning of the Ukrainian War on the abnormal rates of returns on the main stock indexes. *Oliveira* and *Anunciacao* examine information system governance with some dimensions to management. *Esteves* and *Anunciacao* examine a framework proposal for enterprise managers with information governance.

Anunciacao, *Penalver* and *Esteves* examine Setúbal and Cartagena in smart tourism within the frame of smart tourism. *Platon*, *Constantinescu*, *Antonescu*, *Frone* and *Popa* examine the drivers in enhancing municipal waste recycling by analysing statistically the evidence concerning the importance of innovation (more specifically eco-innovation) and eco-investment. *Gunesch* investigates "against the motion" of administrative and institutional assistance in cultural and art economics, when analysed from macroeconomic, sociopolitical and philosophical aspects. *Staniuliene* and *Miliordou* analyse the stress management for professional athletes in sport organisations. *Cebeci* examines selected twelve scenes which reflect the 1929 Depression in the movie Cinderella Man.

"All papers have been peer reviewed"

Table of Contents

List of Contributors

Daniela Antonescu
Institute of National Economy, Romanian Academy, Romania

Pedro Fernandes da Anunciação
CICE-ESCE/IPS (Research Centre in Business Sciences) – Polytechnic Institute of Setúbal, Setúbal, Portugal

Ibrahim Aytekin
Bitlis Eren University, Bitlis/Türkiye

Kemal Cebeci
Faculty of Economics, Marmara University, Istanbul, Türkiye

Constantinos Challoumis
National and Kapodistrian University of Athens (N.K.U.A.), Greece

Patrycja Chodnicka-Jaworska
University of Warsaw, Faculty of Management, Warsaw, Poland

Andreea Constantinescu
Institute of National Economy, Romanian Academy, Romania

Anthony D'Andrea
Marymount University, USA

Francisco Joaquim Madeira Esteves
CICE-ESCE/IPS (Research Centre in Business Sciences) – Polytechnic Institute of Setúbal, Setúbal, Portugal

Renato G. Flôres Jr.
FGV IIU and FGV EPGE, Rio de Janeiro, Brazil

Maria Paula Fontoura
ISEG-Lisbon School of Economics and Management, UECE-Research Unit on Complexity and Economics and REM- Research in Economics and Mathematics, Universidade de Lisboa, Portugal

Simona Frone
Institute of National Economy, Romanian Academy, Romania

Konrad Gunesch
London Centre for Interdisciplinary Research, London, United Kingdom

Piotr Jaworski
University of Warsaw, Faculty of Management, Warsaw, Poland

Sabrina Leo
Sapienza University of Rome, Faculty of Economics, Rome

Chrysi Miliordou
Vytautas Magnus University, Kaunas, Lithuania

Almiro de Oliveira
Vice-President of Information Systems Governance European Club, Porto, Portugal

Ida Claudia Panetta
Sapienza University of Rome, Faculty of Economics, Rome

António Juan Briones Peñalver
Polytechnic University of Cartagena, Cartagena, Spain

Victor Platon
Institute of National Economy, Romanian Academy, Romania

Florina Popa
Institute of National Economy, Romanian Academy, Romania

Sonata Staniuliene
Vytautas Magnus University, Kaunas, Lithuania

Alexandru Trifu
University "Petre Andrei", Iaşi, Romania

Margaret Tseng
Marymount University, USA

Susana Vieira
ISEG-Lisbon School of Economics and Management, Universidade de Lisboa, Portugal

Ozkan Zulfuoglu
Faculty of Economics, Marmara University, Istanbul, Türkiye

Constantinos Challoumis

Conditions of the CM (Cycle of Money)

1. Introduction

The transition from GDP into CM (Cycle of Money) is responsible for the determination of the structure of the economy. CM comes from the GDP and indicates if an economy has the appropriate structure. The structure of an economy could be identified by the distribution and use/reuse of money. This chapter shows the theoretical background of the theory of the cycle of money, hinged on the Keynesian and Neoclassical concepts. CM is the only theory that achieves control of an economy and identifies its condition, as the velocity of the cycle of money reveals the structure of an economy.

2. Cycle of Money Mathematical Background

Controlled transactions meant transactions between companies of the same interest group that refer indicatively to issues such as tax avoidance, tax evasion, transfer of profits from the business to business, fictitious transactions between them, the pricing policy of cost savings to maximize their profits, the transfer of profits from a business based in a country with unfavorable tax regime to other countries with more favorable, and generally the accounting and financial practices that each company uses in its relation with the other companies to establish a favorable tax environment. Controlled transactions include transfer pricing, triangular transactions, and any form of internal control aimed at achieving profits. A thorough analysis of their operation shows the way they affect the economies of the countries regardless of whether they are established in them or not. The current work also deals with concepts such as the cycle of money, the velocity of money, and the velocity of escaped savings, in each economy. The cycle of money refers to the difference between the rate of the volume of transactions carried out in an economy and the volume of transactions that escaped outside that economy, $c_y = c_m - c_\alpha$. The velocity of money (liquidity) expresses the inflation or deceleration of the volume of transactions within an economy, $c_m = \frac{dx_m}{dm}$. The velocity of escaped savings indicates the volume of transactions that go beyond an economy, $c_{\alpha} = \frac{dx_m}{da}$ (Challoumis, 2021a, 2021b, 2021c, 2021d, 2021e).

Therefore, the velocity of money refers to the first-order differential equation of the state of an economy, i.e. in quantitative terms, GDP, with the volume of transactions in that economy. The velocity of escaped savings refers to a first-order differential equation of the state of an economy, i.e. in quantitative terms, GDP and the volume of money that goes beyond it. The difference between the velocity of money and the velocity of escaped savings constitutes the cycle of money. A relevant concept bibliographically can be found in M. Friedman's monetarist approach, in the sense that M expresses the supply of money and V the cash flow. Thus, to make the existing framework easier to understand, the M of monetarist theory concerns in this case m, with the difference that M refers to the amount of money on offer, while m refers to the existing money of the economy without the need to implement a monetary policy. As far as the cash flow, V, of the monetarist theory concerns the cash flow which is expressed, in this case, with the velocity of money. Therefore, according to the above, an approximation of the theoretical framework of the money cycle is expressed in quantitative terms through partial differential equations, $\frac{\partial(GDP)}{\partial(S+I+\mathrm{X})}$. and - $\frac{\partial(GDP)}{\partial(S'+I'+\mathrm{M})}$, where S means savings, I is investments, and X is about exports. S' is savings that go beyond the economy, i.e. saved abroad, I' is money raised from the economy and invested in other economies, and M is imports. So, $c_y = \frac{\partial(GDP)}{\partial(S+I+\mathrm{X})} d(\mathrm{S}+\mathrm{I}+\S\,)$

$c_y = \frac{\partial(GDP)}{\partial(S+I+\mathrm{X})} d(\mathrm{S}+\mathrm{I}+\S\,) - \frac{\partial(GDP)}{\partial(S'+I'+\mathrm{M})} d(\mathrm{S'}+\mathrm{I'}+\mathrm{M})$. The reason that used S=C is because in the CM (Cycle of Money) S*=I, then Stot.=S+S*=C+I, as any amount of money not used in the economy is considered as savings. With S being the supporting savings and S' (=C'), then, Stot.' = S'+S*'= C'+I' is the escaped savings. Thus, it is considered that the concept of the cycle of money is directly linked to consumption, and investments, when they do not take active place by consumption or investments. For example, albeit in quantitative terms that m = S + I + X, with S = C, S = 50m, I = 10m, X = 20m and $x_m = GDP$ = (S-S') + (I-I') + (X-M), where S' are the savings that are lost from the economy due to controlled transactions. By analogy, I' also refers to money that is lost and is not invested in the state from which these sums of money were drawn, but are directed to other economies. X is about exports and M is about imports. Essentially what has been done here is the breakdown of GDP in individual terms, in the light of amounts lost due to controlled transactions. So the result of this numerical example is $c_{\alpha} = \frac{dx_m}{da} = 60.$

For example, regarding escaped savings, suppose α = S' + I' + X, με S' = C', S' = 20α, I' = 10α, X = 30α and $x_m = GDP$ = (S-S') + (I-I') + (X-M), where $c_{\alpha} = \frac{dx_m}{da} = 60$. So, in this example, the money cycle is, $c_y = c_m - c_{\alpha} = 20$. Therefore, the second partial differential equation of the first order concerns the amount that is lost from the economy. However, to be able to carry out a comparative study of the inputs and outputs in tax havens and offshore banks, it is necessary to have comprehensive supervision of the amounts of money moving, but this is not possible in the current circumstances. They are not recorded in any official body, because they are hidden amounts. Indicators are used to enable the formulation of an economic policy. The problem with money and controlled transactions, in general, is that there are no records of official financial data. In other words, through the money that goes beyond an economy, both controlled transactions and a broader tax policy can be approached.

3. Fixed Length Principle

Based on this reasoning, controlled transactions are also achieved, with the inability to record the exact amount to be taxed. Thus, the theory of the money cycle has provided for the application of a minimum tax, through the so-called Fixed Length Principle, to cover de facto the economic loss from controlled transactions. In this way, controlled transactions become manageable within the framework of the existing theory. In this way, the formulation of economic and fiscal policy was defined. The correctness of the theory of the money cycle is reflected in the G7 decision, as the application of a minimum fixed tax in the countries, in this case, is 15 %, but in the future, it must be made larger to completely remove the controlled transactions. The theory of the cycle of money (money cycle) analyzes the dynamics of each economy to maximize the well-being of its population. It is about maximizing prosperity in the economy in the conduct of public economic policies, both from the point of view of the country and from the point of view of businesses that carry out controlled transactions, and also of other economic units that do not engage in these practices (Bergquist, Mildenberger, & Stokes, 2020; Goldsztejn, Schwartzman, & Nehorai, 2020;

GVELESIANI, 2019; Kamradt-Scott & McInnes, 2012; Sultana, Or Rashid, Akter Eva, & Sultana, 2020; Ustinovich & Kulikov, 2020).

The present work, however, proceeds to the issues of economic policy. It should be noted that ultimately a theoretical framework is given to maximize the benefits to the economy. The gap in the existing literature covered by this work concerns the study of economic models in the light of the use of money in a fragmented economy. It is a fragmented and not closed economy, as this economy is in interaction with other economies, but presents some elements of protectionism and economic elements that make it perceived as a unity that is in interaction with other economies. A "fragmented economy" is called an economy that while it is in interaction with other economies, nevertheless has elements that make it a distinct economic unity. This distinction allows us to investigate the use of money in an economy that has specific liquidity available. This means that using a certain amount of money available, in a certain time frame, it is allowed to determine the frequency of the use of money in an economy. The concept of frequency expresses the rate of increase or decrease in the volume of transactions.

The use of a given amount of money in a specific time frame, without losing this amount of money to the economy, highlights the correctness of the structure of this economy. Structure of the economy is expressed by the money cycle, as an economy with a large volume of transactions and a large dispersion of money between as many businesses and households as possible that indicates it has a good distribution of financial resources throughout the economy.

Therefore, if in an economy a certain amount of money is used several times, then the use of money is maximized, with an impact on both social well-being and the appropriate structure of the economy. The maintenance of a quantity of money in an economy and its use with great frequency ensures the smooth functioning of the economic system and the robustness of the economy. In general, as the spread of money in several economic units increases, so does the money cycle. In a hypothetical economy where there are neither inflows nor outflows, the economy that has a money cycle ratio equal to one will continue to have the same dynamics; it will not be affected in this ideal case.

It is observed that no country operates under these conditions of the perfect case, to a money cycle index equal to one, except for some cases approaching the price of one. Economies that have a high index of the money cycle can cope directly with a temporary, but also a global crisis. These economies have a good indicator, which means that there is a good dispersion of money, in their society and therefore a good economic structure. Therefore, the theory of the cycle of money allows the investigation of the resilience of an economy, through the dispersion of money, its preservation, and the rate of its reuse. In this way, conclusions are drawn both about the structure of an economy and its resilience to economic crises. Within this framework, it is possible to determine the persistence and frequency of use of money in an economy. The higher the money cycle ratio an economy has the more good economic structure it has, as it can have a greater frequency of the use of money due to the greater dispersion of money. In other words, good money dispersion also indicates a good structure of the economy. Appropriate policies in taxation, but also the fiscal policy of an economy, make it possible to maximize its benefits. The existing literature, regardless of whether it is a Classical, Keynesian, Neoclassical, or Marxist theory, leave this field of research out of the study, and the current work fills this bibliographic gap. In other words, the resilience of an economy and its structure through the reuse of money is studied. Ultimately, a classification is made for the correctness of the structure of economies by state.

It should be noted that the proposed theory aims to set out the dynamics of an economy, which has an impact on its characteristics and structure. Thus, this work aims to link the money in an economy with the structure of the economy, making it essentially a single economic system, formed through the frequency of reuse and preservation of money, with this reuse of money being linked to the characteristics of the economy.

The proposed theory cites economics as a single mechanism, that is, how often a quantity of money is used, indicating the characteristics of the economy. In other words, the development of the given theoretical schema was made possible, thanks to the conceptual demarcations provided by organisms like OECD and World Bank publications. It should be noted, however, that the aim of the present work, apart from the aforementioned, is to render a way of imprinting the "body of the economy", i.e. to connect its variable part, which is money, to its static part, which is its structural characteristics in a given time frame (of course, the structural characteristics of an economy are in a dynamic condition).

4. Characteristics of the Economy

Also, a bibliographic gap that this theory comes to fill is the issue that the economy, apart from being a "single body", which is revealed by the dispersion of money in it, is that it generally has a natural social character, as it emerges in this case that society is the economy. The resilience of the economy is not only linked to GDP, the deficit or surplus, and the related economic aggregates, as these are the results of an economic situation and not its causes. Therefore, the causes of an economy are identified in the current economic theory in sizes such as imports, exports, and generally variables that cannot on their own describe the structure of an economy over a certain period, so they do not reflect the structure of economies but the situation in which they find themselves. For example, using the case of the crisis in Greece, Ireland, and Cyprus, their deficit has been reduced at certain given times; it does not reflect whether these results have been achieved either by a reduction in paid employment or by an increase in investment, but they reflect, regardless of the structure of their economy, that an economic situation has been achieved (Challoumis, 2018, 2020). The structure of the economy differs from the state of an economy, as it is implicitly linked to the way that money is distributed and, by extension, to social welfare. Ultimately, in this way, conclusions can be drawn about the resilience of economies standing on the money cycle and the corresponding indicators for each economy. The aforementioned indicators, however, reflect the economic situation of an economy, but there is no theory oriented in itself on the structural characteristics of economies in combination with the way money is used, because otherwise all theories and indicators aim to express certain characteristics of economies. GDP relates to imports, exports, investment, taxes, and many other sub-economic aggregates, but none of these figures describes the structure of an economy, but its current situation, as opposed to the dispersion of money, which can show the appropriateness of the structure of an economy.

Bibliographically, this theory is based on the arm's length concept, with elements of an intrusive policy of regulatory content. Broadening the tax base is possible by reducing unemployment, by limiting taxation on small and medium-sized enterprises. The reduction of taxation in the industrial sector is an interventionist tax policy, which combats unemployment and directs large companies to activities that smaller companies cannot cover because of the limited capital they have. The theory of the money cycle is drawn up in a specific way with full competition and with the concept of interventionist policy, not necessarily through expenditure, but based on regulatory policies that allow for a low tax policy, but under the conditions of the available capital available to each company. Coming up with a scheme of interventionist policy about the capital of companies, but in the other elements of the economy, the concept of arm's length competition and the free functioning of the market is being followed (Commission, 2021; Meyer D., 2021; Rolle, 2012; Taylor, 2021; Viegas M., 2021).

5. Interventionist Fiscal Regulatory Policy

Fiscal regulatory policy has the advantage that apart from improving the structural characteristics of an economy, and the way money is managed within it, on the other hand, it has no cost the interventionist policies are based on expenditure, and this is an important advantage hinged on the fact that the proposed interventions concern the structure of the economy itself, leaving it ultimately at arm's length. In this way a tax policy should take into account the capital invested and how to maximize the benefits and functionality of an economy's resources, maximizing consumption and investment, through the maximum dispersion and reuse of money. Thus, this approach achieves the effects of a socialist type economy in the early stage of the economy, through a Keynesian regulatory interventionist policy, and after that leaves the economy to free competition in the light of the Neoclassical approach, but free from the consequences of the absorption of smaller enterprises by the larger ones, as described in Marxist literature. It is in this option, that an expansionary Keynesian-style fiscal policy is achieved, based on a regulatory framework and not on budgetary expenditure. This theory, however, does not exclude either Keynesian-style fiscal policies or the monetary policies of the Neoclassical approach, as these may be carried out unhindered under the constraints mentioned above, but focus on the structural characteristics of the economy, with the degree of reuse of money determining consumer power and direct investment. It is the investments of small and medium-sized enterprises, as well as the economic activity of citizens other than large enterprises which carry out activities that replace smaller enterprises, that shape the economy and the largest part of GDP. The importance of maximizing the dispersion of money and its reuse is of major importance, as they also shape the resilience of an economy.

It is indicative that the diagrams of the Keynesian as well as the Neoclassical approach, whereby improving the structural characteristics of an economy is not altered, but remains as they are, and the only thing that changes is the order of magnitude of their variables in a similar way. When an economy has an inflated money cycle then its size increases; while when they are smaller it has a shrinking money cycle, and this translates into weaker structural features of the economy.

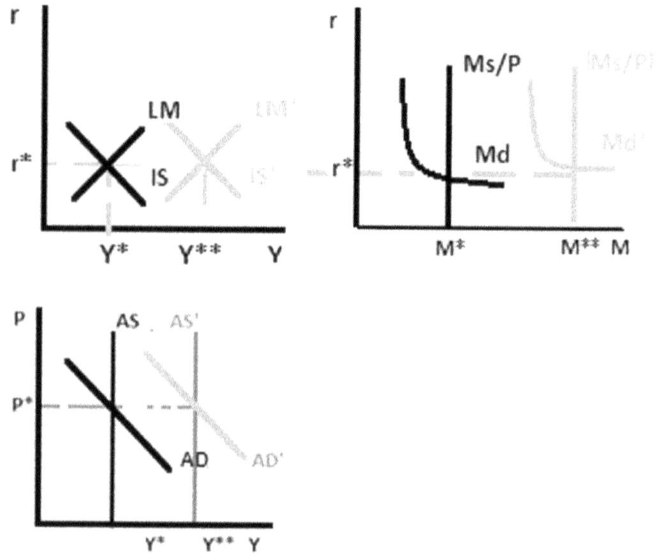

Fig. 1: IS-LM model according to CM

Therefore, both diagrammatically and in terms of existing theoretical schemes, there is no modification of them, but what changes are that it delineates not the state of an economy, as it is mainly expressed through GDP and the growth rate, but its structural characteristics, which are inextricably linked to social welfare, as large reuse of money affects the IS curve, which increases the size of consumption, and investment, while income increases, thus increasing the aggregate demand curve, AD, without changing prices and interest rate. Demand as well as supply are increasing without changing prices. It is important to mention that the changes occur with the growth of the figures in proportion, without disproportionate shifts being there in the curves; hence, it emerges that the structural characteristics of the economy are changing and not economic policy.

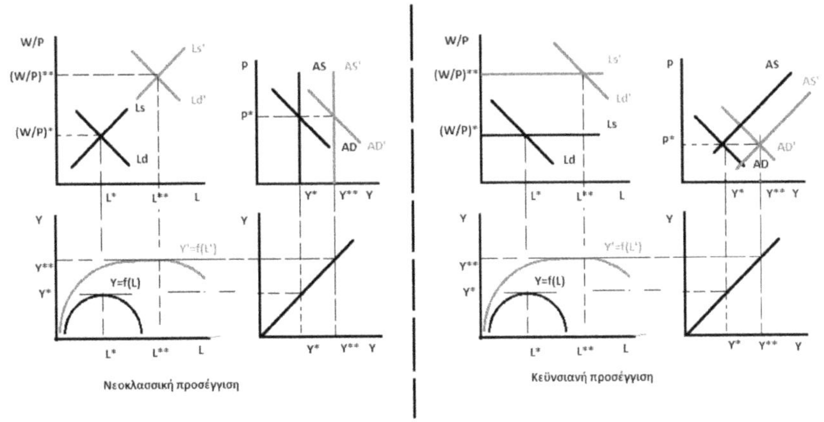

Fig. 2: Characteristics of the money cycle in the neoclassical and Keynesian approaches

Therefore, the above analysis in the case of the Neoclassical and Keynesian models is reflected in Figure 2. Economies which have high index of the cycle of their money, achieve better dispersion of money, have greater consumption and investments, leading to an increase in income, a higher GDP is achieved, through a regulatory tax policy that changes the structural characteristics of the economy, through discrete taxation according to capital and the category of investment, eliminating the consequences that proposed in the Marxist theory of absorption of smaller companies, from larger ones, leaving the economy in conditions of better perfect competition, without the effects of oligopolies and monopolies (Bestari, Sinaga, & Saudi, 2019;Kananen, 2012; Scholvin & Malamud, 2020).

Regulatory means tax policy that makes no use of either fiscal or monetary tools (not only by them), but through the money cycle achieves better economic results. Prices do not change, as demand that is increasing as well as supply is proportional in both sizes, while they are not linked to any fiscal or monetary policy but are the result of a differently structured economy with better use of money, due to its improved economic structure and the better dispersion and reuse of money.

6. Conclusion

It is obtained by analyzing that in one case the neoclassical policy is depicted, and in the other case the fiscal policy, as it is expressed throughout the literature. The difference from the literature is that here the gray curves are the same as the black curves, but that the gray curves reflect more robust economies, since both product and labor, which are the real variables of the economy, are depicted with larger sizes. In general, the neoclassical approach supports the classical dichotomy and flexibility of wages, in contrast to the Keynesian theory that states pecuniary variables influence real variables. In this way, in Keynesian policy, there is a balance between the economy and unemployment, which is why state intervention is necessary, on the demand side. In the present case, in the Fig. 2, it appears that regulatory policy is a policy that makes no use of either fiscal or monetary policy, has the effect of increasing income and reducing unemployment, through greater reuse and greater dispersion of money, by inflating the money cycle. This increase in size is due to the increase in the money cycle, as the volume of transactions in the economy has increased. In this way, the authorities direct large-capital enterprises to industrial production, but also services, and goods with high added value.

Therefore, an economic and fiscal policy with low rates of taxation should be drawn up depending on the investment sector, the size of the capital, and its category. In other words, it is possible to prevent the economic activities of smaller companies and medium companies. The dispersion, maintenance, and reuse of money are increasing, without increasing the money supply or fiscal expansion, but by interfering with the structural features of an economy – in the sense of a regulatory tax policy – social well-being increases, while unemployment decreases.

The regulatory interventionist policy in taxation does not have the subsequent negative consequences of a fiscal or monetary policy as what is achieved is the improvement of the characteristics of the economy themselves. According to Milton Friedman {MV=PY} it does not change prices, as there is no change in the money supply, but an increase in the velocity of money, which monetary policy cannot influence, as these are elements of the economy that depend on its structure; this is where the circulation of money is instilled, as it is observed that there is such a bibliographic gap. Monetary policy in Milton Friedman's theory affects the money supply and prices, not the other two variables.

References

Bergquist, P., Mildenberger, M., & Stokes, L. C. (2020). Combining climate, economic, and social policy builds public support for climate action in the US. *Environmental Research Letters*, 15(5). Retrieved from https://doi.org/10.1088/1748-9326/ab81c1.

Bestari, P., Sinaga, O., & Saudi, M. H. M. (2019). Implementation of online tax system: Implications for the development of a public policy course. *International Journal of Innovation, Creativity and Change*, 6(7).

Challoumis, C. (2018). Methods of controlled transactions and the behavior of companies according to the public and tax policy. *Economics*, 6(1), 33–43. Retrieved from https://doi.org/10.2478/eoik-2018-0003.

Challoumis, C. (2020). The impact factor of education on the public sector – The case of the U.S. *International Journal of Business and Economic Sciences Applied Research*, 13(1), 69–78. Retrieved from https://doi.org/10.25103/ijbesar.131.07.

Challoumis, C. (2021a). Index of the cycle of money – The case of Bulgaria. *Economic Alternatives*, 27(2), 225–234. Retrieved from https://www.unwe.bg/eajournal/en.

Challoumis, C. (2021b). Index of the cycle of money – The case of Greece. *IJBESAR (International Journal of Business and Economic Sciences Applied Research)*, 14(2), 69–78.

Challoumis, C. (2021c). Index of the cycle of money – The case of Serbia. *Open Journal for Research in Economics (OJRE)*, 4(1). Retrieved from https://centerprode.com/ojre.html.

Challoumis, C. (2021d). Index of the cycle of money – The case of Thailand. *Chiang Mai University Journal of Economics*, 25(2), 1–14.

Challoumis, C. (2021e). Index of the cycle of money – The case of Ukraine. *Actual Problems of Economics*, 243(9). Retrieved from https://eco-science.net/en/issue/.

Commission, E. (2021). Taxation and Customs Union. Retrieved from https://ec.europa.eu/taxation_customs/business/company-tax/transfer-pricing-eu-context_en#:~:text=According to international standards individual, made or imposed between …

Goldsztejn, U., Schwartzman, D., & Nehorai, A. (2020). Public policy and economic dynamics of COVID-19 spread: A mathematical modeling study. *PLoS ONE*, 15(12 December). Retrieved from https://doi.org/10.1371/journal.pone.0244174.

Gvelesiani, R. (2019). Compatibility problem of basic public values with economic policy goals and decisions for their implementation. *Globalization and Business*, 4(7). Retrieved from https://doi.org/10.35945/gb.2019.07.004.

Kamradt-Scott, A., & McInnes, C. (2012). The securitisation of pandemic influenza: Framing, security and public policy. *Global Public Health*, 7(2). Retrieved from https://doi.org/10.1080/17441692.2012.725752.

Kananen, J. (2012). International ideas versus national traditions: Nordic economic and public policy as proposed by the OECD. *Journal of Political Power*, 5(3). Retrieved from https://doi.org/10.1080/2158379X.2012.735118.

Meyer D., W. V. (2021). 'Far too low': Tax justice campaigners push back against the G7's 15% minimum tax-rate pact. *Fortune*. Retrieved from https://fortune.com/2021/06/07/global-minimum-corporate-tax-rate-g7-15-percent-pact/.

Rolle, G. (2012). Arm's length principle and EU law. *Jean Monnet Roundtable*. Retrieved from https://limo.libis.be/primo-explore/fulldisplay?docid=LIRIAS1844422&context=L&vid=Lirias&search_scope=Lirias&tab=default_tab&lang=en_US&fromSitemap=1.

Scholvin, S., & Malamud, A. (2020). Is Brazil a geoeconomic node? Geography, public policy, and the failure of economic integration in South America. *Brazilian Political Science Review*, 14(2). Retrieved from https://doi.org/10.1590/1981-3821202000020004.

Sultana, A., Or Rashid, M. H., Akter Eva, S., & Sultana, A. (2020). Assessment of relationship among regional economic development policy, urban development policy and public policy. *Sumerianz Journal of Economics and Finance*, 3 (10), 171–177. Retrieved from https://doi.org/10.47752/sjef.310.171.177.

Taylor, C. (2021). US makes new offer on setting global minimum corporate tax rate at 15%. Retrieved from https://www.irishtimes.com/business/economy/g7-agreement-means-ireland-s-12-5-per-cent-corporate-tax-rate-is-under-threat-1.4586043.

Ustinovich, E., & Kulikov, M. (2020). National projects, socio-economic policy and public equilibrium. *Social'naja Politika i Social'noe Partnerstvo (Social Policy and Social Partnership)*, 6(1), 17–25. Retrieved from https://doi.org/10.33920/pol-01-2006-01.

Viegas M. D. A. (2021). Country-by-country reporting: A step towards unitary taxation? *Intereconomics*, 56(3), 167–173. Retrieved from https://doi.org/10.1007/s10272-021-0974-9.

Susana Vieira, Renato G. Flôres Jr., Maria Paula Fontoura

The Upstream and Downstream Integration of Global Value Chains in the XXI Century

1. Introduction

Global Value Chains (GVCs) translate the principle of labor division on an international or global scale. The idea behind the concept – the breakup of production into several stages, with at least one occurring in a different country – has gained popularity over the last decades, due to an ever-increasing fragmentation of production which has been promoted by advances in transportation, information, and communication technologies, and in services in general. Similarly, multinationals play a vital role in GVCs in the form of the outsourcing of their production to third countries.

The literature on GVCs is already extensive and basically follows two different lines: (i) the impacts for GVC-participating countries, and (ii) the appropriate measurement of GVC participation. The former includes a vast range of case studies on the economic spillovers of GVC participation, regarding either technology (Brach and Kappel, 2009), productivity (Baldwin and Yan, 2014), knowledge diffusion (Saliola and Zanfei, 2009), or foreign direct investment (Martinez-Galán and Fontoura, 2019). A wide range of references focus on the impact of GVC participation in development (Taglioni and Winkler, 2016), especially for countries in later stages of development. The latter – which is more methodological – is based on the premise that, by not accounting for the import content of a country's exports, traditional trade statistics do not fully capture the fragmentation of international production and are thus responsible for double-counting in import and export data. Departing from internationally linked Input-Output (IO) tables, several authors have attempted to build measures for value-added imbedded in trade to properly identify production linkages between economies and country´s participation in GVCs. Their studies differ according to the value-added components of domestic production exported and the decomposition method of value-added adopted[1].

1 See, for instance, Martinez-Galán and Fontoura (2019), Figure 1, for a picture of different GVC metrics, and Borin and Mancini (2019) for a general toolkit of

This chapter uses data from the latest release of the World Input-Output Database (WIOD), which was launched by the University of Groningen (see Timmer et al., 2016, for an explanation of the database) and network analysis to map the trade in value-added amongst countries worldwide in the XXI century, namely in 2000 and the most recent year covered by the WIOD database (2014). The second release in 2016[2] includes data for 43 countries (covering the 27 EU countries and 6 other major countries in the world) and 56 sectors, and covers 85 % of the world trade, which represents an enhancement on the first one (2013) that only included data from 40 countries and 35 sectors. This database has been widely used by scholars, partly because it permits the study of the international fragmentation of production, as well as environmental and socio-economic issues.

This chapter builds the GVC world network by considering bilateral relations amongst countries with two views: the upstream integration (with buyers of value-added), via forward linkages; and the downstream integration (with suppliers of value-added), via backward linkages. Specifically, we consider the appropriation of value-added by domestic agents of a given economy due to the foreign demand of domestic intermediates (hereinafter designated as "domestic value-added", or DVA) and also the appropriation of value-added by foreign agents due to the domestic demand of foreign intermediates used as inputs in domestic production exported (hereinafter designated as "foreign value-added", or FVA). The former captures the domestic value-added "exported" (to be processed abroad) and can be considered a buying (demand) view; the latter is the value-added "imported" (to be processed abroad and imbedded in the country´s own exports) and can be interpreted as a supply-chain view. Santoni and Taglioni (2015) also adopted a similar approach but focused on sectoral trade relations and, as shown in detail by Borin and Mancini (2019), the sectoral-geographical perimeters of the analysis matter for the metrics of the trade related to GVCs.

The destination of domestic value-added is useful to assess the structural position of a country with respect to foreign demand and the origin of foreign value-added used in domestic production exported helps in identifying potential sources of technology/ productivity spillovers through intra-firm and arm's-length transfers (Santoni and Taglioni, 2015: 71). Together, they convey

methodologies for value-added accounting of trade flows at the country, bilateral and sectoral levels.

2 See wiod.org/release16

information regarding the degree of a country's embedment into GVC links and the potential economic spillovers of GVC participation (idem).

To better explore the backbone of the GVC dynamics, special attention is paid to the analysis of the "most relevant flows", and to compute the network by large production regions. Previous studies have shown that a small number of countries occupy central positions in the international production chains, with concentration being the rule in a few major production regions (cf., for instance, Amador and Cabral, 2017; Amador et al., 2018; Li et al., 2019; Xiao et al., 2020). This work highlights to what degree the GVC process is regional and also the main users and suppliers by regional hub.

The results obtained consolidate some of the most relevant conclusions from previous research, despite the methodological differences with regards to tracing trade in value-added. Considering the trend observed, they allow to conclude that without Germany, Europe would lose its pumping engine, with the same for Asia without China, and, for the whole world, without the US.

The article is organized as follows: The Section 2 briefly explains the adopted network methodology, namely the graph visualization, the centrality concepts of Node and Eigenvector, and the use of filters for unveiling the backbone of the world GVC network. The section 3 analyses the world GVC network in both 2000 and 2014 with some descriptive statistics and centrality indicators. The Section 4 uses graph visualization built with network analysis to uncover the GVC dynamics and explore the regional hubs' contribution to the GVC network. Finally, the Section 5 concludes.

2. Networks of Trade in Value-Added: A Brief Comment on the Tools and Statistics Used

Graph theory is a widely recognized field in mathematics, which is also adopted by social sciences on account of its potentialities in assessing social phenomena. In the field of international economics, trade flows between economies (countries/country-sectors) can be naturally represented by a straight line (edges) connecting two points (nodes).

It is possible to add complexity to the nodes and edges by weighting them according to the importance of trade flows. The result is a directed network which captures not only the direction but also the magnitude of bilateral trade relationships, while the weighting of nodes highlights the importance of trade for each economy.

Based on the idea that an IO matrix can be associated with a weighted-directed network, through the weighted nodes and edges, it is possible to gain a picture of the real-world network of suppliers and users of trade in value-added.

In the networks described in this chapter, nodes represent countries, and they are weighted by their total trade in value-added (TTVA), i.e., the sum of (total) DVA with (total) FVA, where larger diameters represent higher TTVA values.

The edges or links connecting each country to its suppliers and users of value-added are weighted according to the size of the bilateral flows, with greater thickness representing higher flows. As the networks are directed, they enable the visualization of the trajectory of bilateral value-added flows (with arrows pointing to the destination – the user country), more specifically of the split between domestic value-added (DVA) and foreign value-added (FVA) in the world's economy.

Two important concepts are associated with the world production network, namely: the *indegree*, which refers to the number of incoming edges (user country); and the *outdegree*, which refers to the number of outgoing edges (supplier country).

The computation of network-based measures of connectivity and centrality is crucial for the network analysis, as they enable the identification of connection partners and of key hubs inside the network. There is a wide range of such measure, whose formulas vary in presence of a weighted/unweighted network. Barabási (2016) is a standard reference for them.

Considering a trade in value-added network of countries, connectivity includes Node Degree (ND), i.e., the number of a country's users and suppliers, and Node Strength (NS), i.e., the value (intensity) of a country's relationships in terms of trade in value-added (TTVA). In the case of directed networks, the ND is divided into indegree (number of suppliers) and outdegree (number of users), and the NS is divided into in-strength (a country's total FVA) and out-strength (a country's total DVA).

NS and ND are often referred to as Node Centrality in the literature, although centrality includes a wide range of measures depending on whether they are only first order, one-step links (e.g., closeness, betweenness), as it is the case, or also secondary, where more remote links are considered (e.g., Eigenvector Centrality, as explained below).

NS and ND centrality only capture straight links and neglect indirect linkages. To better understand a country's role in the users and suppliers' network, Eigenvector Centrality, as formulated by Bonacich (1987), is a finer node-related measure, which is also adopted in this study. The rationale behind it is that nearby high-scoring nodes contribute to the score of the node in question.

The measure thus contemplates further, multiple-steps away linkages, and thus differs from other centrality indexes, such as closeness or betweenness, which disregard the non-adjacent neighbors' score. The Eigenvector Centrality index uses Tang et al. (2015) for all nodes, with a cystoscope plugin that is based on the Bonacich (1987) formula.

Kali and Reyes (2007) stress another feature of network visualization: the possibility of adding a threshold that not only enables a clearer visualization but also reveals the backbone structure of the world's trade. To arrive at a basic structure for the world network of value-added embodied in trade, links (flows) were progressively eliminated in this study, according to a sequence of minimal thresholds. This eventually produced a new set of highly informative graphs on the backbone of the world's GVC mesh.

3. The World GVC Network in the XXI Century: An Overview Given by Descriptive Statistics and Centrality Measures

To obtain a picture of the world GVC network, this section analyses some descriptive statistics and centrality measures for the 43 countries available in the WIOD (2nd release) in both 2000 and 2014. Even though the WIOD includes the RoW, it has been excluded from the network-based calculations and visualization because, as an aggregate of economies, it would profoundly influence the weights of the nodes and edges, as it embodies a disproportionate number of economies for which trade in value-added data is not specified. To facilitate visual insights without blurring the "most relevant flows", whilst not excluding any of the 43 countries, a threshold has been defined: only those flows accounting for at least 1 % of TTVA of one of the countries involved in the bilateral relation are considered, hereinafter designated as "relevant flows".

Tab. 1 presents some descriptive statistics and centrality measures for the trade in value-added under scrutiny.

Tab. 1: Value-added flows: Descriptive statistics

	2000	2014
Total No. of Countries	43	43
Total No. of trade flows	713	730
Total value of TTVA* *(Billion US dollars)*	2408.7	6790.7
Lowest value of TTVA *(Billion US dollars)*	2.1	7.0
Highest value of TTVA *(Billion US dollars)*	874.1	1885.2
Average, TTVA *(Billion US dollars)*	3.4	9.3
Median, TTVA *(Billion US dollars)*	1.0	3.4
No. of countries making up 50 % of TTVA	17	23
No. of flows making up 50 % of TTVA	45	57
No. of countries making up 90 % of TTVA	34	35
No. of flows making up 90 % of TTVA	260	316
% of TTVA belonging to the top 10 % flows	61.7 %	56.3 %
% of TTVA belonging to the top 10 % flows	23.2 %	19.5 %

*TTVA is total trade in value-added (see text for definition). Values in billion US dollars.
Source: Own calculations for "relevant flows" (see text for definition) using data from WIOD (2nd release).

In Tab. 1, it is evident of an increase in participation in GVC networks over time: the number of flows have (slightly) grown from 2000 to 2014 and total TTVA has more than trebled. Both mean and median values are low and are close to the lowest value of TTVA; the distribution of average TTVA is left-skewed, as shown by a mean that is higher than the median. The left bias of the distribution is further supported by the flows' intensities, as a small number of flows accounts for most of total TTVA flows. The results differ, however, (even slightly) between 2000 and 2014. For in 2000, only 17 countries made up 50 % of the world's TTVA, whereas in 2014, more than half of the countries (23) under analysis accounted for half of the world TTVA. Despite this, a small number of countries still do not have a substantial place in the global production networks, as 34 and 35 of the 43 countries at stake accounted for 90 % of the TTVA, respectively, in 2000 and 2014.

More specific centrality measures facilitate a more in-depth analysis. The users and suppliers' networks exhibit a strong correlation between ND and NS (≈0.75) for both periods, which means that countries with a higher number of partners have higher TTVA values. The correlation of in-strength and out-strength, with a value of 0.85 and 0.92 in 2011 and 2014, respectively, tell us that great suppliers of trade in value-added also tend to be great users.

As expected from previous statistics, the distribution of ND is highly left-skewed, as shown in Graph 1 with most of the countries in 2000 and 2014 having between 15 and 45 (out of 84) partners for inward and outward flows, with no bimodality. It is even more left-skewed when values are considered (NS), as shown in Graph 2. Indeed, most of the countries in the network hold weak trade in value-added relationships, with only a few accountings for high values. The middle classes are empty or bear low frequencies in both periods, which reinforces the uneven distribution of the production chains. Nevertheless, in 2014, a few more countries feature in the higher classes than in 2000.

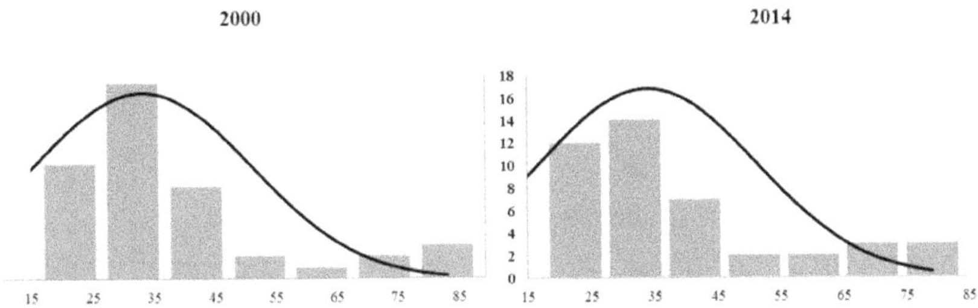

Graph 1: Distribution of Node Degree in 2000 and 2014

Source: In the horizontal axis, the number of a country's partners. Own calculations for "relevant flows" (see text for definition) using data from WIOD (2nd release).

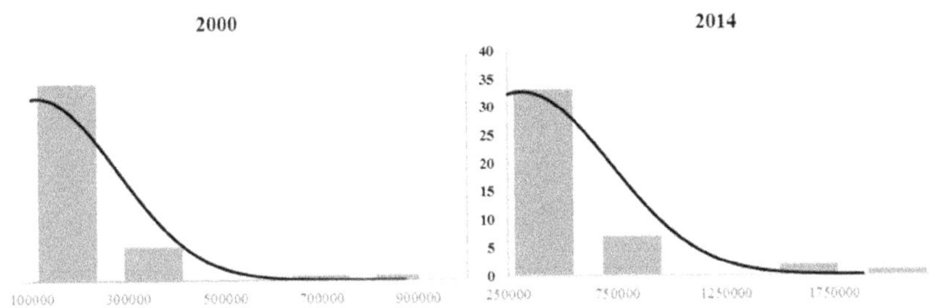

Graph 2: Distribution of Node Strength in 2000 and 2014

Source: In the horizontal axis, the value of a country´s total trade in value added (TTVA), in million US dollars. Own calculations for "relevant flows" (see text for definition) using data from WIOD (2nd release).

The correlation between Node and Eigenvector Centrality is positive in both years, which means that more intense direct supply-use relationships contribute to a more central position within the network. An interesting aspect is that the correlation with NS is much higher than that with ND (0.92 and 0.59 in 2014, and 0.94 and 0.58 in 2000, respectively) which emphasizes the character of this measure that plays down the number of partners in favor of their importance within the network. For instance, countries such as Canada and Mexico have a low number of partners, but are strongly connected to the US, which has a high centrality; accordingly, they also account for a high Eigenvector Centrality (respectively, 0.381 and 0.231, in 2014). The opposite occurs in countries such as Belgium and Italy, which have a relatively high number of trade partners that are only moderately central within the network (0.119 and 0.133, respectively, in 2014).

Tab. 2 lists the countries with the highest and lowest values of in-strength and out-strength[3]. As the above correlation between both indicators would predict, the top 5 countries for in-strength are virtually the same as the top 5 ones for out-strength. This applies for both periods considered, as well as for the bottom 5 countries.

Tab. 2: Top 5 and bottom 5 countries in in-strength and out-strength

	In-strength (Foreign value-added, FVA*)		**Out-strength (Domestic value-added, DVA)***	
	2000	**2014**	**2000**	**2014**
Top 5	USA	USA	USA	USA
	DEU	DEU	DEU	DEU
	FRA	CHN	JPN	CHN
	GBR	FRA	GBR	NLD
	JPN	GBR	FRA	GBR
Bottom 5	BGR	LTU	CYP	HRV
	CYP	MLT	LTU	MLT
	LTU	EST	EST	EST
	LVA	LVA	LVA	CYP
	EST	CYP	BGR	LVA

*See text for definition.
Source: Own calculations for "relevant flows" (see text for definition) using data from WIOD (2nd release). Country abbreviations based on the International Naming Convention (ISO - International Organization for Standardization 3166).

It is enlightening to compare the top and bottom economies in Tab. 2 with a similar rank analysis with the Eigenvector Centrality measure (not shown but available upon request). One noticeable difference between the NS ranking and

3 Full rank analysis available upon request.

that of the Eigenvector Centrality Index is that Canada is now in the second position in both periods, due to its connection to the US. China is in fourth position in 2014, which means that the country is well established in the supply-use networks; however, a comparison with its NS third position suggests that China's relevance is bigger when the intensities of the flows with its direct partners are taken into consideration. Another significant change is the entrance of the Netherlands to fifth position. From the NS analysis, one could see that this centrality is mostly due to the Netherlands upstream position in the production chain, as it accounts for a higher out-strength than in-strength centrality. At the same time, the strong tie with Germany also contributes to this high rank. Nearly the same small European countries occupy the bottom positions in both rankings, showing that the two parameters convey similar information. Once again, the importance of size is stressed out and, furthermore, Malta's and Cyprus' small dimension, combined with their insular position, has an effect of increasing freight rates due to the distance between main trading partners and the small size of individual shipments, World Bank (2017). In addition, an extended look at the full NS and Eigenvector Centrality rankings enables one to draw conclusions for countries outside the top and bottom positions. Almost all emerging economies have increased their centrality in GVCs. Indonesia and India are noteworthy evolutions, where both are improving their positioning as suppliers of value-added. Russia has impressively progressed both as a supplier and importer of value-added. Türkiye is also gaining momentum in the international GVC scene, but still lags its emerging partners.

4. The Backbone of World GVC Network: A Graph Visualization

To better grasp the backbone of the GVC networks, we restrict the analysis by applying to the previous data a threshold that only permits the visualization of flows above the 90th percentile of the distribution of value-added flows, which are hereinafter designated as the "most relevant flows". Figs. 1 and 2 represent those "most relevant" users and suppliers of the world GVC network in 2000 and 2014, respectively[4]. Two elements are key for the network: the nodes, i.e., the 43 countries available in the WIOD; and the edges, i.e., the bilateral value-added flows (DVA and FVA) amongst the nodes.

By comparing both networks, in 2014 there is a greater number of relevant flows, and more countries such as Russia, India, Luxembourg, Czech Republic

4 A network analysis with flows considered in previous section is available upon request.

and Brazil enter this more restricted trade scene. A broad pattern is common to both periods: three clear hubs exist (the so-called regional "Factories", Baldwin and Lopez-Gonzalez, 2015), namely, North America, a European cluster, and a sparser Asian one, with Indonesia and India further apart. In the denser but also more concentrated 2014 network, Türkiye gets more GVC embedded with the EU and Australia with Asia. The Asian cluster becomes somewhat tighter, as India and Indonesia move closer to the other countries in it. Geography indeed plays a role: in 2000, 38 % of the "most relevant flows" were between countries that share territorial borders, such as the cases of Canada, Mexico and the US, and the Netherlands with Germany, whereas in 2014 this increased to more than 40 %.

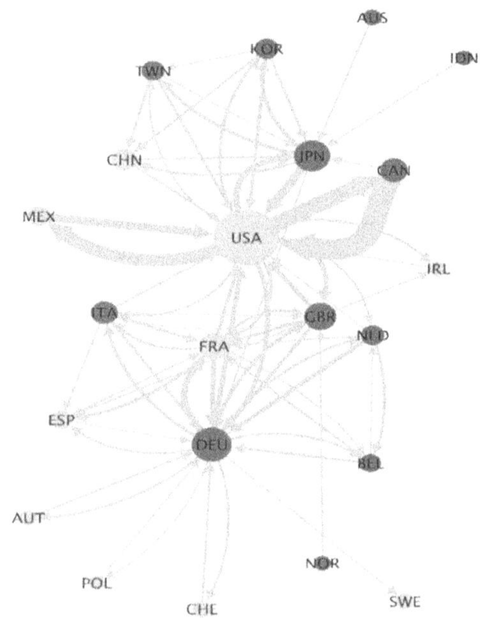

Fig. 1: The world GVC network, in 2000

Note: Light nodes and dark nodes represent, respectively, net importers and net exporters of intermediates.

Source: Own calculations for the "most relevant flows" (see text for definition) using data from WIOD (2nd release). Country abbreviations based on the International Naming Convention (ISO – International Organization for Standardization 3166).

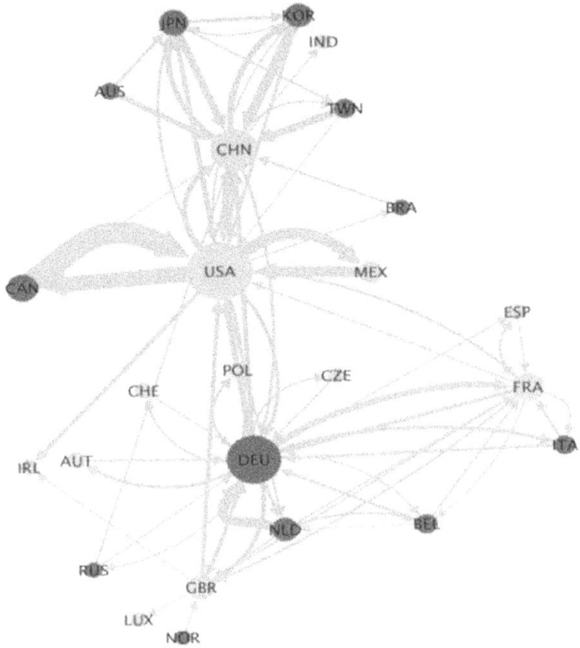

Fig. 2: The world GVC network, in 2014

Note: Light nodes and dark nodes represent, respectively, net importers and net exporters of intermediates.

Source: Own calculations for the "most relevant flows" (see text for definition) using data from WIOD (2nd release). Country abbreviations based on the International Naming Convention (ISO-International Organization for Standardization 3166).

Focusing now with more detail on each regional "Factory", Factory America is clearly dominated by the US, which is not only the country at worldwide level with the biggest node (TTVA equals 874.1billion and 1885.2 billion US dollars in 2000 and 2014, respectively) but also accounts for the thickest intra- and inter-regional flows. Over the period analyzed, the bilateral flow with the highest value was by far that from Canada to the US (126.7 billion and 247.6 US dollars in 2000 and 2014, respectively), with the opposite flow in the second position (94.4 billion and 187.7 billion US dollars in 2000 and 2014, respectively). Mexico has been gradually increasing its role as a supplier of value-added to the US, especially in the automotive sector. It has even supplanted Canada as the main provider of automotive components to the US, World Bank (2017). Also noteworthy is the fact that in 2014 the outward flow from China to the US (130.2 billion US dollars) is higher than the opposite flow (66.5 billion US dollars), which means that China is a net supplier of value-added to the US. Notwithstanding Brazil's still modest participation in the global production networks – it mostly trades with its MERCOSUL neighbors – the country entered the world's "most relevant flows" in 2014 as a net importer of value-added from the US and a net exporter of value-added to China.

Turning to Factory Europe, Germany was the country of the region in both periods with the highest TTVA (538.4 billion US dollars in 2000 and 1556.7 billion in 2014), although other West European economies are relevant players as well. The highest regional flows were those among Western European countries. Germany maintained an important supply and use relationship with bordering countries such as Switzerland, as does with Austria, Belgium, and especially with the Netherlands, one of its net suppliers. Germany is also responsible for the presence of Poland in the "most relevant flows" in 2000 and 2014, as well as the Czech Republic's emergence in 2014. Finally, Germany is also a net supplier of valued added to the US and China, although the flows between this hub and the US have comparatively lost relevance within the world flows, as they no longer figure amongst the "most relevant" in 2014. The UK holds a steady trade link with Norway, mainly due to its imports of primary commodities. In turn, Ireland and Luxembourg are importers of value-added from the UK, what is consistent with the role of Luxembourg as a financial center and that of Ireland as a location for headquarters of multinational corporations. As regards Ireland, the country also maintains a strong tie with the US, whereas France remains essentially European in its production networks, with a somewhat robust input link with North America.

Russia has emerged in the global production scene in the end of the period at the upstream margin of GVCs, as is typical of those countries that specialize in primary commodities. The country's most valuable exports go to Germany, which is also an important supplier of value-added to Russia.

Factory Asia underwent the biggest changes during the period: not only the central position shifted from Japan to China but also the density of intra- and inter-regional trade has increased substantially. In 2000, Japan was the country of this region with the highest TTVA (306.3 billion US dollars), as well as the center of intra-regional flows. However, Japan's centrality within Factory Asia was not as visually evident as the US one in Factory America, as other Asian countries such as China, South Korea (the thickest intra-regional flow) and Taiwan already exhibited strong positions within the region. In 2014, China is the center of the hub (with a TTVA of 1338.3 billion US dollars, which corresponds to an increase of 1208 billion US dollars relatively to 2000), seemingly adopting the model of those of its Asian neighbors which have entered the GVCs in the final stages of the manufacturing process. South Korea, a former major player in Japanese production chains, still maintains strong trade in value-added links with Japan, albeit it has evolved as a crucial supplier and user of China's inputs. This model is the core of intra-Asian production chains, which helps explain why China has become a supplier of value-added to India. In 2000, Australia was already an important supplier of production inputs to Japan, with this link remaining strong in 2014, but a new one with China had by then surpassed it. In 2014, 9 % of Asia's TTVA was with Australia, a country that is profoundly integrated in the Asian production processes.

Finally, to better grasp the existence of regional hubs, in Figs. 3 and 4 we aggregate nodes and flows in each GVC-linked regional hub, in 2000 and 2014, respectively. Namely, we consider Asia, which includes China, South Korea, Japan, India, Indonesia and Taiwan; Europe, which includes all 27 countries of the current European Union, plus Great Britain, Switzerland and Norway; and North America, which corresponds to the 3 NAFTA countries.

Figs. 3 and 4 confirm that an important part of the GVC activities take place within regions, especially in Factory Europe, as can be seen from the width of the regional self-loops which capture the intensity of intra-regional flows. In fact, the share of intra-European flows in total TTVA of this region is well above 60 % in both periods and it has only slightly decreased from 66 % to 65 % over the period analyzed. In the other two regions, intra-regional flows predominate when compared to inter-regional flows with each of the other regions.

Asia is the region where the weight of intra-regional flows was lower in 2000, but it has increased from 34 % to 36 % of TTVA of the region between 2000 and 2014, in contra cycle with the other regions and surpassing North America share in the last year (35 %). Another salient characteristic of this region is the increased intensity of the links with the remaining hubs as supplier (from 5 to 7 % and 20 to 25 % of the total TTVA of the user, respectively, in Europe and North America), which is mainly due to China. Also of note is the fact that the share of North America in Asian TTVA decreased (from 38 % to 26 % in the 15 years under analysis), which is explained by a decreasing dependence of Asia on "imported" value-added from North America.

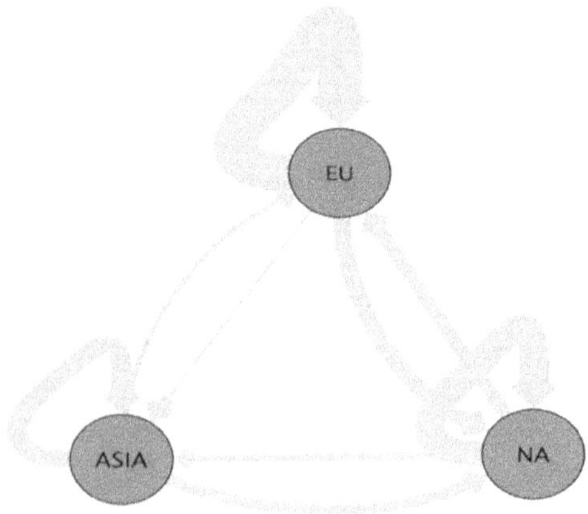

Fig. 3: The world GVC network' s regional hubs, in 2000

Note: Asia: China, South Korea, Japan, India, Indonesia and Taiwan; Europe (EU): all 27 countries of the current European Union, plus Great Britain, Switzerland and Norway; North America (NA): the three NAFTA countries.

Source: Authors' calculations for the "most relevant flows" (see text for definition) based on WIOD (2nd release).

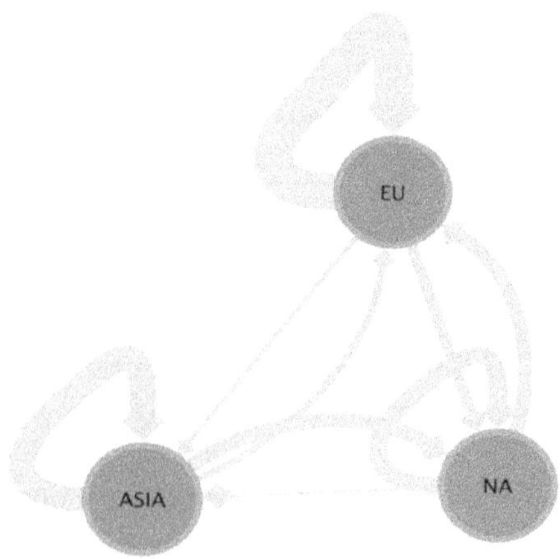

Fig. 4: The world GVC network' s regional hubs, in 2014

Note: Asia: China, South Korea, Japan, India, Indonesia and Taiwan; Europe (EU): all 27 countries of the current European Union, plus Great Britain, Switzerland and Norway; North America (NA): the three NAFTA countries.

Source: Authors' calculations for the "most relevant flows"(see text for definition) based on WIOD (2nd release).

5. Concluding Remarks

Our results show that the world's trade in value-added has more than trebled during the period 2000–2014, and its geographical spread has become less unequal, with more countries and bilateral flows relevant for the GVCs. Countries with a larger number of partners also account for higher values of trade in value-added, with major suppliers also tending to be major users. However, most of the countries do not maintain a meaningful GVC relationship with a significant number of partners. Accordingly, the distribution of all centrality parameters is left-skewed.

Globally, the GVCs phenomenon remains regionalized, as shown by the distribution of the several centrality measures, which are highly asymmetric, even though it is evident that a certain diversification of world production is taking place.

It is hard to conceive the GVCs phenomenon without the initial contracting out trend in the US and the steady industrial capacity of Germany. The networks associated with the two timeframes which were analyzed in this study clearly support this point, as well as how crucial Asia is, with its virtuous dynamics, combining the evolving roles of Japan, South Korea, and China (besides less important players, such as Vietnam and Thailand, which are not included in the WIOD). Despite this, the US still appears to be maintaining its position as the global winner from this phenomenon. Emerging countries have intensified their positioning in the world production network from 2000 to 2014, driven by an increase in the intensity of their previous relationships with the key hubs.

Is the world production fragmentation model sustainable without strong regional hubs experiencing the possibility of linkages to other major markets, as observed in the period under analysis and in other similar previous studies?

We venture that with only a strictly regional market, or a fully globalized one, GVCs would perhaps be unfeasible or, at least, less frequent. The regional hub provides a basis for a process of continuous outsourcing and supply that feeds the growth and upgrading of the center, while the linkages to other major markets multiply the fragmentation options. The regional dimension is also key for the smaller firms, given the greater impact of transportation and logistics costs on these firms.

It is important to note that the international production and GVC network may well undergo significant changes in the future, which cannot yet be fully captured with the available IO internationally linked databases. Firstly, there is the swing from liberal trade and investment policies towards a return to protectionism and more interventionism in national economic policies, compounded by the digital transformation of the supply chains of firms and the sustainability concerns that led many MNEs to re-examine their supply chain resilience (UNCTAD, 2020). Next, we are facing the COVID-19-induced crisis, which has led to a slowdown of international production since mid-2020 and severe supply chain disruptions across many industries (the 1,000 largest global MNEs and their supplies own more than 12,000 facilities in the areas that were first affected by mobility restrictions, UNCTAD, 2020, chap., 4), followed by the adoption of trade protectionist and domestic security-related investment policies and support for the repatriation of international supply chains as a way to mitigate the risks of the geographical concentration in the production of certain critical supplies. For instance, the European Parliament declared on 17 April 2020 that it "supports the reintegration of supply chains inside the EU" (European Parliament, 2020). As multi-country production networks have become more complex and more sensitive to trade-linked contagion, policies to restraint supply-chain trade can prove costly, especially for those countries whose output relies more on each other countries' inputs (Baldwin and Freeman, 2020; Bekkers et al., 2020).

Even if it is extremely difficult to make economic predictions in the face of the pervasive uncertainty of the evolution of key variables of worldwide economic activity, the key point that GVC trade is regionalized suggests that the main transmission in terms of disrupting complex production networks will be regional (Baldwin and Freeman, 2020). An acceleration of the trend towards regionalism is even possible, as it is likely that countries will place a premium on the diversification of trading partners and that MNEs will look to reinforce the geographical concentration of value-added (UNCTAD, 2020). In any case, the consequent loss of momentum in international production will not necessarily decrease the interdependence between countries and the use of intermediates. As China is rapidly scaling up its production and exports (Bown, 2020), while its major partners are still facing the consequences of an unprecedented collapse of output, the developments described above – including the increasing dependence of North America and Europe on Chinese intermediates – lead us to ask the question: will China eventually absorb and/or dominate the other hubs, and consequently become the new central node of the world GVC network?

♠ The authors are grateful for the comments received at the 92nd International Atlantic Economic Conference and acknowledge financial Support from FCT – Fundação para a Ciência e Tecnologia (Portugal), national funding through research grant UIDB/05069/2020.

References

Amador, J., & Cabral, S. (2017). Networks of Value-added Trade. *The World Economy*, *40*(7), 1291–1313. doi.org/10.1111/twec.12469.

Amador, J., Cabral, S., Mastrandrea, R., & Ruzzenenti, F. (2018). Who's Who in Global Value Chains? A Weighted Network Approach. *Open Economies Review*, *29*, 1039–1059. doi.org/10.1007/s11079-018-9499-7

Baldwin, R., & Freeman, R. (2020). Trade Conflict in the Age of Covid-19. *VoxEU*, 22 May. Available at: <https://voxeu.org/article/trade-conflict-age-covid-19> [Accessed on July 2021].

Baldwin, R., & Lopez-Gonzalez, J. (2015). Supply-chain Trade: A Portrait of Global Patterns and Several Testable Hypotheses. *The World Economy*, *38*(11), 1682–1721.

Baldwin, J., & Yan, B. (2014). Global Value Chains and the Productivity of Canadian Firms. *Economic Analysis (EA) Research Paper Series*, Economic Analysis Division, Statistics Canada. Available at: <Global Value Chains and the Productivity of Canadian Manufacturing Firms - ARCHIVED (statcan.gc.ca)> [Accessed on December 2020].

Barabási, A.-L. (2016). *Network Science*. Cambridge, England: Cambridge University Press.

Bekkers, E., Keck, A., Koopman, R., & Nee, C. (2020). Trade and COVID-19: The WTO's 2020 and 2021 Trade Forecast. *CEPR*, VOX^{EU}. Available at: <Simulating the trade effects of the COVID-19 pandemic – Bekkers – 2022 – The World Economy – Wiley Online Library> [Accessed on July 2021].

Bonacich, P. (1987). Power and Centrality: A Family of Measures. *American Journal of Sociology*, *92*, 1170–1182.

Borin, A., & Mancini, M. (2019). Measuring What Matters in Global Value Chains and Value-Added Trade. *Policy Research Working Paper*, *8*, World Bank Group.

Brach, J., & Kappel, R. T. (2009). Global Value Chains, Technology Transfer and Local Firm Upgrading in Non-OECD Countries. *GIGA* Working Paper, *110*.

Brown, C. P. (2020). *COVID-19: China's Exports of Medical Supplies Provide a Ray of Hope*. Trade and Investment Policy Watch. Massachusetts: Peterson Institute for International Economics. Available at: <https://www.piie.com/blogs/trade-and-investment-policy-watch/COVID-19-chinas-exports-medical-supplies-provide-ray-hope> [Accessed on July 2021].

European Parliament (2020). European Parliament Resolution of 17 April 2020 on EU Coordinated Action to Combat the COVID 19 Pandemic and Its Consequences. (2020/2616(RSP)). Available at: <European Parliament resolution of 17 April 2020 on EU coordinated action to combat the COVID-19

pandemic and its consequences (2020/2616(RSP)) – Publications Office of the EU (europa.eu) > [Accessed on July 2021].

Kali, R., & Reyes, J. (2007). The Architecture of Globalization: A Network Approach to International Economic Integration. *Journal of International Business Studies*, *38*, 595–620. doi.org/10.1057/palgrave.jibs.8400286.

Li, A., Meng, B., & Wang, Z. (2019). Recent Patterns of Global Production and GVC Participation. In D. Dollat, E. Gabbe, V. Stolzenburg, & Z. Wang (Eds.), *Global Value Chain Development Report 2019: Technical Innovation, Supply Chain Trade and Workers in a Globalized World* (pp. 9–43). The World Bank Group and WTO, Available at: < gvc_dev_report_2019_e_ch1.pdf (wto.org) > [Accessed on November 2020].

Martinez-Galán, E., & Fontoura, M. P. (2019). Global Value Chains and Inward Foreign Direct Investment in the 2000s. *The World Economy*, *42*(1), 175–96. doi.org/10.1111/twec.12660.

Saliola, F., & Zanfei, A. (2009). Multinational Firms, Global Value Chains and the Organization of Knowledge Transfer. *Research Policy*, *38*(2), 369–381. doi.org/10.1016/j.respol.2008.11.003.

Santoni, G., & Taglioni, D. (2015). Networks and Structural Integration in Global Value Chains. In J. Amador & F. di. Mauro (Eds.), *The Age of Global Value Chains: Maps and Policy Issues* (pp. 68–84). London: Centre for Economic Policy Research.

Taglioni, D., & Winkler, D. (2016). *Making Global Value Chains Work for Development.* Washington, DC: World Bank.

Tang, Y., Li, M., Wang, J., & Wu, F.-X. (2015). CytoNCA: A Cytoscape Plugin for Centrality Analysis and Evaluation of Protein Interaction Networks. *ByoSystems*, *127*, 67–72. doi.org/10.1016/j.biosystems.2014.11.005.

Timmer, P. M., Los, B., Stehrer, R., & de Vries, J. G. (2016). An Anatomy of the Global Trade Slowdown Based on the WIOD 2016 Release. *New Economic Papers*, Groningen Growth and Development Centre, University of Groningen, GGDC Research Memoranda, *162*.

UNCTAD (2020). *World Investment Report.* New York and Geneva: United Nations.

World Bank (2017). *Measuring and Analyzing the Impact of GVCs on Economic Development.* Global Value Chain Development Report. Washington, D.C. Available at: < Measuring and analyzing the impact of GVCs on economic development (un.org):~:text=Measuring%20and%20analyzing%20the%20impact%20of%20GVCs%20on,discrete%20tasks%20or%20phases%20in%20the%20production%20process. > [Accessed on October 2020].

Xiao, H., Meng, B., Ye, J., & Li, S. (2020). Are Global Value Chains Truly Global?. *Economic Systems Research*, *32*(4), 540–564.

Ida Claudia Panetta, Sabrina Leo

Why Are M-Payment Platforms So Attractive? M-Payment as the Entry Level to the Digital Financial Era

1. Introduction

Mobile technologies have opened opportunities for innovative financial technology solutions for storing money and payment instruments (e.g., digital wallets) and performing transactions (e.g., Apple Pay). Mobile Payments (M-Payments) allow making payments in a simple, fast, and low-cost way to purchase goods and services using smartphones or wearable devices. The advantages are based on the speed with which identities can be verified and transactions completed, not just on the prospect of being linked everywhere.

M-Payments provide additional benefits to market players on both the demand and supply sides.

On the demand side, the M-Payments system combines old and new technology to "connect" clients to the financial system, even those who were previously unable to do so (Korovkin et al., 2015). Furthermore, it influences client behaviour and increases their belief in machine-based transactions, undermining trust, one of the financial intermediation's pillars (Dhar and Stein, 2017). On the supply side, M-Payments, in fuelling commercial transactions in the real sector, hasten processes and modify the operating domain of the financial system. Payments via mobile devices have also opened new business opportunities for various players belonging to diverse sectors involved in the supply side, leading to less-defined borderlines between the financial and the real sectors. In this panorama, financial Payment Service Providers (PSPs) and those others outside the financial sector (i.e., Telco, GAFA) further foster collaborative or competitive relationships, breaking down traditional business models (BMs), creating unique, previously non-existent ones.

Platform-based BMs (Evans et al., 2006), which have been successful in other industries, might provide value to the financial industry by facilitating direct connections between more diverse users and offering a new means of expanding a company that benefits all parties involved.

This work focuses on how M-Payments have made the financial system more permeable to new players, highlighting the financial system changes brought on by mobile devices and applications. This indicates that services previously supplied by banks may be fragmented into a variety of commercial activities that FinTech organizations can perform more simply and disseminate through a mobile-based platform. As clients acquire confidence in technology, it may be used to create more convenient, low-cost digital apps. Furthermore, in this situation, M-Payments Apps may play a role as catalysts and distributors of information that may be utilized to provide additional financial goods and services.

2. Backgrounds

2.1 Mobile Payments: A Brief Definition

Despite its apparent simplicity, M-Payments are based on extremely complicated and variable operational structures, making it impossible to identify and categorize M-Payments using the "dimensions" often employed in so-called traditional payment systems (ECB, 2010). Traditional categorization methods for M-Payments ignore important aspects of the phenomena, such as technology and the types of operators engaged. In addition, some categories might quickly become obsolete. Differently, we've broken down the system into its constituent pieces to describe M-Payments: technology, operational structures, players engaged, and so on.

As part of this work with M-Payments, we refer to all payment services initiated via mobile devices (by the user) according to the ECB's most complete and – in our opinion – valid definition.

Besides, when we talk about M-Payments systems or digital/mobile money, we frequently confuse money as a store of value with the usage of digital infrastructure that allows value to be transferred using bank deposit money. This creates a perplexing scenario where the terms "money" and "payment system" are becoming more difficult to distinguish in the digital world. While the term "M-payments" refers to the M-Payments system, the term "M-Payments industry" refers to the economic system and "space" in which the operators play a role. In particular, considering the role assumed by technology and innovation to indentify the industry we refer to: (i) hardware components (basically M-device), (ii) software user enablers (M-Apps), and (iii) the improvement in the connections (Wi-Fi, 5G, NFC). By analysing them, it is possible to deeply understand and distinguish the main operating mechanisms that populate the sector and identify the peculiarity of the ecosystem created within this industry (Panetta and Leo, 2017).

Despite the seeming rapidity of moving money between accounts using M-devices, few directnesses identify this financial movement. Looking at M-Payments transactions, we can see that between the payer and the payee, there are a variety of actors from various industries, creating a great illustration of a complex ecosystem. Moore (1993, 1996) defined a "business ecosystem" as "an economic community sustained by a foundation of interacting firms and individuals," and it perfectly matches the M-Payments sector as well. Depending on the prevalence of the role assumed by one or more subjects and their interaction, it is possible to identify the TechFinNet Ecosys (Panetta and Leo, 2017) to analyse strategies and BMs that vary rapidly over time and space. The ecosystem can be divided into the following subsets:

- Tech-Ecosys, i.e., the set of products, services, and subjects that recognizes, interacts, and evolves around a particular product or technology, which, with a close network of relationships and interactions that produce value, give life to the ecosystem (e.g., M-Device manufacturer, Hardware provider);
- Fin-Ecosys, which coincides with the space defined by identifying players who provide payment services in favour of the user via M-Device. This is a broader set of PSP: the "Fin" dimension is due to the content of the services, not to the nature of the servicer, which can belong to very different sectors (e.g., Telco, 2P2 money transfer);
- Net-Ecosys, namely the vast area of the subjects that compete and collaborate in providing inter-communication services via M-Device (e.g., SIM-card providers, Instant Messaging Providers).

In our ecosystem, it is possible to identify three macro-categories of new actors treading the scenes. We refer at:

- New players, the subject that is recently involved in financial activity (Zetsche et al., 2017);
- FinTech firms that supply financial products through the most advanced information and communication technologies;
- BigTech, or OTT, whose BMs rely on tech innovation; they have big moves in payments for a variety of reasons: accessing new revenue streams and protecting core products (Apple Pay), improving margins of existing revenue streams (Amazon credit cards), acquiring new customers (WeChat), and deepening loyalty of existing customers (Alipay's Zhima).

The existence of an ecosystem as described above implies that all components must develop relationships with multiple stakeholders such as suppliers, demanders, and even competitors, focusing on those which enable more value-added.

2.2 Platform-Based Business Model

By facilitating direct contact between two (two-sided platform) or more (multi-sided platform) types of clients, the platform BMs is considered a key breakthrough in the field of BMs for a variety of sectors (Evans et al., 2006). A platform is made up of two theoretical ideas in terms of an economic standpoint:

- two-sided networks, in which two separate user groups benefit from each other's network;
- network effects (same-side and cross-side) in which a product or service's value depends on the number of people who use it (Shapiro and Varian, 1998).

Differently from linear BMs, platform-based BMs gather various revenue sources from stakeholders and count on multilateral profit structures.

Platform-based businesses contribute to creating a business ecosystem because they can build and amplify network effects among players, allowing them to gain additional benefits such as an installed base of users or the availability of complementary goods. Platform owners (e.g., Apple) and complementors (e.g., developers) cooperate to build firm-specific components to co-create valuable platform derivatives (Kazan et al., 2018).

The platformisation of digital goods (e.g., Google Play) and services (e.g., payments) is layered modular IT architectures embedded within business networks. Digital platforms, according to Kazan et al. (2018), serve as innovation hubs by providing services that emphasize mediation and modularity.

Considering the foregoing, the TechFinNet ecosystem may be classified as a platform-based business since it relies on platforms to link networks, content, services, and communication tools. The fundamental point is that the platform's payment service is modular and based on the technological and economic interfaces required for: (i) the provision of the service, (ii) its combination with other products, and (iii) the definition of ways for players involved in the commercial process to interact.

3. Major Changes Operating by M-Payments to the Financial System

3.1 Levels of Transformation in the Supply Side

To analyse how different waves of IT innovations have affected the banking industry, we have:

- considered three phases of IT innovations (Fig. 1). The first two are inspired by Alt et al. (2018), who dates to the beginning of financial institutions (FIs) and the FinTech phase that started around 2008. The third, from 2014, is considered by us to distinguish among other FinTech innovations those induced by M-Payments;
- used Venkatraman's framework (1994) to represent the degrees of transformation of the banking business over time.

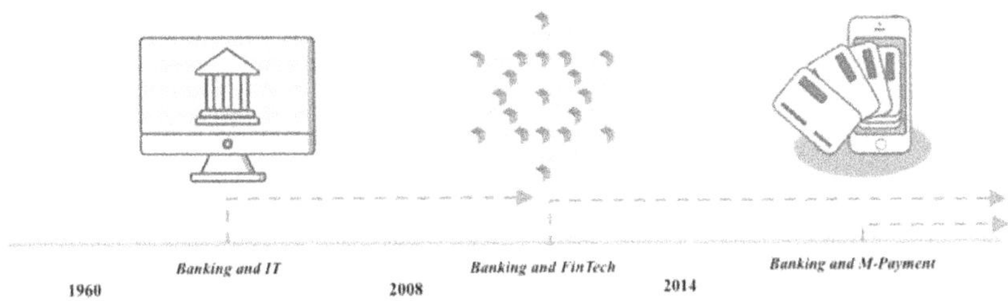

Fig. 1: Banking sector's IT evolution

This diagram aims to demonstrate how the M-Payments Era differs from previous waves of banking IT innovation and digitalization. M-Payments, in our opinion, assist in promoting engagement with business network participants and impacting the logic of business relationships inside the extended business network (Venkatraman, 1994), whereas other innovations improve internal activities and procedures.

According to Venkatraman's model (1994), we see localized exploitation and internal integration as evolutionary phases, with three revolutionary levels more relevant to banking business aspects (business process redesign, network redesign, and scope redefinition).

As Alt et al. (2018) refer to IT-induced change in the financial industry, the intra-organizational levels may be summarized in three levels: external organization, business network organization, and internal organization (Tab. 1).

	Transformation level	Banking and IT (up to 2008)	Banking and FinTech effect (after 2008)	Banking and M-Payment effect (after 2014)
External organization	Regulators	Equity requirements Deregulation Discretionality at regional level	Stricter rules on capital requirement Awareness of new risk and new players Harmonization	Stricter rules; less protection
	Supervisors	Emphasis on microprudential supervision Harmonisation in supervising conduct	Emphasis on macroprudential supervision Harmonisation in supervising conduct	
	Policymakers	War on cash	War on cash	Non-cash payments increase
	Consumers	Use of cash		
	Business Model Innovation		Online services distribution of tasks	Mobile services distribution of tasks
Business Network organization	Networking	Small number of network partners	Many specialized partners	Many specialized partners from different sectors
	Margins and cost structure	High margins in core business	Lower margins, Higher competition	Lower margins, Higher competition also different sectors
	Competitors	Other traditional financial service providers	Newcomers, lateral entrants	Start-ups, lateral entrants, BigTech
	Culture/Customer retention	Hierarchical/ High customer loyalty	Cooperative, agile reduced switching costs	Co-opetition
Internal organization	Business focus	Process-oriented; provider processes focused	Customer-centric;	Information-centric
	Customer interaction - Core competencies	Offline first; individual channel	Online first, omni-channel online distribution;	Mobile Channel, hybrid interaction with customers, Platforms and peer to peer, business model,
	Vertical integration	Distribution, products, transactions high integration	Low integration; External financial services provider systems integration	De-integration, platformization External non-financial services provider systems integration

Tab. 1: IT-induced change in the financial industry

The first transformation level considered is the changed context in which banks operate, the external organizational level; the key changes occurring after (and because of) the financial crisis can be classified from the perspective of regulators, supervisors, policymakers, and consumers.

Tighter requirements for equity holdings (e.g., Basel III), consumer protection (e.g., EU GDPR), payment systems (e.g., EU PSD2), and protection against new risks (NIS Directive) were key regulatory reforms. Innovation offers new company potential and poses unknown risks that must be controlled. Regulatory restrictions have been relaxed in specific sectors to allow innovative players to experiment and expand quickly (Ringe and Ruof, 2019; EBA, 2017). FinTech regulatory initiatives emerge primarily after the 2008 financial crisis (Lee and Shin, 2018) and vary from country to country. They depend on the country's economic development plans (Lee and Shin), bringing a trade-off between competition and financial stability.

Supervisors on the banking system seem to show, especially in some areas, a greater and pervasive level of supervision, with less protection offered by national laws towards a more international level of control (FSB, 2017).

Policymakers are fine-tuning policies designed to tackle cash at the regional level, with significant variances among nations, leading to the continued growth of electronic payments. These shifts in policymakers' attitudes impact payment system participants' relationships, affecting them and redefining their BMs as a result. Consumer payment habits are evolving due to a mix of policymaker prescriptions, attitudes towards new technology, and the ongoing demand for ease in shopping expeditions (par. 3.2).

There are also some resulting from BMs developments in the non-financial system that have imposed pressure on the banking system at the external organization level, in particular:

- the new BM that uses network and IT-driven disruption tested in the real sector (e.g., platform-based BM, cloud-based services) is now inspiring FIs;
- the use of the digital channel to sell products and services that also cross-border and cross-sector ask for new financial services and payment instruments;
- Pay-per-view, micro/pico payment, and subscription are examples of novel selling and pricing strategies that force FIs to re-evaluate their commercial and production practices (Puschmann and Alt, 2016; Zetsche et al., 2017).

The second degree of transformation described is the business network organization redesign produced by IT innovation; it refers to reshaping the nature of interchange among various members in a business network via the effective deployment of IT capabilities (Venkatraman, 1994). One of the most evident consequences of the FinTech Era at the business network level is that firms are increasingly networked with specialized external partners, and competition is fiercer, affecting margins and other variables as regulatory pressure (Puschmann and Alt, 2016). In today's FinTech sector, new firms have a different dynamic mindset than incumbents in the traditional financial services market. On the one hand, we refer to newcomers and, on the other, to new digital entrants (Zetsche et al., 2017). The latter are players that offer specific products/services, especially appreciated by digital-inclined customers. The combined effect of customer research on convenience and the reduced switching costs among FinTech providers determines lower customer retention (Pousttchi and Dehnert, 2018) and more intense competitive pressure. To adapt to the competitive scenario, participants' (including incumbents and newcomers) relationships swiftly transition from:

- competition for both input (e.g., HR and technology) and output (e.g., market share and contracts);
- cooperation in search of mutual gains.

Often, incumbents and new players define a co-opetition scenario as a binary relationship (cooperative and competitive) between two players that should occur at the same time, i.e., that players should compete and cooperate rather than individuals cooperating in some activities while they compete in others. According to Gnyawali and Park (2011), co-opetition is rising, with more than half of all collaborative and competitive B2B partnerships in the same industry.

In the TechFinNet ecosystem, relationships in business networks are more complex and diverse than those reported in the FinTech space. Unlike other fields, the M-Commerce and M-Payments domain favours players who can develop platforms that can meet the needs of upstream content and application sources and downstream consumers who need access to financial services. BigTech, such as GAFA, demonstrate the relevance of this approach.

Finally, we look at the internal organizational level, which is likely a result of the first two. The redesign of business processes may be seen as a response to the FinTech and mobile payments revolution. It examines the shift in focus from internal corporate procedures to a "customer-centre" (Pousttchi and Dehnert, 2018). Since M-Payments are a two-sided market, business operations are focused on two different types of customers: end-users and merchants. This allows players to experiment with new BMs based on current pricing policies (usually asymmetric) and different interfaces/processes to connect with different categories of customers.

On the user side, there are two major IT developments affecting bank clients and their internal organizations: the proliferation of smartphones, touchscreens, wearables, and other hardware; a range of community-based software solutions (users-generated content, UGC sites). Because of the technical infrastructure, types of web applications, and user experience, UGC websites offer a paradigm shift in the creation, management, and distribution of information and media, as well as social interactions among users.

These shifts are reshaping all organizations and enterprises' consumer-supplier interactions, including the banking industry. Previous studies have found societal pressure on firms to swiftly embrace social web technologies in banking-related online apps for consumer engagement. The development of the "platform-as-a-service" idea, as well as the growth of M-Device access points to these platforms, has paved the way for novel distribution platforms that currently provide a diverse range of financial services.

To take advantage of the changes in the reference framework mentioned, banks must first consider the following:

- the correct balance of distribution channels based on mobile and social technologies. The IT advancements allowed for the complementing and substituting of physical branch offices in terms of various aligned online channels (Shim and Shin, 2016), which included handling towards the administration of multiple channels. Interactions, settings, and knowledge should be available across all channels, and switching channels should be feasible without loss of information or duplicate operations, according to cross-channel management;
- the most efficient technique to filter through all sorts of large data (Puschmann and Alt, 2016).

M-Devices and the IoT are generating a vast amount of transactional data, making it easier for customers to contact businesses, research products, and conduct online transactions (and even banking). This large, diverse body of data, which is growing exponentially, allows banks to create customer profiles that follow patterns, anticipate actions, and, when used correctly, help banks better understand their customers.

This is accompanied by an increase in digitized (automated) processes, which are less connected to core banking systems and often on their own with agile approaches with specified API interfaces (Puschmann and Alt, 2016) both via web and mobile channel.

In the digital ecosystem considered, the relevance of customer information is to reshape and redefine the user, form a prosumer entity, and move from a customer-centric approach to an information-centric approach. This becomes more apparent with digital money, which generates data in a cash-free way. The underlying potential value may be used to create money and offer users information about their financial activities through inventive BMs. The current inside-out product-centric logic (Puschmann, 2017) for a new ecosystem introduced by non-financial service providers outside the financial industry and the creation of peer-to-peer BMs are determined by new customer-centric applications. In the past, banks' highly vertically integrated value chains were moving to non-linear multi-sided (Evans et al., 2006) and platform-based representations (Panetta and Leo, 2017).

3.2 Major Changes in the Demand Side: Focus on User Behaviour

In the user-end market, the increased penetration of M-devices enables flexibility and ubiquity, allowing users to run flexible ways to share and/or search information. On the other hand, new mobile applications allow users to perform activities quickly at their convenience while simultaneously generating and consuming massive amounts of digital data that can exploit. Since the introduction of digital services and mobile applications in commercial and social contexts, people's interactions have changed dramatically (Singh et al., 2017). In this context M-Payments have shown to be disruptive. They increased the number of transactions and users and shifted people's attitudes towards the financial system. M-Payments have the merit of promising frictionless transactions, transforming the perception of financial interactions – thanks to modern (i.e., contactless) technology – enabling faster and easier transactions. The ability to access mobile money accounts quickly and easily gives users access to a broader range of services (e.g., healthcare, education, employment), increasing demand for M-Payments services. Furthermore, mobile money accounts enable financial excluded to gain access to the financial system (Korovkin et al., 2015). Users can also transfer money directly to accounts via P2P transfer technology, bypassing traditional intermediaries. In addition to the settlement of economic exchanges, payments technology can create new ways of connecting people and using money to drive social activities.

In terms of financial service characteristics and relationships with FIs, changes in client habits have the most disruptive and promising impact on M-Payments demand. Customers are looking for rapid, easy-to-use, and accessible solutions to meet their financial needs because of their use of M-Payments. Customers now have ubiquitous access to financial information, thanks to the widespread adoption of mobile devices (and digital financial services), which provides functionality previously only available to professional financial advisors. Customers' loyalty to their primary bank is being eroded, and they are favouring relationships with various financial service providers (Rigby and Bilodeau, 2007). As EBA (2017) points out, this component accelerates financial services providers' attention to clients and flexibility, which have become important factors for customers when selecting suppliers.

The regular attendance of FinTech and BigTech, especially for payment services, seems to be diverting part of the consumer level of trust from banks to new players. This is not only testified by the frequency of use of the new players' services but also by the ease with which they leave access to their own (payments) data. A recent survey on US digital payments (Bansal et al., 2018) demonstrates how consumers have become more and more confident in nonbank-branded models for their financial transactions. The latter is due to regulators who have embraced further lowering the barrier to entry in the market through so-called open banking; this is the case, for example, with the EU's PSD2 initiative, which allows for the enhancement of APIs and software development kits (SDKs) to create an interface with banks. This circumstance removes one of the most significant barriers to new players acquiring customers, perhaps resulting in infeasible payment options for the user. These regulatory changes are motivated by the idea that a client should have open access to all their account information from different institutions in one place, independent of who their financial service provider is.

Given the previous, the relationship between customers and banks looks to be fading; users' confidence in technologies, mainly through M-Payments services, has begun to erode trust, one of the financial system's pillars (Dhar and Stein, 2017; Lee and Shin, 2018). The more banks are unaware of this pattern, the more ground they lose in the race.

4. Why Are M-Payment Platforms So Attractive?

Non-financial companies (NFCs) and non-bank financial corporations have entered the payments system in recent years. This is because newcomers have a competitive advantage over banks, which stems from the ability to pay higher interest rates on their accounts, allowing them to compensate for the difficulties of gaining benefits from fractional reserve and maturities transformation; activities that banks provide. This is feasible due to three factors:

- Regulatory standards are less strict. New participants are not bound by the same regulatory restrictions as banking intermediaries, allowing them to

operate in the M-Payments market. Imagine the MNOs, who provide a payment service through Direct Carrier Billing (albeit a small amount);
- use of more performing technologies. NFCs may now offer payment services like those provided by banks at a cheaper cost because of the deployment of more performant technology. When new firms can enter the market and leverage their finest technology, they gain a huge advantage in the short term. The difference in responsiveness in the adoption of new technologies is that banks must carry considerable legacy expenses that affect the shift to new technologies;
- economies of scope other than banks.

Newcomers can achieve economies of scope between payment services and other commercial activities that banks cannot exploit. As reported above, the economy of scope would express its potential only if both sides of the market reached a sufficiently large pool of players. Cross-border differences in consumer credit and other traditional banking services are the primary cause for BigTech to start acting as payment providers. Crucial in these areas is the management of data targeted at analysing the credit risk of their clients similar – or potentially better – than banks.

Another possibility to make the most of economies of scope is related to cross-network externalities and interlinked pricing strategies. Even if lending activities are subject to regulatory restrictions, these operators can do it anyway, inserting in the group NFCs or making agreements with other financial operators.

The gradual development of so-called Payment-as-a-service BMs has attracted several participants who make the most of the platform connection. Payment platforms are increasingly evolving into complicated systems that respond to the demands of their customers, providing possibilities that go well beyond faster payments and more convenient services. The platform providers can play different roles, such as:

- provider of a cloud-native platform that allows users to get access to data via straightforward APIs for developers gradually;
- supplier of modular service offerings, allowing customers to pick and choose the goods and services they want at any moment;
- delivery channel for other financial products offered by a distinct player;
- data collector who converts data into information;
- provider of information processing services (i.e., credit scoring).

Platform-based BMs result in new operators such as "platform integrators", which are third parties whose payments are the "ram's head" for an integrated offer of products/services tailored to the demands of specific consumers or segments. They increase the efficiency of interactions between platforms and providers in the ecosystem. The challenge for both old and new actors is to figure out how to earn profits from the reinvention of the financial intermediation model.

5. Concluding Remarks: From M-Payment Platform to M-Financial Store?

The M-Payments sector designs a range of BMs in response to changing demographics and consumer behaviour, increasingly preferring automated services over a typical bank-customer human contact (Lee and Shin, 2018). As more people trust technology, they might use it to create more accessible, low-cost digital Apps to create and deliver all financial services. The rise in trust in non-bank M-financial Apps has facilitated the growth of an alternative financial system based on "automatic, machine-based trust" to meet major financial needs such as investment (i.e., online trading Apps), funding (i.e., crowdfunding platforms), and so on.

M-Payments Apps have undoubtedly operated as catalysts, acting as a data distributor that can help offer various financial goods and services and a gateway for FinTech and NFCs to join and colonize the financial system. Many banking products, such as savings accounts or loans, are information-based commodities that can be accessed from any device and purchased from any financial service provider.

FinTech is based on the breakdown of production processes resulting in specialized products being offered via digital platforms (direct financial circuits) and other technological solutions. The entry of operators outside the financial system and new financial operators causes reflection on the processes underlying the supply of financial services. This indicates that banks' services may be fragmented into various commercial activities that FinTech organizations can more easily perform and disseminate via a digital platform (mobile-based). The supply of technology-based financial services has grown more modular and commoditized as banks increasingly rely on third-party service providers for operational assistance (BCBS, 2018).

In this context, it's not unexpected that the banking discussion has shifted to whether banks will continue to focus on direct connections with customers or delegate that responsibility to others and merely provide the pipelines to build on. How may M-payments assist banks in this phase of financial system transformation? Two significant options have become available to banks, in our opinion. The first is the ability to get the most out of the M-Payments system by internalizing income that has been lost in previous years; the second is the ability to utilize the M-Payments platform as a springboard to engage in financial system reformation actively.

According to the first strategic choice, banks can offer their customers faster and cheaper transactions by leveraging the higher level of efficiency provided by M-Payments: digital payments, for example, have lower administrative and security costs, as well as no transportation costs, providing significant benefits. Furthermore, because digital money involves interactions rather than just transactions, banks may be able to exploit it as a source of information. From this perspective, it is meant to draw attention to a potential strategic route for banks that strengthens the proactive involvement of users/customers/prosumers while utilizing tremendous scale advantages based on a solid balance sheet and access to massive amounts of data.

The transposition of platform-based strategies from social media networks to the banking sector is probably the most relevant point of discontinuity: it's a matter of enhancing all the contents of the relationships that, through the (payment) platform, the customer creates by interacting with the platform and its stakeholders.

Banks would thus serve as an appealing platform for producers of financial and NFCs, which would be distributed through an "M-Financial Store".

References

Alt, R., Beck, R., & Smits, M. T. (2018). FinTech and the transformation of the financial industry. *Electronic markets*, *28*(3), 235–243.

Bansal, S., Bruno, P., Denecker, O., Goparaju, M., & Niederkorn, M. (2018). Global payments 2018: A dynamic industry continues to break new ground. *Global Banking McKinsey*, pp. 1–27.

Basel Committee on Banking Supervision – BCBS (2017), "Sound practices: implications of fintech developments for banks and bank supervisors", available at: www.bis.org/bcbs/publ/d415.pdf.

Dhar, V., & Stein, R. M. (2017). FinTech platforms and strategy. *Communications of the ACM*, *60*(10), 32–35.

EBA (2017). Discussion paper on the EBA's approach to financial technology (FinTech). EBA/DP/2017/02.

ECB (2010). The payment system, payments, securities and derivatives, and the role of the eurosystem, Francoforte.

Evans DS, Hagiu A, Schmalensee R. 2006. Invisible Engines: How Software Platforms Drive Innovation and Transform Industries. MIT Press: Cambridge, MA.

Financial Stability Board - FSB (2017). Financial Stability Implications from FinTech Supervisory and Regulatory Issues that Merit Authorities' Attention, Retrieved from: https://www.fsb.org/wp-content/uploads/R270617.pdf.

Gnyawali, D. R., & Park, B. J. R. (2011). Co-opetition between giants: Collaboration with competitors for technological innovation. *Research Policy*, *40*(5), 650–663.

Kazan, E., Tan, C. W., Lim, E. T., Sørensen, C., & Damsgaard, J. (2018). Disentangling digital platform competition: The case of UK mobile payment platforms. *Journal of Management Information Systems*, *35*(1), 180–219.

Korovkin, V., Plaksenkov, E., & Smirnova, O. (2015). Digital platforms and the ecosystems of financial inclusion. The Russian experience. *The Russian Experience (January 18, 2018). The Moscow School of Management SKOLKOVO.*

Lee, I., & Shin, Y. J. (2018). Fintech: Ecosystem, business models, investment decisions, and challenges. *Business horizons*, *61*(1), 35–46.

Mooer, J. F. (1996). *The death of competition: Leadership and strategy in the age of business ecosystem*. NewYork, NY: Harper Business.

Moore, J. F. (1993). Predators and prey: A new ecology of competition. *Harvard Business Review*, *71*(3), 75–86.

Panetta I. C., & Leo, S. (2017). *Mobile payment industry: Caratteristiche operative e modelli di business*. F. Angeli, Milan.

Pousttchi, K., & Dehnert, M. (2018). Exploring the digitalization impact on consumer decision-making in retail banking. *Electronic Markets*, *28*(3), 265–286.

Puschmann, T. (2017). Fintech. *Business & Information Systems Engineering*, *59*(1), 69–76.

Puschmann, T., & Alt, R. (2016). Sharing economy. *Business & Information Systems Engineering*, *58*(1), 93–99.

Rigby, D., & Bilodeau, B. (2007). Bain's global 2007 management tools and trends survey. *Strategy & Leadership*, *35*(5), 9–16.

Ringe, W. G., & Ruof, C. (2019). Keeping up with innovation: Designing a European sandbox for Fintech. CEPS ECMI Commentary no 58| January 2019.

Shapiro, C., & Varian, H. R. (1998). Versioning: The smart way to. *Harvard Business Review*, *107*(6), 107.

Shim, Y., & Shin, D. H. (2016). Analyzing China's fintech industry from the perspective of actor–network theory. *Telecommunications Policy*, *40*(2–3), 168–181.

Singh, B. P., Grover, P., & Kar, A. K. (2017). Quality in Mobile Payment Service in India. In: Digital Nations – Smart Cities, Innovation, and Sustainability.

I3E 2017. Lecture Notes in Computer Science, vol. 10595. Springer, Cham. https://doi.org/10.1007/978-3-319-68557-1_17

Venkatraman, N. (1994). IT-enabled business transformation: From automation to business scope redefinition. *Sloan Management Review*, *35*, 73–73.

Zetsche, D. A., Buckley, R. P., Arner, D. W., & Barberis, J. N. (2017). From FinTech to TechFin: The regulatory challenges of data-driven finance. *NYUJL & Bus.*, *14*, 393.

Patrycja Chodnicka-Jaworska

European Sanctions Impact on the Energy Sector Stock Prices: The Ukrainian War Effect

1. Introduction

The Ukrainian War, the first one after the World War II, has begun on February 24, 2022. This situation created the panic on the stock exchanges during the initial days. The most reacted were stock prices from countries, which are in the neighborhood of Russia and Ukraine. As a result, the European Commission introduced the five packages of sanctions in April 2022. These have been threatened as one of the most significant sanctions. Three of them were introduced before the Ukrainian War. On January 13, 2022 the European Union renewed economic sanctions, when the Council prolong the restrictive measures currently targeting specific economic sectors of the Russian Federation by six months, that was an effect of the do not obey the Minsk agreements. On February 21, 2022, personal sanctions were put on five people. The first from the five package relies on the extend the personal sanctions on the 351 members of the Russian State Duma and an additional 27 individuals, restrictions on economic relations with the non-government controlled areas of Donetsk and Luhansk oblasts and restrictions relies on the Russia's access the EU's capital and financial markets and services. The first package was implemented on February 23, 2022. On February 24, 2022 EU leaders agreed on further sanctions against Russia. On February 25, 2022 the second package of sanctions that relies on freezing assets of the main members of the Russian government was implemented. The Council also agreed on economic sanctions that cover the finance, energy, transport and technology sectors, as well as visa policy. On February 28, 2022 the European Union presented the third package of sanctions, that included a prohibition on transactions with the Russian Central Bank, a ban on the overflight of the European Union airspace and on access to EU airports, and an extension to the individual sanctions on the new group of people. The Ukrainian army received 500 million Euro support for finance equipment. On March 2, 2022 the European Union excluded seven Russian banks from SWIFT. The following were also prohibited: investments to future projects co-financed by the Russian Direct Investment Fund; turnover Euro banknotes to Russians. On March 3, 2022 asset freezes directed against individuals were extended that was identified as responsible for the misappropriation of Ukrainian state funds or for the abuse of office causing a loss to Ukrainian public funds. On March 9, 2022 the European Union agreed new measures targeting Belarus and Russia relies on: restrict the provision of specialized financial messaging services (SWIFT) to three Belarusian banks, prohibit transactions with the Central Bank of Belarus, prohibit the listing and provision of services in relation to shares of Belarusian state-owned entities on EU trading venues, significantly limit the financial inflows from Belarus to the European Union, prohibit the provision of euro-denominated banknotes to Belarus. The European Union imposes restrictive measures on an additional 160 individuals. On March 10, 2022 the European Union extended sanctions over territorial integrity for a further six months that relies on the travel restrictions, the freezing of assets, and a ban on making funds or other economic resources available to the listed persons and entities. On the March 15, the European Union presented the fourth package of sanctions that relies on the prohibition of all transactions with certain state-owned enterprises, the provision of credit rating services to any Russian person or entity, new investments in the Russian energy sector, trade restrictions for iron, steel and luxury goods, and sanctions on individuals and entities. The fifth package has been implemented on April 8, 2022. It includes ban on imports of coal and other solid fossil fuels from Russia, all Russian vessels from accessing EU ports, road transport operators from entering the EU, ban on imports of other goods such as wood, cement, seafood and liquor, export of jet fuel and other goods to Russia, deposits to crypto-wallets, full transaction with key Russian banks.

These sanctions have had an influence on the abnormal rates of return on stock prices. During the publication an information about sanctions in press are presented for opinions about the situation on the coal and oil and gas market.

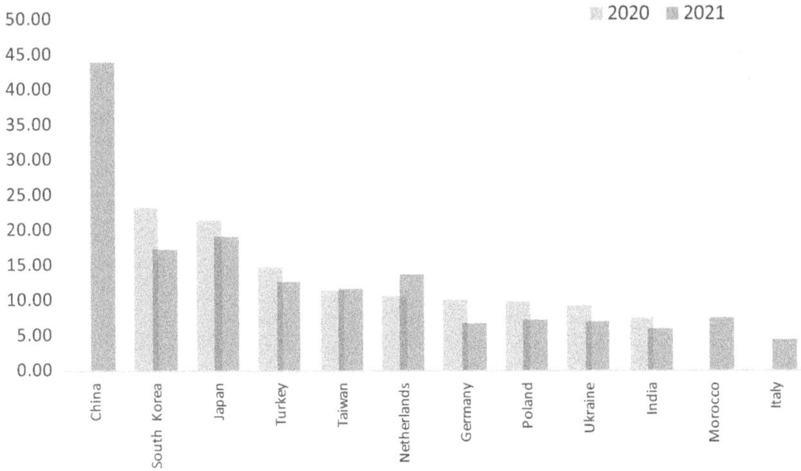

Fig. 1: Volume of coal exports from Russia in 2020 and 2021 in million metric tons
Source: Refinitiv Eikon Database

Fig. 1 presents the volume of coal exports from Russia in 2020 and 2021 to other countries. The main importers are China, South Korea, Japan and Türkiye. In most cases the volume of import from Russia is lower, except Netherlands. Fig. 2 presents the volume of metallurgical coal exports from Russia in 2021 in million metric tons. The main importers belong to China, Ukraine, South Korea, Japan and Vietnam.

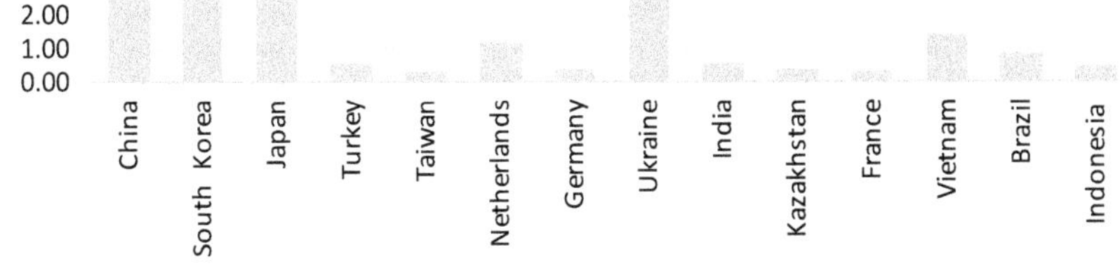

Fig. 2: Volume of metallurgical coal exports from Russia in 2021 in million metric tons
Source: Refinitiv Eikon Database

Fig. 3 presents the dependence on the Russian oil. The main countries that are addicted to Russian oil belong to Lithuania, Finland, Slovakia, Poland, Hungary, Estonia, Germany and Greece. It shows which countries are especially sensitive on the potential sanctions on the prohibition on import from Russia.

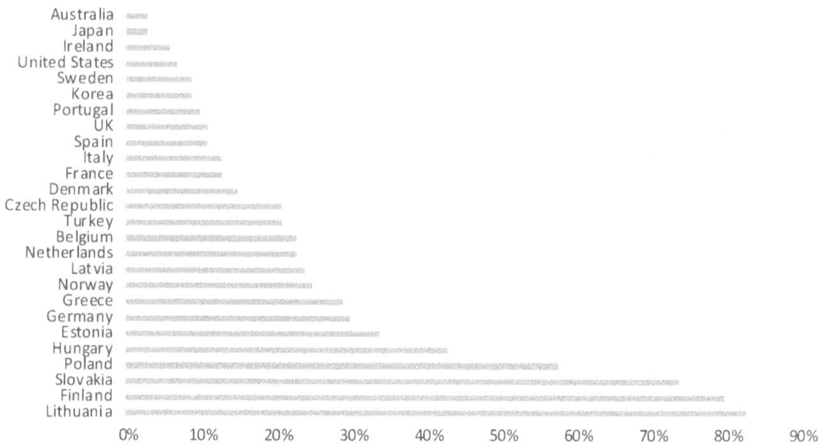

Fig. 3: Dependence on the Russian oil (share of total imports from Russia)
Source: Refinitiv Eikon Database

The crude oil is imported especially by China, Netherlands, South Korea, Italy, Poland and Türkiye (Fig. 4). The fuel oil is imported from Russia especially by USA, Netherlands, Greece, Denmark, Malta and Spain. The Russian diesel is bought by France, UK, Germany, Poland, Belgium and Netherlands. It shows that China is buying crude oil; on the other hand, Singapore, Portugal, UAE, Malta and Denmark import only fuel oil, whereas Belgium, for example, is buying diesel.

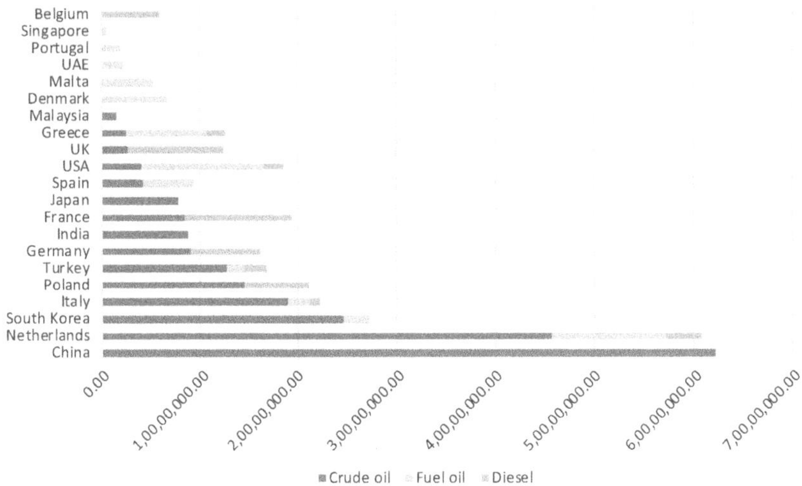

Fig. 4: Russian crude oil, fuel oil and diesel by loan region
Source: Refinitiv Eikon Database

The natural gas according to region import volume from Russia is presented in Fig. 5. Main importers are Japan, China, France, South Korea, Spain and UK.

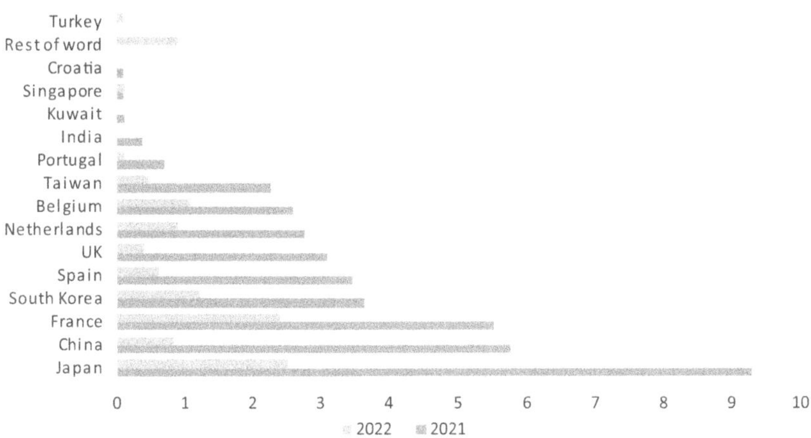

Fig. 5: Natural gas in region import volume from Russia
Source: Refinitiv Eikon Database

The presented data suggest the direction of the influence of the sanctions on the stock prices. In previous literature sanctions and their impact on the financial market was varied, some of them threaten sanctions as an ineffective tool (Galtung, 1967; Lindsay, 1986), but others suggested that most of them brought the intended effect (Hufbauer et al., 1990; Weber & Schneider 2022). Weber and Schneider (2022) compared sanctions imposed by UE, UN and USA, and suggested that the most effective were sanctions given by EU and UN. The impact on the quality and sanctions' effectiveness relates to the relationship between countries that impose sanctions and target it. This situation is also connected with economic and political relationship (Jing et al., 2003; Smeets, 2018).

The analyses presented by Schmıdbauer et al. (2016) suggest that sanctions reduced the significance of the Russian market but increased its significance as a propagator of volatility shocks in international financial markets. Stone (2017) also confirmed the increasing volatility on the Russian financial market and reduction of the rates of return as an effect of sanctions.

Some of studies tested the impact of sanctions on the oil prices. Tyll et al. (2018) proved that sanctions have rendered the exchange rate of the ruble firmly bound to oil price changes. Previous sanctions coincided with a considerable fall in the price of oil in the international energy market and the consequent decrease in income from fuel exports. Hence, studies assessing the sanctions' impact have considered decline in oil prices an essential factor behind the economic deterioration (Dreger et al. 2015; Tyll et al. 2018). Sultonov (2021) shows that the sanctions have a significant positive short-term impact on exchange rate returns. He suggested that the economic sanctions have a significant negative long-term impact on the returns and variance of the exchange rate and a significant positive long-term impact on the returns of the stock price index. Financial sanctions have a positive/negative long-term impact on the returns of the exchange rate/stock price index and a positive long-term impact on the variance of the exchange rate and the stock price index. Corporate sanctions have a positive long-term impact on exchange rate returns. Ahn and Ludema (2020) found that US and EU "smart sanctions" on specific Russian companies, and their shareholders, managers and directors, have had substantial negative effects on those firms' performance. The analysis prepared on the French market by Kirat and Rezaee (2019) shows that the market reacts negatively when a sanction is announced in the press. After the financial crisis of 2008, a plethora of news on financial wrongdoings has desensitized markets to announcements of sanctions against large companies. Reputational losses are nearly nine times the size of fines, and are associated with misconduct harming customers or investors, but not third parties.

Draca et al. (2019) found that the stock returns of firms owned by targeted political elites respond especially sharply to such news, though other listed firms unconnected to these elites also benefit from progress towards sanctions relief. These results not only indicate the "bluntness" of sanctions on Iran but also provide evidence of their effectiveness in generating economic incentives for elite policymakers to negotiate a deal for sanctions relief.

The theoretical impact of sanctions on the stock market has been presented by Webb (2020).

Sanctions and sanctions threats create market uncertainty that is reflected in stock price volatility for firms with commercial interests in targeted states. Comparisons are made using stock price data for firms within sectors at the same point in time, within sectors over time and across sectors over time. The stock prices for firms with commercial interests in targeted states are more volatile than stock prices for comparable firms without commercial interests in targeted states. These spells of uncertainty not only reflect the costs of sanctions and sanctions threats for firms caused by interruptions in commercial activities but also represent important costs for firms in-and-of themselves.

The presented literature and practical knowledge create the need to analyze the impact of the sanctions implemented by EU as a result of the beginning the Ukrainian War event on the abnormal rates of return on the stock prices of companies from the energy sector. This topic has not been tested on the literature. It has been put on the following hypothesis: the EU sanctions cause the negative abnormal rates return on the stock prices of companies from the energy sector at the moment of their implementation by taking into consideration the type of the subsector.

2. Methodology

The analysis was prepared by using the panel data event study methodology. Data have been collected from the Refinitiv Eikon Database. To the analysis, daily data of the companies from the energy sector listed on the stock exchanges from 1 November 2021 to 20 April 2022 have been used. The energy sector has been divided into four subsectors: oil and gas, coal, uranium and the renewable energy. Next, the sample has been divided into two groups: countries which are dependent on the oil and gas import from Russia and those that are free of the mentioned problem. Events are connected with the implementation of sanctions by EU. To the analysis the following event data have been used:

- 02/24/2022 – EU leaders agree on further sanctions against Russia
- 02/25/2022 – Second package of sanctions

- 02/28/2022 – Third package of sanctions – first stage
- 03/02/2022 – Third package of sanctions – second stage
- 03/03/2022 – EU prolongs restrictive measure
- 03/09/2022 – Restrictive measures on individuals and new measures targeting Belarus and Russia
- 03/10/2022 – Extended sanctions over territorial integrity
- 03/15/2022 – Fourth package of sanctions
- 04/08/2022 – Fifth package of sanctions

The analysis has been made for the event window, that is, the moment of publication of sanctions plus one day after. The research has not been prepared for the pre-event window and post-event window because of the high frequency of the events. To the presented model logarithmized daily rates of return on the stock prices have been used. As a basic model the market model described by the following equation was used:

$$R_{i,t} = \alpha_{i,t} + \beta_{i,t} RM_{i,t} + \varepsilon_{i,t}$$

where $R_{i,t}$ are the logarithmized rates of return on the stock prices of the company i in period$t$; $R_{i,t}$ are the logarithmized rates of return on the benchmark for the company i in period t.

$$\hat{R}_{i,t} = \bar{R}_{i,t}$$

$$\hat{\alpha}_{i,t} = \frac{1}{T-1}\left(\sum_{t=1}^{T-1} R_{i,t} - \hat{\beta}_{i,t}\sum_{t=1}^{T-1} RM_{i,t}\right)$$

$$\hat{\beta}_{i,t} = \frac{\sum_{t=1}^{T-1}\left(R_{i,t} - \bar{R}_{i,t}\right)\left(RM_{i,t} - \overline{RM}_{i,t}\right)}{\sum_{t=1}^{T-1}\left(R_{i,t} - \bar{R}_{i,t}\right)\left(RM_{i,t} - \overline{RM}_{i,t}\right)}$$

In the next step the abnormal stock rates of return on the stock prices were defined as a difference between the real and the forecast value (limited by the information set in the estimating window Ω_{EW}).

$$AR_{i,t} = R_{i,t} - E\left(R_{i,t} | \Omega_{EW}\right)$$

The average abnormal rates of return during *t* period is estimated according to:

$$\overline{AR_{i,t}} = \frac{\sum_{t=1}^{N} AR_{i,t}}{N}$$

where *N* is the size of the research sample. The standard deviation $\hat{\sigma}_{AR}$ is estimated by:

$$\hat{\sigma}_{AR} = \sqrt{\frac{1}{N-1}\sum_{t=1}^{N}\left(\overline{AR_{i,t}} - \overline{\overline{AR_{i,t}}}\right)}$$

Next, in the pre-event window, event window and post-event window the hypothesis was tested. To verify the hypothesis the t-Student test has been used.

$$t_{STAT} = \frac{\frac{1}{N}\sum_{t=1}^{N} AR_{i,t}}{\breve{\sigma}_{AR}}$$

The use of a more advanced model, taking into account the heterogeneity of the variance of the random component and the autocorrelation, would require a longer estimation window.

3. Findings

Results of the impact of the neighborhood on the abnormal rates of return on the stock prices of companies from the energy subsectors have been presented in Tab. 1. The European Union sanctions have got a significant negative impact on the abnormal rates of return on the stock prices for the whole period of sanctions, in comparison to the local benchmark index. The positive reaction has been noticed only for the uranium subsector. The companies form coal subsector form the direct neighborhood of military conflict react negatively on the sanctions, that have been announced on as a result of beginning of war (February, 24), second package of sanctions and fourth package of sanctions (March, 15) and positive on the third package of sanctions. The individual restrictive measures were insignificant. The stronger reaction has been noticed on the second package of sanctions in the case of US and Japan. It was connected with own sanctions prepared by these countries. The weaker effect has been observed in the case of fourth package of sanctions.

The abnormal rates of return has been noticed in the oil and gas subsector, in the case of the direct neighborhood of war. As an effect of the beginning of war and the second package of sanctions announcement the higher positive abnormal rates of return have been observed in comparison to the local benchmark index. Because on the beginning of March in press and local governments was published information on the potential sanctions on oil and gas import form Russia, the stock prices react negative to the benchmark. During the same time stock prices of renewable energy's entities that are not in the neighborhood of war react positive. In the case of US and Japan the significant negative abnormal rates of return are observed during the period of the fourth sanctions announcement.

In the case of US and Japan companies from the renewable energy sector's stock prices react strongly negative on the third and fourth package of sanctions. The same reaction has been observed for companies from the direct neighborhood of military conflict as an effect of the fourth package of sanctions announcement.

The companies from the uranium sector that are not from neighborhood of war react positive on these sanctions, except the moment when there was an attack on the Zaporozhe power plant. This situation confirms the reaction of the American and Japanese companies.

The received results suggest few findings. First, it shows that some of the stock prices of the group of the entities react stronger than the local benchmark. The presented situation is strictly connected with the direct neighborhood of the military conflict and the type of the subsector. The relationship between countries that are the sides of the military conflict and countries in the neighborhood confirms opinion presented by Weber and Schneider (2022), the same like the economic and political relationship (see Jing et al., 2003; Smeets, 2018). On the significance of sanctions have got influence also news published in press, the type of information presented by local governments, the frequency of meetings by the heads of states and representatives of the main organizations. Not without of the significance is the impact of situation in Russia and Ukraine, which example is the attack and fire in the Zaporozhe power plant or taking the exclusion zone and power plant in Chernobyl.

The analysis of the impact on the Russia stock market suggest that sanctions have not got the significant impact on the stock prices. The mentioned situation is consistent with the Galtung (1967) and Lindsay (1986) studies. It will be truth if the Russian stock exchange will be open. We should remember that the mentioned stock exchange generated very high decreases as an effect of the beginning of war and strong outflow of the international capital, that caused the closing of the stock exchange. The reduction of the volatility will not bring such a valuable finding. The effect of them can be analyzed in longer future, when we could assess if they brought the intended effect like in Hufbauer et al. (1990), Weber and Schneider (2022) and Stone (2017) studies. Sanctions reduced the significance of the Russian market but increased its significance as a propagator of volatility shocks in international financial markets, that confirm the opinion presented by Schmıdbauer et al. (2016).

The impact of European sanctions has been noticed only in the case of oil and gas subsector during the beginning of war and the publication of the information about the second package of sanctions. It can be connected with few reasons. First, the presented study has been prepared on the market model taking into consideration the relationship to benchmark. As a result, the stock prices of the mentioned companies do not react different than index. Next is the long-term contracts and finding a new market to selling the natural sources.

The presented results suggest that we can observe some winners of this situation. One of them is the coal subsector in countries that are in the direct neighborhood of war. This region is still based on coal, as a source of the energy, especially Poland. The next sector is the renewable energy in countries that are not in the neighborhood of the military conflict. Also, the uranium subsector generated abnormal rates of return, but this sector is very sensitive on the nuclear war, or the catastrophe risk connected with the military attack on the power plant. The negative abnormal rates of return are noticed for the oil and gas subsector. According to Tyll et al. (2018) the mentioned group of entities are also connected with the oil prices changes. Previous sanctions coincided with a considerable fall in the price of oil in the international energy market and the consequent decrease in income from fuel exports.

The significance of sanctions will be observed in the long period. Assessing them in a short period bring the information about sensitiveness in comparison to the local benchmarks and assess the impact of the behavioral finance, but they do not give the final information about their effectiveness.

Tab. 1: Impact of neighborhood on the abnormal rates of return on the stock prices of companies from the energy subsectors

	all	**Coal**				**oil&gas**				**renewable energy**			**uranium**	
	0	**0**	**1**	**2**	**3**	**0**	**1**	**2**	**3**	**0**	**1**	**2**	**0**	**2**
Total														
_cons	**-4.259***	-0,0707	-0,00132	0,0128	-0,0045	-0,546	0,0929	-21,92	-0,00154	0,0719	-0,103	-0,246	**0.0154****	0,00373
t-student	**(-2.05)**	(-1.90)	(-0.40)	-1,56	(-1.16)	(-1.22)	-0,82	(-1.95)	(-1.13)	-0,62	(-1.69)	(-1.65)	**-3,01**	-0,27
N	**15102**	894	306	108	36	5562	882	2790	378	888	342	738	**396**	36
24.02-26.02														
_cons	-6,819	-0,153	**-0.0290*****	-0,0201	-0,00567	-0,0235	**0.0141***	-36,66	**-0.0129***	**0.0119***	-0,047	-0,601	**0.0405*****	0,0314
t-student	(-1.01)	(-0.98)	**(-6.36)**	(-1.56)	(-0.25)	(-1.21)	**-2,6**	(-1.01)	**(-2.05)**	**-2,14**	(-0.86)	(-1.70)	**-4,01**	-2,09
N	2517	149	**51**	18	6	927	**147**	465	**63**	**148**	57	123	**66**	6
28.02-1.03														
_cons	-6,819	0,00336	**0.0318****	**0.0457***	-0,0025	-0,0129	-0,00113	-25,16	-0,000543	0,698	-0,183	-0,0391	**0.105*****	**0.129***
t-student	(-1.01)	-0,21	**-3,36**	**-2,86**	(-1.55)	(-0.83)	(-0.30)	(-1.01)	(-1.27)	-1,04	(-0.86)	(-0.39)	**-7,62**	**-2,96**
N	2517	149	**51**	**18**	6	927	147	465	63	148	57	123	**66**	**6**
03.03-4.03														
_cons	-6,819	-0,0512	**0.0299*****	0,0353	-0,00159	-0,0132	0,695	-27,24	-0,0018	0,00331	0,0259	**-0.325***	**-0.0631*****	**-0.0276***
t-student	(-1.01)	(-0.60)	**-4,92**	-1,46	(-0.80)	(-0.73)	-1,03	(-0.99)	(-0.95)	-0,35	-1,07	**(-2.11)**	**(-8.13)**	**(-2.86)**
N	2517	149	**51**	18	6	927	147	465	63	148	57	**123**	**66**	**6**
09.03-11.03														
_cons	-6,819	-0,126	-0,000967	-0,0201	-0,0067	0,0525	**-0.0406*****	-42	0,000745	**0.0160***	-0,282	**-0.602***	**0.0525*****	-0,0328
t-student	(-1.01)	(-1.22)	(-0.17)	(-1.56)	(-1.64)	-0,48	**(-6.24)**	(-0.98)	-0,7	**-2,13**	(-1.01)	**(-2.24)**	**-3,9**	(-1.40)
N	2517	149	51	18	6	927	**147**	465	63	**148**	57	**123**	**66**	6
15.03-16.03														
_cons	-6,819	-0,1	**-0.0446*****	**-0.0261***	-0,00503	-2,642	**-0.0279*****	-0,216	0,000577	-0,0582	-0,112	**-0.474***	**0.0398*****	-0,0608
t-student	(-1.01)	(-1.19)	**(-5.52)**	**(-2.45)**	(-1.76)	(-1.01)	**(-5.35)**	(-1.70)	-0,92	(-1.15)	(-1.11)	**(-2.02)**	**(5.11)**	(-2.30)
N	2517	149	**51**	**18**	6	927	**147**	465	63	148	57	**123**	**66**	6

	all	Coal				oil&gas				renewable energy			uranium	
08.04-09.04														
_cons	-6,819	0,00283	0,00499	0,0167	-0,00549	-0,636	-0,0822	**-0.251****	0,00462	-0,24	**-0.0229****	0,563	-0,00285	-0,0169
t-student	(-1.01)	-0,63	-0,61	-1,18	(-0.58)	(-1.06)	(-1.04)	**(-3.20)**	-1,01	(-1.39)	**(-3.46)**	-0,78	(-0.38)	(-1.83)
N	2517	149	51	18	6	927	147	**465**	63	148	**57**	123	66	6

Legend: 0- countries that are not in the Russia and Ukraine neighborhoods; 1 - countries in the direct Russia and Ukraine neighborhoods, i.e. Norway, Finland, Estonia, Latvia, Ukraine, Georgia, Azerbaijan, Kazakhstan, China, Mongolia, Lithuania, Poland, Slovakia, Hungary, Romania, Moldova; 2 - USA and Japan; 3 - Russia and Ukraine.

Source: Own elaborations.

4. Conclusions

The aim of this chapter is to analyze the impact of the sanctions implemented by EU as a result of the beginning the Ukrainian War event on the abnormal rates of return on the stock prices of companies from the energy sector. The hypothesis has been proposed as follows: the EU sanctions cause the negative abnormal rates return on the stock prices of companies from the energy sector during the moment of their implementation by taking into consideration the type of the subsector. The presented hypothesis has been partially fulfilled. The significance and strength of the reaction of the stock prices is strictly connected with the direct neighborhood of the described military conflict. Something that was interesting is that the companies from Russia and Ukraine do not react on European sanctions, except the oils and gas subsector during the beginning of war and the publication of the information about the second package of sanctions. It can be connected with few reasons. First, the presented study has been prepared on the market model with taking into consideration the relationship to benchmark. As a result, the stock prices of the mentioned companies do not react different than index. Next is the long-term contracts and finding a new market to selling the natural sources. The Russian stock exchange was partially closed that has got the impact on the received findings. Mostly, the lower rates of return on the stock prices than local benchmark are noticed in the case of the companies that are in the direct neighborhood of the military conflict. The mentioned situations suggest that sanctions can be significant for countries that impose them. On the significance of sanctions have got influence also news published in press, the type of information presented by local governments, the frequency of meetings by the heads of states and representatives of the main organizations. Not without of the significance is the impact of situation in Russia and Ukraine, which example is the attack and fire in the Zaporozhe power plant or taking the exclusion zone and power plant in Chernobyl.

The received findings can be useful for regulatory and governments because they show which of the subsectors are the most sensitive on presented group of sanctions. They also present the effect of sanctions on the countries which imposed them. This study can be also used by the investors, because it given answer on the question which type of the energy subsector and when generate the higher abnormal rates of return on the stock prices than local benchmark. it is useful for building the portfolio. They can show which companies can generate abnormal rates of return as an effect of closing sanctions.

The presented study has also got some limitations. In future it should be rebuilt on the other sanctions. The interesting results will also give the comparison of the rates of return on the stock prices effect between particular sectors. It can be also extended on the other sanctions presented by, for example, the United States of America. The useful information will also get the analysis on the average to verify the impact of the mentioned sanctions on generating the abnormal rates of return to average value of them before the war.

References

Ahn, D. P., & Ludema, R. D. (2020). The sword and the shield: The economics of targeted sanctions. *European Economic Review*, 130.

Draca, M., Garred, J., Stickland, L., & Warrinnier, N. (2019). *On Target? The Incidence of Sanctions Across Listed Firms in Iran*. LICOS Discussion Paper Series Discussion Paper 413/2019.

Dreger, C., Fidrmuc, J., Kholodilin, K., & Ulbricht, D. (2015). *The Ruble between the Hammer and the Anvil: Oil Prices and Economic Sanctions*. Discussion Papers 1488. Berlin: DIW Berlin, German Institute for Economic Research.

Galtung, J. (1967). On the effects of international economic sanctions, with examples from the case of Rhodesia. *World Politics, 19*, 378–416.

Hufbauer, G., Schott, J., & Elliott, K. (1990). *Economic Sanctions Reconsidered: History and Current Policy*, 2nd ed. Washington: Institute for International Economics.

Jing, C., Kaempfer, W., & Lowenberg, A. (2003). Instrument choice and the effectiveness of international sanctions: A simultaneous equations approach. *Journal of Peace Research*, *40*, 519–35.

Kirat, T., & Rezaee, A. (2019). How stock markets react to regulatory sanctions? Evidence from France. *Applied Economics, 51*(60), 6558–6566.

Lindsay, J. (1986). Trade sanctions as policy instruments: A re-examination. *International Studies Quarterly, 30*, 153–73.

Schmıdbauer, H., Rösch, A., Uluceviz, E., & Erkol, N. (2016). The Russian stock market during the Ukrainian crisis: A network perspective. *Journal of Economics and Finance*, *66*, 478–509.

Smeets, M. (2018). *Can Economic Sanctions Be Effective? Staff Working Paper ERSD-2018-03*, Economic Research and Statistics Division. Geneva: World Trade Organization.

Stone, M. (2017). *The Response of Russian Security Prices to Economic Sanctions: Policy Effectiveness and Transmission*. Working Paper February 2017; Washington: Office of the Chief Economist, U.S. Department of State.

Sultonov, M. (2021). The impact of international sanctions on Russian financial markets. *Economies*, *8*(4), 107.

Tyll, L., Pernica, K., & Arltová, M. (2018). The impact of economic sanctions on Russian economy and the RUB/USD exchange rate. *Journal of International Studies, 11*, 21–33.

Webb, C. (2020). Re-examining the costs of sanctions and sanctions threats using stock market data. *International Interactions, 46*, 749–777.

Weber, P., & Schneider, G. (2022). Post-cold war sanctioning by the EU, the UN, and the US: Introducing the EUSANCT dataset. *Conflict Management and Peace Science*, *39*(1), 97–114.

Margaret Tseng, Anthony D'Andrea

Digital Technology and Social Capital in the Era of Covid-19

1. Introduction

Discussions of social capital created by networks, communities, and associations of people in the United States have largely focused on traditional in-person gatherings for the past two centuries. However, the greater availability of digital technology in the twenty-first century has created a new landscape of digital services and platforms that facilitate online networks of community, while associations that involve in-person gatherings have seen a decline in participation. In addition, the COVID-19 pandemic exacerbated this decline due to social isolation practices. Conventional wisdom posits that these in-person networks of community are critical for social, political, and economic actions that are imperative for the proper functioning of society. This chapter chronicles three case studies examining Peloton, Reddit, and Twitter during the COVID-19 pandemic and illustrates how these digital services and platforms facilitated forms of social capital despite being solely online. As online communities continue to grow, additional research is needed to examine whether online networks can fully replicate the social capital created by in-person networks and also have the profit potential companies and stock holders desire.

2. Association and Social Capital

When the young lawyer, Alexis de Tocqueville, came to the United States in 1831, he found that "Americans of all ages, all conditions, and all minds are constantly joining together in groups" (Tocqueville, 2004). Tocqueville (2004) observed that the right of association in the United States was relied upon daily by Americans, who were members of political, economic, moral, and religious associations that influenced all aspects of social life. People collaborated to create public places like hospitals and schools or to spread a shared idea that was held among others. "In America I came across types of associations which I confess I had no idea existed, and I frequently admired the boundless skill of Americans in setting large numbers of people a common goal and inducing them to strive toward that goal voluntarily," said Tocqueville (2004), noting how associations allowed Americans to solve collective problems and act upon their vast interests.

In 1904, German sociologist and political economist, Max Weber, on his own trip to the United States found that "in the past and up to the present, it has been a characteristic precisely of the specifically American democracy that it did not constitute a formless sandheap of individuals, but rather a buzzing complex of strictly exclusive, yet voluntary associations" (as cited in Kalberg, 1997). These voluntary associations would continue to be defined in the twentieth century. In 1969, sociologists Daniel Bell and Virginia Held described three types of communal systems: civic associations (e.g., the Commerce and Industry Association), fraternal and service organizations (e.g., the Protestant Council, the Catholic Charities, and the Federation of Jewish Philanthropies), and neighborhood organizations (e.g., parent-teachers associations, block associations, tenant associations, local churches, and synagogues) (Bell and Held, 1969).

Although it is clear that associations have been a key aspect of the American tradition, Robert Putnam in *Bowling Alone* chronicled how social capital and engagement in the United States was starting to wane in areas, such as political participation, civic engagement, religious participation, connections in the workplace, informal social connections, altruism, and reciprocity towards the end of the twentieth century. According to Putnam (2000) 53 % of baby boomers in 1989 found that their parents' generation was better "in terms of being a concerned citizen, involved in helping others in the community." In addition, "fully 77 percent said the nation was worse off because of 'less involvement in community activities,'" and in 1992, "three quarters of the U.S. workforce said that 'the breakdown of community' and 'selfishness' were 'serious' or 'extremely serious' problems in America" (Putnam, 2000). In 1999, several surveys found that Americans said, "America's civic life had weakened in recent years, that social and moral values were higher when they were growing up, and that our society was focused more on the individual than the community" (Putnam, 2000).

However, Putnam (2000) emphasized that the decline in community in the United States is not particular to the end of the twentieth century, but has rather ebbed and flowed throughout the nation's history. Moreover, Putnam argued in the concluding pages of *Bowling Alone* that the United States can reverse the decline of social capital by multiple means, but most significantly, through the use of mass media and the Internet, if deployed with the right intention. Putnam (2000) wrote: "If we are to reverse the adverse trends of the last three decades in any fundamental way, the electronic entertainment and telecommunications industry must become a big part of the solution instead of a big part of the problem."

Since *Bowling Alone*, the Internet and digital technology have become home to a vast new array of social networks and digital services compared to the early platforms of the 1990s. Today, information and communication flow through apps, such as Facebook, Instagram, TikTok, Twitter, Twitch, Reddit, Discord, and Snapchat. Instead of sending a letter or making a phone call, it's likely that individuals are sending a message through the social infrastructure of the twenty-first century. In addition to changing how individuals communicate with one another, it has also become the primary way society participates in the economy. The Internet has allowed markets to succeed in ways that could never be possible. A key feature of the Internet is that it allows people to connect with others sharing those same interests, and those connections are not disrupted by physical location. But Putnam (2000) noted: "The tougher question is whether that flow of information itself fosters social capital and genuine community."

The capabilities of the Internet and Big Tech were put to the test at the start of a new decade. On January 29, 2020, the White House established the Coronavirus Task Force, chaired by the U.S. Health and Human Services Secretary, Alex Azar, in response to an increase in 2019-nCoV cases across the world ("COVID-19 Timeline," CDC). A few weeks later on February 11, the World Health Organization (WHO) announced an official name for the disease: COVID-19; and in a month's time, on March 11, the WHO declared the coronavirus disease a pandemic ("COVID-19 Timeline," CDC). At the time of writing, the coronavirus pandemic has persisted for two years since it was first classified as such by the WHO. It has changed all social, political, and economic aspects of society. But perhaps most significantly, society has had to rely on digital services and platforms more than ever before and likely accelerated this trend that was gaining momentum since the early 2010s, with the greater availability of cell phones and computers with advanced computing capabilities. Social isolation practices with the intent of maintaining public health would be expected to have severely diminished social capital, especially in a society where social connections have already been waning. However, digital services and platforms enabled people to connect with one another in ways that at least met their bare needs of connection. In this chapter, we will discuss three examples of digital services and platforms that are replicating the traditional form of associations and facilitating the growth of social capital through contemporary mechanisms: Peloton, Reddit, and Twitter.

3. Peloton Interactive, Inc.

In December of 2019, Peloton Interactive, Inc. stock plummeted by over a billion dollars. The culprit, a cringe-inducing commercial about a husband gifting his wife a Peloton stationary bike for Christmas. Critics deemed the ad "sexist" and "tone-deaf" (Belam and Partridge, 2019). Some even predicted the end of Peloton all together. Fast forward to March 2020 with the start of the pandemic lockdown, Peloton found itself in a particularly advantageous position as gyms closed across the country. With live trainers as well as on-demand videos, Peloton was on the cusp of an exercise revolution. Sales of Peloton bikes and treadmills surged as state governments extended lockdowns. Membership jumped to 3.1 million pushing revenue up 172 % (*Peloton Sales Surge As* Virus Boosts Home Workouts, 2020). Peloton logged its first profitable quarter from the pandemic-induced surge with a profit of $89 million and its stock price jumped from $30 to $158 (Owens, 2020).

Peloton is a connective fitness company with over 6.6 million members and a 12-month retention rate of 92 %, as of December 31, 2022 (*Investor Relations*, Peloton, n.d.). The company's instructors teach live classes daily in indoor cycling, indoor/outdoor running and walking, bootcamp, yoga, strength training, high intensity interval training (HIIT) cardio, stretching, and meditation. In Q2 2022, members completed over 123 million workouts and quarterly revenues totaled $1,133.9 million (*Investor Relations*, Peloton, n.d.). The key to their initial success relied heavily on community building features that provided encouragement, collective fitness goals, and ultimately brand loyalty. "The level of emotional loyalty that our members have with the brand, with our instructors, with one another is so beyond anything I've seen anywhere," said Brad Olson, Peloton's Chief Membership Officer (Peloton's Ride Forward, 2021). While convenience might have initially drawn in users, the carefully cultivated features have helped Peloton build a devoted and faithful community.

Peloton's platform has integral community-building features to grow and expand member connectivity. These features include the leaderboard, badges, the capability to follow other users, and official/unofficial social media pages dedicated to the Peloton community. While the leaderboard shows your ranking in relation to the rest of the class, it also serves as a medium for connection and accountability. The leaderboard for a live class allows you to access a list of community members who are also taking the class with you. A user can also have a leaderboard tag, such as #MentalHealthWarriors or #PeloDoctors, underneath their leaderboard name to promote and self-identify with groups in the community. With a simple touch of the screen, you also can provide encouragement through virtual "high fives." If you hit certain milestones (i.e. 100 workouts, birthdays, etc.), instructors reference the leaderboard to give shout-outs during class. These virtual and real-time acknowledgments provide the encouragement members need to come back day after day.

Studies have shown that individuals seeking to lose weight and maintain healthy lifestyles in communal settings are far more successful than individuals who tackle it alone. The communal setting goes beyond virtual high fives with long-term accountability. The "follow" feature allows members to add one another on the platform and review each other's profiles, which highlights how many classes that member has taken in each of Peloton's offerings. Once connected, Peloton will alert you when your friends are working out in case you are interested in taking the class with them. For even greater connectivity, those with the Peloton bikes and treadmills (versus the digital app) can request to video chat with friends in the Peloton community during a ride or run.

Peloton recognized early on the importance of community and building social capital by finding ways to reward those who initiate and seek out group connection. Members can earn social badges for initiating group workouts, cleverly labeled "dynamic duo," "three's company," "pack," "squad," "flock," and "swarm." In order to earn these unique badges, members must connect and coordinate which classes to work out together in groups. And while all these activities take place during actual rides, the Peloton community extends outside the boundaries of workouts in a multitude of social outlets (official and unofficial).

Peloton only hosts one official account on Instagram, Twitter, and Facebook. However, there are thousands of unofficial accounts dedicated to the Peloton community. Groups including Peloton Moms/Dads, Peloton Teachers, Peloton Riders for Christ, Peloton Craft Beer Riders, and Black Girl Magic: The Peloton Edition are only a small sample of vibrant unofficial Peloton community groups. In these groups, there are discussions that vary from favorite rides to personal fitness goals.

The software and user experience and interface design of the Peloton platform is instrumental in encouraging users to come back, but arguably, the instructors of Peloton are a key part to the company's success and part of Peloton's larger strategy to become a global entertainment brand; "a media company akin to Netflix" as CEO and Co-Founder, John Foley described in 2018 (Rubin, 2021). The top Peloton instructors are widely followed across social media, and their classes are produced by an Emmy-award winning team (Rubin, 2021). As of March 2022, Robin Arzon has over 950,000 Instagram followers, Kendall Tool has over 650,000 Instagram followers, Alex Toussaint has over 550,000 followers, and Tunde Oyeneyin has over 500,000. In an SEC filing, the company stated: "If we fail to produce and provide our Members with interesting and attractive content led by instructors who they can relate to, then our business, financial condition, and operating results may be adversely affected." In addition, there are fan groups for each of Peloton's 50 instructors, such as Becs Beasts for instructor

Becs Gentry, Denis's Menaces for instructor Dennis Morton, and the You Get To (Do Hard Things) Crew for instructor Jess Sims. Members within these groups often coordinate taking one of the instructor's on demand or live classes together. Before the COVID-19 pandemic, groups would also plan in-person meetups at the Peloton studio to take classes with their favorite instructor. With this, the Peloton community is not just a virtual community. This is critical, as it may address one of Putnam's (2000) noted risks of computer-mediated communication: "drive-by relationships" compared to "dense and bounded" face-to-face networks. Peloton members may be taking classes physically alone and connecting afterwards online, but it is also leading to the development of face-to-face communities outside of the service.

During the 30th season of Dancing with the Stars, we saw these groups demonstrate the power of collective action when Peloton instructor Cody Rigsby competed as a celebrity dancer. Dancing with the Stars is an American dance competition series based on the British show Strictly Come Dancing. The reality TV dancing show pairs celebrities with professional dancers. Each week, the dancing couples perform one to two dances for the judges and TV audience. Scores from the judges and voting public are combined to determine eliminations each week. While the show favors celebrities with dancing prowess, it also provides advantages to celebrities with a wide and deep following.

Many people outside of the Peloton community may not know Cody Rigsby, but his Peloton fame and social media following made him an ideal candidate for Dancing with the Stars. Rigsby's Instagram following sat under 300,000 at the start of the pandemic and tripled to nearly a million a year into the pandemic (Abad-Santos, 2021). His loyal followers known as his "Boo Crew" showed up in massive numbers during his stint on Dancing with the Stars to the chagrin of many loyal Dancing with the Stars fans. Cody Rigsby is known as a charismatic motivating Peloton instructor, but his dancing abilities were a big unknown coming into the 30th season of Dancing with the Stars. For his first dance, judges criticized him for a lackluster performance giving him low scores that dropped him into the bottom three. The official and unofficial Peloton social media outlets went to work after an abysmal start. Calling on Rigsby's Boo Crew, thousands of posts went out reminding fellow Peloton members to vote CODY. Week after week, the Peloton community showed up to vote, ultimately catapulting him into a third place win. The Peloton case study highlights not only the power of virtual and digital platform communities to grow a business, but it also demonstrates the power of collective action to help one of its own.

4. Reddit

In 2005, college roommates, Steve Huffman and Alexis Ohanian, created Reddit and dubbed it "the front page of the internet" (*Reddit: Managing the "Front Page of the Internet,"* 2017). Since then, it has grown into one of the largest online communities in the world. As of January 2021, Reddit had over "50 million daily active unique viewers, 100,000 active communities, and 13 billion posts and comments" (*Reddit by the Numbers*, n.d.). The power of Reddit comes directly from its members, as they create and manage subreddits, which are communities within the online digital platform based on shared interests. Subreddits can center around anything from politics and music to celebrity news and stocks. These communities can have over millions of members or less than 100 users. Members upload content to a subreddit and fellow community members up or down vote the post. As a post gains more up votes, it climbs to the top page of the subreddit. This voting mechanism also serves as a mechanism of moderation by community members. However, this form of self-governance is also supplemented by community moderators that review the community's activity and ensure alignment with the community's editorial guidelines. Reddit allows users to participate in subreddits that align with their interests. They can not only have discussions around certain aspects of their interests but also find resources about subjects they are more interested in. There are subreddits for financial, legal, academic, and interpersonal relationship advice.

In these subreddits, members can grow their reputation. Members frequently post and comment in hopes to gain greater credibility and increase their Karma. Reddit Karma must be earned through up votes and cannot be purchased on the digital platform. As you earn more up votes, your Karma increases. Reddit uses a special algorithm to calculate your up votes to Karma ratio. Karma unlocks a myriad of features which entices members to continue to post and comment to reach certain goals. For instance, at a particular Karma level members can join exclusive subreddits. In addition, increased Karma can allow members to post and comment as much as possible. When members first join Reddit, they are limited on the number and frequencies of their posts depending on the subreddit. Reddit's unique community design draws in millions of members and users a month and keeps them continually engaged.

When the pandemic hit, Reddit activity surged as people all around the world looked to better understand Covid-19 and find greater connection to other members as countries went into lockdown. In 2020, Reddit experienced over a 25 % jump in the number of monthly users – climbing to an all-time high of over 37 million users (Goetzen, 2020). Much of the activity in the United States was fueled by discussions about Covid-19 and the 2020 presidential election. Other subreddit discussions circled around the uncertainty of the economy as the stock market plunged. In March 2020, the Dow Jones Industrial (DJIA) dropped over 25 % in just four days only to see a record breaking rebound months later. As financial institutions made money off the record breaking prices of Zoom, Netflix, and Amazon, they also made money off shorting retail stocks flailing during the pandemic lockdowns. These institutions targeted retail outlets like GameStop Corp. and AMC Entertainment Holdings.

GameStop is a video game electronics retailer based in the United States. GameStop experienced wild success from 2004 to 2016, but its profits began to flounder as the gaming industry shifted to downloadable formatted games. In 2018, GameStop posted its biggest financial loss, with a net loss of nearly $700 million (Roberts, 2021). GameStop struggled to find its footing after the financial loss and then hit an even bigger roadblock when the Covid-19 lockdowns started. Sensing a potential monetary windfall, financial institutions started to target vulnerable retail outlets by taking short positions against retailers like GameStop and AMC.

The subreddit group WallStreetBets saw financial institutions accumulating short positions on GameStop. In order to short a stock, a shorter must purchase borrowed shares of stocks with the anticipation that the stock price will decrease. If the stock price decreases, the shorter makes money off of the price difference. However, shorting stocks carries high risk because if a stock price unexpectedly goes up, the shorter must cover the difference by purchasing the stock at the higher market price. In January 2021, members of WallStreetBets noted unusually high short positions on GameStop by financial institutions. Out of defiance, the three million strong community collectively targeted GameStop stock for purchase consequently driving the stock price up 600 % in four days (Roberts, 2021). The "short squeeze" left financial institutions scrambling as they lost billions of dollars.

As the price of GameStop started to increase, shorters panicked in a buying frenzy in order to cover their shorts. The panic "covering" coupled with the WallStreetBets stock purchases drove GameStop to its highest historical value of $490. The short squeeze left hedge funds like Melvin Capital Management in dire straits seeking out a nearly $3 billion infusion to cover its losses (Li, 2021). With the success of GameStop short squeeze, the members of WallStreetBets looked for its next investment.

AMC Entertainment Holdings was a natural target for shorters. AMC is the world's largest theater chain in the world. Since governments deemed movie theaters non-essential, they were the last retail outfits to re-open in most states; shorters saw its deep vulnerability. The fear of spreading Covid-19 in large congregations at the theater coupled with a wider range of streaming movie options put AMC on its figurative death bed. WallStreetBets literally gave AMC a lifeline, giving ape retail investors ownership of AMC. The ape movement is a reference to the movie Rise of the Planet of the Apes where apes work collectively to fight human oppression and adopt the mantra "Apes Together Strong" (*How The "Apes" Took Over AMC – The Journal.* – WSJ Podcasts, 2021). A year into the pandemic, AMC stock hovered slightly above $2. As the ape movement gained traction, in a matter of months, AMC stock shot up to its peak value of $72. Adam Aron, AMC's CEO, recognized the power of the ape movement that the Reddit community helped facilitate and quickly embraced it. "At the beginning, all of us weren't necessarily getting into AMC because we liked AMC. What Adam did is he kept people here. He came in, saw an opportunity, connected and started listening to what people were saying" (*How The "Apes" Took Over AMC – The Journal.* – WSJ Podcasts, 2021).

Ultimately, the GameStop and AMC examples demonstrate the power of digital platforms like Reddit to create connection amongst its members and to provide a means to collective action. In this particular case, the collective action of WallStreetBets led to financial gains for some investors and significant losses for financial institutions.

5. Twitter

Twitter originally started as an SMS-based communication platform, but it has evolved into one of the most popular social media outlets in the world. Jack Dorsey and Evan Williams co-founded Twitter in 2006 to build community and help friends keep in touch. Twitter differentiated itself from other platforms like Facebook by creating a 140 character limit for posts known as tweets. The 140 characters limit on tweets was not by design, but rather because mobile carriers on the SMS platform imposed those limits (as of 2022, the character limit is now 280). Over the years, celebrities, politicians, and influencers have gravitated towards the social media platform because of the ability to connect with followers in a fast and efficient manner. The brevity of the tweets is appealing to users because it allows for a quick intake of information in a short amount of time.

Like other social media outlets, Twitter experienced a massive surge in users during the start of the pandemic and their ad revenue followed suit. A year into the pandemic, Twitter boasted nearly 200 million active daily users, which was a 20 % increase in growth from the previous year (Wong, 2021). Advertisers eagerly increased their presence on the social media outlet as they saw the surge in popularity. Twitter's revenue jumped 28 % earning over $1 billion (Wong, 2021).

As people stayed home during the pandemic lockdown, a captive audience fixated their eyes on TV and smartphone screens. This was no different for the stans (stalker fans) of K-Pop (Korean pop music) who favor Twitter to communicate with K-Pop musicians and with fellow K-Pop stans. While K-Pop started in the 1990s, its global growth in popularity started in the 2000s around the time Twitter was created (Oak, 2013). The synergistic relationship grew from there.

In 2021 alone, K-Pop stans sent out over 7.5 billion tweets related to anything and everything related to Korean pop music (*K-Pop Sets Another Record on Twitter with 7.5 Billion Tweets in a* Year, 2021). "When K-pop artists want to reach a global audience, they go on Twitter to connect with their passionate fans who want to be the first to see and talk about what's happening. These fans – many who are young and based all over the world – are flocking to Twitter to join these fun #KpopTwitter conversations to feel connected to a global fan community" (*K-Pop Sets Another Record on Twitter with 7.5 Billion Tweets in a* Year, 2021). Some say that K-Pop stans go beyond community to the brink of obsessive behavior. Consider what stan actually means. It is the merging of the word stalker and fan. Stanning requires collective action by millions of stans across the world for one common goal. These goals can be anything from public votes for a music award to watching YouTube music videos to catapult a song to the number spot. It is precisely the global community connection and obsessive behavior that has allowed K-Pop stans to act and coordinate outside the world of K-Pop fandom.

In June 2020, a week after George Floyd's murder by Minneapolis police officers, #WhiteLivesMatter emerged as a trending hashtag in response to the Black Lives Matter (BLM) protests. In Nashville, six young women met over Twitter and created the organization Teens for Equality. These six organizers led a youth march of over 10,000 people, which became one of the largest demonstrations in Nashville's history. "We all met on Twitter…that's how easy it is to do something like this" (Wanshel, 2020). An estimated 500,000 participated in protests in 550 places across the United States (Wanshel, 2020). As these protests grew in size and numbers, counter-protestors showed up in person and on digital platforms with the hashtag #WhiteLivesMatter.

According to the Anti-Defamation League, "White Lives Matter" is a phrase that was created in response to the BLM movement in 2015 (*White Lives Matter*, Anti-Defamation League, n.d.). White supremacist groups like the Aryan Renaissance Society and the Ku Klux Klan have adopted the slogan. As the hashtag gained popularity when the protests continued, K-Pop stans all around the world collectively worked together to drown out the racist hashtag and replace it with photos and videos of their favorite K-Pop musicians. Likewise, K-Pop stans collectively worked together to sabotage the Dallas Police Department's efforts to arrest protestors engaged in illegal activities. The department created an app called iWatch Dallas and tweeted out a call for assistance by the public to send videos of illegal activity from protestors. K-Pop stans flooded the app with content from their favorite K-Pop artists. Within 24 hours, the Dallas police disabled the app.

Two weeks into the protests, BTS (K-Pop's most successful boy band) tweeted to its 26 million followers: "We Stand against racial discrimination. We Condemn violence, You, I and we all have the right to be respected. We will stand together. #BlackLivesMatter." BTS and their management company Big Hit Entertainment donated $1 million to Black Lives Matter (Turak, 2020). K-Pop stans around the world saw the gesture as a call to action galvanizing them to #MatchAMillion. Within a little over 24 hours, K-Pop stans around world had successfully matched the million dollar donation (Turak, 2020). The unlikely intersection of K-Pop and Black Lives Matter during the pandemic showed the world the power of Twitter and the power of collective action by K-Pop stans and BLM protestors.

6. Conclusion

Overall, these platforms were heavily relied upon before the pandemic, but have been particularly essential for maintaining social connections across communities during this time period and have become a daily part of people's lives today. In these case studies, Peloton and the connected fitness industry is helping people create healthy habits, and Reddit and Twitter are platforms facilitating collective social, political, and economic action. These digital services and platforms are facilitating the growth of social capital despite not resembling the forms of associations that Tocqueville first saw when he visited America or having the same face-to-face features of the associations Putnam analyzed. The case studies demonstrate that although social capital may look different, interactions through digital technology can still be just as valuable.

However, as Putnam (2000, p. 21) noted, there are negative forms of social capital. While enabling new markets, products, and services, the Internet is also attributed to the dangers of contemporary society. Peloton had to recall its Tread+ after the U.S. Consumer Product Safety Commission issued an urgent warning for the machine, that it poses "serious risks" to children and pets and that the agency was "aware of 39 incidents including one death" ("CPSC Warns Consumers: Stop Using the Peloton Tread+," 2021). The company's stock has lost all of the gains associated with the growth of at-home workouts during the COVID-19 pandemic and its CEO and Co-Founder, John Foley, resigned after activist investor Blackwells Capital LLC claimed that Foley was unsuccessful in handling the company (Lombardo, 2022). Some members of the subreddit WallStreetBets lost thousands of dollars after failing to time their trades at the rally's peak for GameStop (Phillips et al., 2021). In addition, the number of text posts and total comments across WallStreet Bets has decreased since 2020 (Banerji and McCabe, 2022). Twitter, along with fellow tech companies Facebook and Google, had to testify before Congress to explain how the platforms handled the online extremism that led to the siege on the U.S. Capitol on January 6 and misinformation related to COVID-19 cures and vaccines (Bond, 2021). Jack Dorsey's written testimony described that "a trust deficit has been building over the last several years, and it has created uncertainty – here in the United States and globally" (Disinformation Nation, 2021).

These platforms have become integrated into society, serving as a new infrastructure for our social, political, and economic behaviors. Despite the related dangers of these platforms, people will still rely on them, particularly younger generations, as they have no memory of a world without the Internet and digital technology. As Putnam posed in 2000, Big Tech must consider how their services and platforms can be mechanisms for positive social capital, to the extent that is possible, if they are to be the infrastructure for associations in contemporary and future societies.

References

Abad-Santos, A. (2021). Why Peloton's Cody Rigsby Is a Dancing with the Stars Favorite. *Vox*. Available at: <https://www.vox.com/the-goods/22678193/cody-rigsby-dwts-peloton-boo-crew> [Accessed March 2022].

Banerji, G., & McCabe, C. (2022). Reddit's wall street bets was the game stop kingmaker, but longtime users say the thrill is gone. *The Wall Street Journal*. Available at: <https://www.wsj.com/articles/reddits-wallstreetbets-was-the-gamestop-kingmaker-but-longtime-users-say-the-thrill-is-gone-11643025602> [Accessed March 2022].

Belam, M., & Partridge, J. (2019). Peloton loses $1.5bn in value over "dystopian, sexist" exercise bike ad. *The Guardian*. Available at: <https://www.theguardian.com/media/2019/dec/04/peloton-backlash-sexist-dystopian-exercise-bike-> [Accessed March 2022].

Bell, D., & Held, V. (1969). The community revolution. *The Public Interest, 16*, 142–176. Available at: <https://www.nationalaffairs.com/public_interest/detail/the-community-revolution> [Accessed March 2022].

Bond, S. (2021, March 25). Facebook, Twitter, Google CEOs Testify Before Congress: 4 Things To Know. *National Public Radio (NPR)*. Available at: <https://www.npr.org/2021/03/25/980510388/facebook-twitter-google-ceos-testify-before-congress-4-things-to-know> [Accessed March 2022].

Disinformation Nation: Social Media's Role in Promoting Extremism and Misinformation. Hearing before the Subcommittee on Communications and Technology and the Subcommittee on Commerce of the House Committee on Energy and Commerce, 117th Cong. (2021) (Testimony of Jack Dorsey). Available at: <https://energycommerce.house.gov/sites/democrats.energycommerce.house.gov/files/documents/Witness_Testimony_Dorsey_CAT_CPC_2021.03.25.pdf> [Accessed March 2022].

Goetzen, N. (2020). Reddit User Base Will Grow This Year Amid Pandemic And Election News. *Business Insider*. Available at: <https://www.businessinsider.com/reddit-user-base-will-grow-amid-pandemic-election-news-2020-11> [Accessed March 2022].

How The "Apes" Took Over AMC - The Journal. - WSJ Podcasts. (2021). *The Wall Street Journal*. Available at: <https://www.wsj.com/podcasts/the-journal/how-the-apes-took-over-amc/a7366483-a497-4cf6-99b1-25128c890ecd> [Accessed March 2022].

Investor Relations. (n.d.). *Peloton Interactive*, Inc. Available at: < https://investor.onepeloton.com/> [Accessed March 2022].

K-Pop Sets Another Record On Twitter With 7.5 Billion Tweets In A Year. (2021). *T zwitter Blog*. Available at: <https://blog.twitter.com/en_us/topics/insights/2021/kpop-sets-another-record-on-twitter-with-7-billion-tweets-in-a-year> [Accessed March 2022].

Kalberg, S. (1997). Tocqueville and Weber on the sociological origins of citizenship: The political culture of American democracy. *Citizenship Studies, 1*(2), 199–222. Available at: <https://doi.org/10.1080/13621029708420655> [Accessed March 2022].

Li, Y. (2021). Melvin Capital, Hedge Fund Targeted By Reddit Board, Closes Out Of GameStop Short Position. *CNBC*. Available at: <https://www.cnbc.com/2021/01/27/hedge-fund-targeted-by-reddit-board-melvin-capital-closed-out-of-gamestop-short-position-tuesday.html> [Accessed March 2022].

Lombardo, C. (2022). Peloton CEO John Foley to Step Down, Firm to Cut 2,800 Jobs. *The Wall Street Journal*. Available at: <https://www.wsj.com/articles/peloton-ceo-john-foley-to-step-down-become-executive-chair-11644314403> [Accessed March 2022].

Oak, J. (2013). The Root of K-Pop: The Influences of Today's Biggest Acts – Billboard. *Billboard*. Available at: <https://www.billboard.com/music/music-news/the-root-of-k-pop-the-influences-of-todays-biggest-acts-5638224/> [Accessed March 2022].

Owens, J. C. (2020). Peloton Produces Profit For The First Time Amid Pandemic-Demand Spike, Stock Pushes Toward New Record. *MarketWatch*. Available at: <https://www.marketwatch.com/Story/Peloton-Produces-Profit-For-The-First-Time-Amid-Pandemic-Demand-Spike-Stock-Heads-Toward-New-High-11599768987> [Accessed March 2022].

Peloton's Ride Forward. (2021). *Forbes*. Available at: <https://www.forbes.com/video/6226398486001/pelotons-ride-forward/?sh=4f26aa5238c6> [Accessed March 2022].

Peloton Sales Surge As Virus Boosts Home Workouts. (2020). BBC News. Available at: https://www.bbc.com/news/business-54112461 [Accessed March 2022].

Phillips, M., Lorenz, T., Bernard, T. S., & Friedman, G. (2021). The Hopes That Rose and Fell With GameStop. *The New York Times*. Available at: <https://www.nytimes.com/2021/02/07/business/gamestop-stock-losses.html> [Accessed March 2022].

Putnam, R. (2000). *Bowling Alone: The Collapse and Revival of American Community*. New York: Simon and Schuster Paperbacks.

Reddit: Managing the "Front Page of the Internet." (2017). *Digital Innovation and Transformation*. Available at: <https://digital.hbs.edu/platform-digit/submission/reddit-managing-the-front-page-of-the-internet/> [Accessed March 2022].

Reddit by the Numbers. (n.d.). *Reddit*. Available at: <https://www.redditinc.com/> [Accessed March 2022].

Roberts, J. J. (2021). GameStop Shares Hit New Heights, Battering Short Sellers. *Fortune*. Available at: <https://Fortune.Com/2021/01/25/Gamestop-Stock-Yolo-Rally-Short-Sellers/> [Accessed March 2022].

Rubin, C. (2021). "The Netflix of Wellness": Inside the Hollywoodization of Peloton. The Hollywood Reporter. *The Hollywood Reporter*. <https://www.hollywoodreporter.com/business/business-news/hollywoodization-of-peloton-1234964386/> [Accessed March 2022].

Tocqueville, A. (2004). *Democracy in America* (A. Goldhammer, Trans.) (O. Zunz, Ed.). The Library of America. (Original work published 1835).

Turak, N. (2020, June 8). K-Pop's BTS Donated $1 Million to Black Lives Matter. *CNBC*. Available at: <https://www.cnbc.com/2020/06/08/bts-donated-1-million-to-black-lives-matter-its-fans-matched-it-in-a-day.html> [Accessed March 2022].

U.S. Centers for Disease Control (CDC). (n.d.). COVID-19 Timeline. *U.S. Centers for Disease Control (CDC).* Available at: <https://www.cdc.gov/museum/timeline/covid19.html> [Accessed March 2022].

U.S. Consumer Product Safety Commission (CPSC). (2021). *CPSC Warns Consumers: Stop Using the Peloton Tread+. U.S. Consumer Product Safety Commission.* Available at: <https://www.cpsc.gov/Newsroom/News-Releases/2021/CPSC-Warns-Consumers-Stop-Using-the-Peloton-Tread> [Accessed March 2022].

Wanshel, E. (2020). Teen Girls Organized A 10,000-Person Black Lives Matter Protest in Nashville. *HuffPost.* Available at: <https://www.huffpost.com/entry/teen-girls-organized-10000-person-black-lives-matter-protest-nashville_n_5eda8f78c5b62f530c799daa> [Accessed March 2022].

White Lives Matter, Anti-Defamation League. (n.d.). *Anti-Defamation League.* Available at: <https://www.adl.org/education/references/hate-symbols/white-lives-matter> [Accessed March 2022].

Wong, Q. (2021). Twitter Shows Strong User, Revenue Growth in Second Quarter. *CNET.* <https://www.cnet.com/tech/mobile/twitter-shows-strong-user-revenue-growth-in-second-quarter/> [Accessed March 2022].

Ibrahim Aytekin

The Econometric Analysis of the Relationship Between Economic Growth and Health Services in Türkiye

1. Introduction

The more important the health services are for a healthy society in a country, the more important the economy. Because, while poverty rates are high in countries with a bad economy and low-income levels, investments in health services may remain at low levels. In such countries, where poverty rates are high and health services are inadequate, people may face serious health problems because they cannot access enough food, hygiene products, and health services. Therefore, the positive developments in the economy support the emergence of healthy individuals and societies by enabling people to eat healthily and receive better health services.

More than one study has been found in the literature examining the relationship between economic growth and health services. Among these studies are Fogel (1994), Arora (2001), Bhargava et al. (2001), Bloom et al. (2004), Taban (2006), Suhrcke et al. (2006), Dağdemir (2009), French (2012), Çalışkan et al. (2013), Öztürk and Uçan (2017) and Some et al. (2019). In the studies conducted by most of them, there was a positive relationship between health services and economic growth. In addition, although limited in the literature - Acemoglu and Johnson (2007), Kaya and Bozkurt (2011), and Cömertler-Şimşir et al. (2015) - such as the studies carried out on health services and economic growth, there is a negative and statistically meaningless relationship.

The aim of this chapter is to analyze the relationship between economic growth and health services in Türkiye for 1967–2019 period. Johansen Cointegration test, which is one of the econometric time series analysis methods, was used, and the method of Granger Causality test was used in the study.

The results obtained in the study showed a meaningful relationship between health services and economic growth in the literature. However, the analysis method, period and variables used in this study distinguish this from other studies and make this study important in terms of filling the gap in the literature.

Thus, the introduction part is included in the first stage of this study. After the introduction, the literature review of the studies on this subject is emphasized.

After the literature review, econometric analysis was initiated, and here, the data set, method, methodology, and empirical findings are included. Then, in line with the findings, the study was completed by giving place to the conclusion and evaluation part.

2. Literature Review

As a result of the literature examination for studies dealing with the relations between economic growth and health services, it was observed that many studies deal with both Türkiye and other countries. While it is determined that these studies in the literature have reached similar and different results, the findings and results of these studies are given in detail.

Fogel (1994) concluded that the economy negatively affects economic growth by reducing the productivity of the economy, not only chronic and other diseases but also low calories in terms of health.

Arora (2001) concluded that improvements in the health system, health investments, and public health during the last 30 years of the world increased the economic growth rate by 30 % to 40 % in the long term.

Bhargava et al. (2001) concluded that the positive developments in health services in their studies increased adult survival rates, and this situation had positive effects on economic growth rates in low-income countries.

Bloom et al. (2004) concluded that good health states and services have a positive and statistically significant effect on economic growth.

In his study, Taban (2006) did not find any causality relationship between the number of health institutions and economic growth, while a bidirectional relationship developed between other health indicators and economic growth.

Suhrcke et al. (2006) concluded that in their studies on the European Union, the improvement of the health system and a good health care system positively affected economic growth activities not only in developed countries but also in poor countries.

In Acemoglu and Johnson (2007), they examined the effects of health developments due to life expectancy on economic growth. In the examination, they observed that the idea that health has a first-degree effect on economic growth is a suspicious phenomenon.

Dağdemir (2009) has observed that improvements in the health systems of developing countries positively affect the economic growth performance of these countries.

Kaya and Bozkurt (2011) in their studies on Türkiye with the smallest frames method stated that there was a positive relationship between unemployment and crime rate and health services (number of green cards) and there was no significant relationship between income and health services (number of green cards).

Swift (2011) examined 13 OECD countries in his study. In the examination, it was found that there was a cointegration relationship between health and economic growth.

French (2012) examined by the panel data method that 30 OECD countries improved the income of health or health in the period between 1960 and 2007. In the examination, in general, it was concluded that a better health state improves income, and in return, income affects health positively.

Çalışkan et al. (2013) in their studies examined Türkiye's period between 1967 and 2010. In their examination of the number of patients per health personnel, it has been found that there is a unidirectional causality relationship between the number of beds and the number of hospitals of health institutions to real GDP. However, there was no causal relationship between life expectancy to real GDP.

Cömertler-Şimşir et al. (2015) in their studies examined Türkiye's period between 1975 and 2012. In this study, they concluded that there is a negative relationship between long and short health indicators and economic growth in Türkiye.

Öztürk and Uçan (2017) studied Türkiye, thanks to increasing health expenditures and investments in the developing health sector in the nursing and doctors' number of patients per nursing, and thus health expenditures have a positive effect on growth in Türkiye.

In the study conducted by Piabuo and Tieguhong (2017), a conclusion is that income is an important element in explaining health expenditures and therefore the increase in the general income level encourages an increase in health expenditures.

Some et al. (2019) analyzed 48 African countries in their studies. In the analysis, in Africa, a positive relationship between mother, baby, and child mortality rates and economic growth was found.

3. Data Set and Method

In the time series analysis of this study, annual frequency variables covering the period between 1967 and 2019 in Türkiye were used. The main reason for choosing the analysis period among these years is to aim for creating a common data period among the variables and the data limitation due to the number of health institutions. All of the variables were obtained from the Turkish Statistical Institute. In this context, the variables used in the analysis, the definitions of these variables, and their shortened versions are given in Tab. 1.

Tab. 1: Variables and description

Variables	Variable Short Name	Variable Description
Economic Growth	GRWT	Gross domestic product
Health Institutions	HINS	It represents the total number of healthy health institutions within the state and the private sector.
Health Personnel	HPER	The university and the private sector include all health personnel. These personnel consist of medical doctors, dentists, nurses, midwives, pharmacists, and other health and support personnel.

In this study, econometric time series analysis was used as a method. In this direction, descriptive statistics of the variables and correlation matrix were created in the first stage of the analysis. Then, Augmented Dickey-Fuller (ADF) and Philips-Perron (PP) unit root tests were applied to the variables to test whether they contain a unit root. In the third stage of the analysis, the Johansen Cointegration test was applied to the variables in line with the results of the unit root tests. The last stage of the analysis was completed by applying the Granger Causality test to the variables.

4. Empirical Findings

Descriptive statistics and correlation matrix constitute the first findings of the empirical analysis made in this study. The descriptive statistics calculated in this context are given in Tab. 2.

Tab. 2: Descriptive statistics

Variable	Observation	Minimum Value	Maximum Value	Median	Stand. Deviation
GRWT	53	111.430	862.740	289.349	294.419
HINS	53	646.00	34.595	8.425	11.789
HPER	53	34.103	664.107	247.127	175.352

When the descriptive statistical values given in Tab. 2 are examined, it is confirmed that the number of observations, standard deviations, averages, and minimum and maximum values of the variables is suitable for the analysis. In the next step, the correlation matrix of the variables was created, and the results are given in Tab. 3.

Tab. 3: Correlation matrix

	GRWT	HINS	HPER
GRWT	1		
HINS	0.939	1	
HPER	0.957	0.931	1

When the correlation matrix given in Tab. 3 is examined, the fact that all variables have positive values and these values are greater than 0.9 shows that there is a very strong correlation between the variables. After the correlation matrix, unit root tests were applied to the variables to determine the stationarity levels of the variables.

4.1. Unit Root Test Results

The variables to be used in a time series analysis should not contain unit roots, that is, they should have a stationary structure. Otherwise, generalization cannot be made in a time series analysis, and it should be said that the regression models created with such variables will not be fake or meaningful (Aytekin, 2022: 25). Unit root tests of the variables used in this study were carried out by Augmented Dickey-Fuller (ADF) developed by Dickey and Fuller (1981) and Philips-Perron (PP) unit root tests developed by Philips and Perron (1988). The unit root test results obtained are given in Tab. 4.

Tab. 4: ADF and PP unit root test findings

Level	Variable Name	ADF		PP	
		With Constant	With Constant & Trend	With Constant	With Constant & Trend
		t-Statistic (Probability)	t-Statistic (Probability)	t-Statistic (Probability)	t-Statistic (Probability)
At Level	GRWT	0.092 (0.962)	-1.777 (0.701)	0.125 (0.965)	-1.765 (0.707)
	HINS	1.150 (0.997)	-0.980 (0.938)	1.121 (0.997)	-0.989 (0.936)
	HPER	7.144 (1.000)	2.280 (1.000)	7.144 (1.000)	2.280 (1.000)
At First Difference	ΔEGRW	-7.470 (0.000)*	-7.535 (0.000)*	-7.465 (0.000)*	-7.533 (0.000)*
	ΔHINS	-6.455 (0.000)*	-6.958 (0.000)*	-6.472 (0.000)*	-6.958 (0.000)*
	ΔHPER	-0.325 (0.913)*	-5.661 (0.000)*	-3.621 (0.000)*	-5.604 (0.000)*

* and ** denote statistical significance at 1 % and 5 % significance levels, respectively, while Δ denotes difference operator.

When the results of the unit root tests given in Tab. 4 are examined, it has been determined that the variables of health personnel, economic growth, and health institutions contain unit root according to the level value constant and constant-trend models of ADF and PP unit root tests. In other words, it is understood that these three variables are not stationary according to both models of ADF and PP unit root tests. After it was understood that the variables were not stationary at the level, the values of the variables in the first difference were examined. In the analysis made according to the first difference, it was understood that the variables of health personnel, economic growth, and health institutions do not contain unit roots according to both fixed and fixed-trend models of ADF and PP unit root tests. In other words, it has been determined that these three variables are stationary in the first difference, that is, I(1).

The determination of all the variables as I(1) indicates that the Johansen Cointegration (1988) test and the Granger Causality test can be used in the analysis. Therefore, in the analysis of this study, the Johansen Cointegration (1988) test and Granger Causality test were used in line with the results of unit root tests. To perform the causality test with the cointegration test, first of all, it is necessary to determine the appropriate number of lag lengths for the variables. Accordingly, in the next step, the appropriate lag length estimation results determined for the variables are included.

4.2. Lag Length Determination

The number of lag lengths is the point at which the stability condition is met in the series (Aytekin, 2021: 44). In this context, to apply the Johansen Cointegration test, it is necessary to determine a lag length number for the variables. This number of lag lengths is determined by considering the minimum lags of the information criteria Likelihood-Ratio (LR), Final Prediction Error (FPE), Akaike (AIC), Schwarz (SC), and Hannan-Quinn (HQ) given in Tab. 4 (Kaya et al., 2018: 87; Aytekin, 2020: 326–327). Based on this, the estimated appropriate lag length test results are given in Tab. 5.

Tab. 5: Lag length criteria test results

Information Criteria						
Lag	**LogL**	**LR**	**FPE**	**AIC**	**SC**	**HQ**
0	-1759.316	NA	3.48e+	71.931	72.047	71.975
1	-1538.956	404.743	6.25e+	63.304	63.767	63.480
2	-1519.779	32.874*	4.14e+	62.889	63.699*	63.196*
3	***-1510.282***	***15.117***	***4.11e+****	***62.869****	***64.027***	***63.308***
4	-1501.671	12.653	4.27e+	62.884	64.390	63.455

*: Indicates the lag length accepted by the information criterion.

When the lag length test results given in Tab. 5 are examined, the appropriate number of lag lengths for this study was determined as three considering the AIC and FPE information criteria, and the analyses were made according to the third lag.

4.3. Johansen Cointegration Test and Results

The Johansen Cointegration test was developed by Johansen (1988) and Johansen and Juselius (1990). This model is a cointegration vector model that accepts each variable as an endogenous variable and is used to test the existence of a long-term (cointegration) relationship between the variables. To apply this model, all of the variables used in the analysis must be stationary at the first difference, that is, I(1). Whether there is a cointegration relationship in the model is determined by looking at the critical values of the trace statistics (λ_{trace}) and the maximum eigenvalue statistics (λ_{max}) (Johansen, 1988: 231–254; Johansen & Juselius, 1990: 169–210). The values of the trace statistic and the maximum eigenvalue statistic are obtained using the Monte Carlo approach. In this direction, the equations of the trace statistics and the maximum eigenvalue statistics are modeled as Equations 1 and 2 given below (Enders, 2015: 378):

$$\lambda_{trace}(r) = -T\sum_{i=r+1}^{n}\ln(1-\lambda'_i) \tag{1}$$

$$\lambda_{max}(r, r+1) = -T\ln(1-\lambda'_i) \tag{2}$$

Here the λ in the equations is the estimated values of the characteristic roots (eigenvalues) obtained from the predicted rank (Π) matrix and T indicates the number of available observations (Enders, 2015: 378). The following hypothesis tests are used to test the largest λ values of the trace statistics and the maximum eigenvalue statistics (Yenisu, 2018: 17):

Hypothesis testing for λ_{trace} testing;

H_0: $\lambda_i = 0$, i= r+1+,.......,n

H_1: there are at most r cointegration vectors.

Hypothesis testing for λ_{max} test;

H_0: $r = r_{0,}$ there are r cointegration vectors.

H_1: $r \neq r_0+1$ it is in the form of “there are r+1 cointegration vectors”.

Thus, the results of the Johansen Cointegration test applied to the variables in this study are given in Tab. 6.

Tab. 6: Johansen Cointegration test results

Trace Statistic	%5 Critical Value	Probability (P)	Hypothesized No. of CE(s)
48.802	29.797	0.000	$r = 0$
19.070	15.494	0.014	$r \leq 1$
1.189	3.841	0.275	$r \leq 2$
Maximum Eigenvalue Statistic	**%5 Critical Value**	**Probability (P)**	**Hypothesized No. of CE(s)**
29.731	21.131	0.002	$r = 0$
17.881	14.265	0.013	$r \leq 1$
1.189	3.841	0.275	$r \leq 2$

r: Cointegration vector number.

When the Johansen Cointegration test results given in Tab. 6 are examined, it is seen that the two values of the trace statistics are greater than the 5 % critical value (48.802>29.797 and 19.070>15.494). This result indicates that there are at least two cointegration relationships between the variables at the 5 % significance level, according to the trace statistics. In other words, this result shows that there is a long-term relationship between the variables according to the trace statistics.

It is seen that the two values of the maximum eigenvalue statistics, which is another statistic in Tab. 6, are greater than the 5 % critical value (29.731>21.131 & 17.881>14.265). Therefore, this result indicates that there are at least two cointegration relationships between the variables at the 5 % significance level, according to the maximum eigenvalue statistic. In other words, this result shows that there is a long-term relationship between the variables according to the eigenvalue statistics.

As a result, according to the Johansen Cointegration test, it has been determined that there is a long-term relationship between economic growth and health services in Türkiye and that these variables can affect each other in the long run.

After determining a long-term relationship between economic growth and health services, an error correction coefficient was estimated to determine whether the established model works well and in what period the fluctuations in the short-term balance will return to the long-term balance (Kaya et al. 2018: 87; Dikkaya & Aytekin, 2020: 270). This estimated error correction coefficient was calculated as -0.239. The fact that this coefficient has a negative value and that this value is statistically significant indicates that the established model works well. In this context, starting from the calculated value of the error correction coefficient, it shows that the short-term imbalances between the economic growth and health services variables in Türkiye will reach the long-term balance again in a period of approximately 1/(|-0.239|) = 4.2 years. After determining a long-term relationship between economic growth and health services, the Granger Causality test was applied to the variables.

4.4. Granger Causality Test and Results

The Granger Causality test is a model developed to determine the cause and effect (causality) relationship between the variables and the direction of this relationship. This causality model was developed by Clive W. J. Granger in 1969. The most important feature and advantage of the Granger Causality test is that it accepts all variables as endogenous variables. Granger Causality is tested in the context of linear regression models. For example, suppose there are two variables, X and Y. The Granger Causality test for these two variables is modeled as in Equation 3 and Equation 4 given below (Granger, 1969: 427):

$$Xt + b_0 Y_t = \sum_{j=1}^{m} a_j X_{t-j} + \sum_{j=1}^{m} b_j Y_{t-j} + \varepsilon_{1t} \quad (3)$$

$$Y_t + c_0 X_t = \sum_{j=1}^{m} c_j X_{t-j} + \sum_{j=1}^{m} d_j Y_{t-j} + \varepsilon_{2t} \quad (4)$$

If the b_0 and c_0 parameters in the equations are equal to 0, the models will be simple causal models. Otherwise, instant causality models will be valid (Granger, 1969: 424–438). In the Granger Causality test, the null and alternative hypotheses needed to determine the causality relationship are formed as follows (Mert & Çağlar, 2019: 340).

H_0: $\sum_{j=1}^{m} a_j = 0$, ie: Y_t is not the cause of X_t;

H_1: $\sum_{j=1}^{m} a_j \neq 0$, ie: Y_t is the cause of X_t,

In addition, four different results emerge from a causality equation for two variables. These results are:

1. X is the Granger cause of Y.
2. Y is the Granger cause of X.
3. There is no Granger Causality between X and Y.

4. There is a feedback process between X and Y. In other words, there is bidirectional Granger Causality between the variables (Mert & Çağlar, 2019: 340).

It is also obtained by applying the Granger Causality test to the error correction model. Therefore, in this study, it has been determined that there is a long-term relationship between economic growth and health services according to the Johansen Cointegration test. In this study, the Granger Causality test was applied to the variables to determine the direction of these relations between economic growth and health services (Gül & Ekinci, 2006: 98–100). Therefore, the findings obtained as a result of the three Granger Causality tests modeled to determine the causality relationship between the variables used in this study are given in Tab. 7.

Tab. 7: VECM Granger Causality test results

Model 1: $\Delta GRWT_t = \mu_0 + \sum_{j=1}^{m} a_{1j}\Delta GRWT_{t-j} + \sum_{j=1}^{m} a_{2j}\Delta HINS_{t-j} + \sum_{j=1}^{m} a_{3j}\Delta HPER_{t-j} + \varepsilon_{1t}$

Model 1	**Dependent Variable:** ΔGRWT				
Independent Variables	**df**	**χ^2 Value**	*P* Value	Decision	Conclusion
ΔHINS	3	6.531	0.088	H_0: Rejection	HINS => GRWT
ΔHPER	3	9.844	0.012	H_0: Rejection	HPER => GRWT
ΔALL	6	50.625	0.047	H_0: Rejection	ALL => GRWT

Model 2: $\Delta HINS_t = \beta_0 + \sum_{j=1}^{m} b_{1j}\Delta HINS_{t-j} + \sum_{j=1}^{m} b_{2j}\Delta GRWT_{t-j} + \sum_{j=1}^{m} b_{3j}\Delta HPER_{t-j} + \varepsilon_{2t}$

Model 2	**Dependent Variable:** ΔHINS				
Independent Variables	**df**	**χ^2 Value**	*P* Value	Decision	Conclusion
ΔGRWT	3	45.905	0.000	H_0: Rejection	GRWT => HINS
ΔHPER	3	13.706	0.003	H_0: Rejection	HPER => HINS
ΔALL	6	50.625	0.000	H_0: Rejection	ALL => HINS

Model 3: $\Delta HPER_t = \lambda_0 + \sum_{j=1}^{m} c_{1j}\Delta HPER_{t-j} + \sum_{j=1}^{m} c_{2j}\Delta GRWT_{t-j} + \sum_{j=1}^{m} c_{3j}\Delta HINS_{t-j} + \varepsilon_{3t}$

Model 3	**Dependent Variable:** ΔHPER				
Independent Variables	**df**	**χ^2 Value**	*P* Value	Decision	Conclusion
ΔGRWT	3	8.741	0.033	H_0: Red	GRWT => HPER
ΔHINS	3	3.999	0.261	$H_{0:}$Acceptance	HINS ≠> HPER
ΔALL	6	9.439	0.150	$H_{0:}$Acceptance	ALL ≠> HPER

χ^2: Chi-sq; =>: Granger is the causality. ≠>: Granger isn't the causality; Δ: Difference processor;

In the equation created for Model 1 from the Granger Causality test results given in Tab. 7, economic growth is considered as the dependent variable, while health personnel and health institutions are considered independent variables. In this context, as a result of the causality test for Model 1, it has been concluded that there is a causal relationship between health institutions and health personnel to economic growth in Türkiye. In other words, it has been determined that there is a causal relationship between health services to economic growth in Türkiye.

In the equation created for Model 2 from the Granger Causality test results given in Tab. 7, health institutions are considered as dependent variables, while economic growth and health personnel are considered independent variables. In this context, as a result of the causality test for Model 2, it has been determined that there is a causal relationship between economic growth and health personnel to health institutions in Türkiye.

In the equation created for Model 3 from the Granger Causality test results given in Tab. 7, health personnel is considered as dependent variables, while economic growth and health institutions are considered as independent variables. In this context, as a result of the causality test conducted for Model 3, a unidirectional causality relationship was found between economic growth to health personnel in Türkiye, while no causality relationship was found from health institutions to health personnel. Thus, according to the results of Model 2 and Model 3, it has been determined that there is a causal relationship between economic growth to health services in Türkiye.

As a result, according to the Granger Causality test, in Türkiye, a bidirectional causality relationship was found between economic growth, health personnel, and health institutions. In addition, it has been observed that there is a unidirectional causality relationship between health personnel to health institutions. The representation in the figural form, which is a summary of the results of the causality test, was created in Fig. 1.

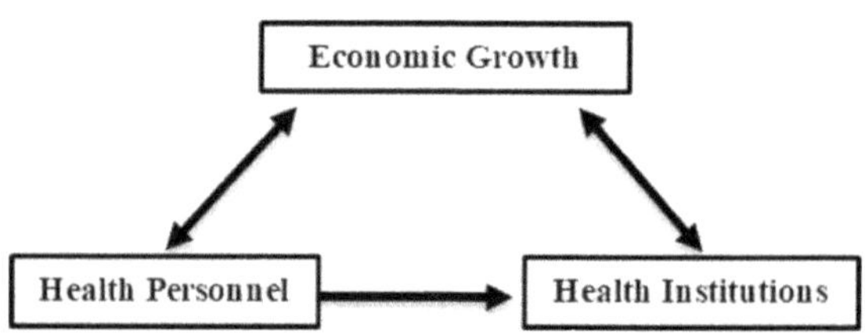

Fig. 1: The association of causality relationship is the formal summary of the test results

The two-way arrows in Fig. 1 show the bidirectional causality relationship between the variables, and the one-way arrows show the unidirectional causality relationship between the variables and the direction of the arrows in this relationship.

5. Conclusion and Discussion

In this study, which examines the relationship between economic growth and health services in Türkiye for the period between 1967 and 2019, it has been determined that there is a long-term relationship between economic growth and health services in Türkiye. In the study, after determining a long-term relationship between economic growth and health services, a causality test was also carried out to determine the direction of this relationship. As a result of the causality test, it was observed that there is a bidirectional causality relationship between economic growth and health services in Türkiye, and this result supports the long-term relationship. Thus, it was determined and confirmed by cointegration and causality tests that there is a close relationship between economic growth and health services in Türkiye.

As a result of the empirical analysis, when the findings that there is a close relationship between economic growth and health services in Türkiye are evaluated, it is seen that as the number of health personnel and health institutions increases in Türkiye, the number of patients per health personnel decreases and better quality and adequate level of health services are provided. Providing health services at adequate levels supports the emergence of a healthy society and generation, as well as the prolongation of the expected life expectancy. Therefore, such positive developments in public health can increase production and productivity by positively affecting other individual and social characteristics that support production, especially the labor force, which is a labor input in Türkiye. Such increases in production and productivity naturally become an important driving force for economic growth and development. On the other hand, it has been observed that health services have improved with the economic growth of Türkiye. Because of the economic growth in Türkiye, in addition to the increase in the employment rate in health, it is possible to say that the increase in investments and reforms in health institutions, the decrease in the poverty rate, the increase in healthy and balanced nutrition opportunities, and similar reasons affect health services and public health positively. Finally, it has been determined that there are mutually positive relations between health services and economic growth in Türkiye.

The results of this study, in which the findings and conclusions that there is a long-term and statistically significant relationship between economic growth and health services in Türkiye are reached, are available in the literature and Fogel (1994), Arora (2001), Bhargava et al. (2001), Bloom et al. (2004), Taban (2006), Suhrcke et al. (2006), Dağdemir (2009), Swift (2011), French (2012), Çalışkan et al. (2013), Öztürk and Uçan (2017), Piabuo and Tieguhong (2017) and Some et al. (2019) support the findings and results of the studies; Acemoglu and Johnson (2007), Kaya and Bozkur (2011) and Cömertler-Şimşir et al. (2015) do not support the findings and results.

In summary, from the results obtained in this study, the improvements in Türkiye's health services affect Türkiye's economic growth performance positively; likewise, it has been shown that the increases in Türkiye's economic growth performance have a positive effect on Türkiye's health services. This result has shown how important the health sector is for the economy and the economy for health.

References

Acemoglu, D., & Johnson, S. (2007). Disease and Development: The Effect of Life Expectancy on Economic Growth. *Journal of Political Economy, 115*(6), 925–985.

Arora, S. (2001). Health, Human Productivity, and Long-Term Economic Growth. *The Journal of Economic History, 61*(3), 699–749.

Aytekin, İ. (2020). Döviz kuru Sanayi Üretimi ve Ekonomik Güven Arasındaki İlişkinin Analizi: Türkiye Örneği. *Bitlis Eren Üniversitesi Sosyal Bilimler Dergisi, 9*(2), 322–330. (in Turkish).

Aytekin, İ. (2021). Kalkınma İnovasyon Ar-Ge Eğitim ve Sağlık Harcamaları Arasındaki İlişkinin Analizi: Türkiye Örneği. *3. Uluslararası Sosyal Bilimler ve İnovasyon Kongresi,* Ankara, Türkiye, 38–53. (in Turkish).

Aytekin, İ. (2022). Türkiye'de Karayolu ve Demiryolu Ulaştırma Hizmetleri ile Kalkınma Arasındaki Nedensellik İlişkisinin Analizi. *Anadolu İktisat ve İşletme Dergisi, 6*(1), 17–35. (in Turkish).

Bhargava, A., Jamison, D. T., Lau, L. J., & Murray, C. J. L. (2001), Modeling the Effects of Health on Economic Growth. *Journal of Health Economics, 20*(2001), 423–440.

Bloom, D. E., Canning, D., & Sevilla, J. (2004). The Effect of Health on Economic Growth: A Production Function Approach. *World Development, 32*(1), 1–13.

Çalışkan, Ş., Karabacak, M., & Meçik, O. (2013). Türkiye'de Sağlık ve Ekonomik Büyüme İlişkisi. *Dumlupınar Üniversitesi Sosyal Bilimler Dergisi, 37*, 123–130. (in Turkish).

Cömertler-Şimşir, N., F. Çondur, F., Bölükbaş, M., & Alataş, S. (2015). Türkiye'de Sağlık ve Ekonomik Büyüme İlişkisi: ARDL Sınır Testi Yaklaşımı. *Finans Politik & Ekonomik Yorumlar, 52*(604), 43–54. (in Turkish).

Dağdemir, Ö. (2009). Sağlık ve Ekonomik Büyüme: 1960–2005 Döneminde Gelişmekte Olan Ülkelerde Sağlık ve Ekonomik Büyüme Arasındaki Karşılıklı İlişkinin Analizi. *Ankara Üniversitesi SBF Dergisi, 64*(2), 75–96. (in Turkish).

Dickey, D. A., & Fuller, W. A. (1981). Likelihood Ratio Statistics for Autoregressive Time Series with a Unit Root. *Econometrica, 49*(4), 1057–1072.

Dikkaya, M., & Aytekin, İ. (2020). İktisadi Büyüme İşsizlik ve Suç Arasında Nedensellik İlişkisi: Türkiye Örneği. *Ekonomi İşletme Siyaset ve Uluslararası İlişkiler Dergisi, 6*(2), 261–274 (in Turkish).

Enders, W. (2015). *Applied Econometric Time Series* (4. Edition). USA: John Wiley & Sons.

Fogel, R. W. (1994). Economic Growth, Population Theory and Physiology: The Bearing of Long-Term Processes on the Making of Economic Policy. *American Economic Review, 84*(3), 369–395.

French, D. (2012). Causation between Health and İncome: A Need to Panic. *Empirical Economics, 42*, 583–601.

Granger, C. W. J. (1969). Investigating Causal Relations by Econometric Models and Cross-Spectral Methods. *Econometrica, 37*(3), 424–438.

Gül, E., & Ekinci, A. (2006). Türkiye"de Enflasyon ve Döviz Kuru Arasındaki Nedensellik İlişkisi: 1984–2003. *Sosyal Bilimler Dergisi, 2006*(1), 91–106. (in Turkish).

Johansen, S. (1988). Statistical Analysis of Cointegration Vectors. *Journal of Economic Dynamics and Control, 12*, 231–254.

Johansen, S., & Juselius, K. (1990). Maximum Likelihood Estimated and İnference on Cointegration with Application to the Demand for Money. *Oxford Bulletin of Economics and Statistics, 52*(2), 169–210.

Kaya, M. V., Aytekin, İ., & Yılmaz, S. S. (2018). Income, Unemployment and Crime in Turkey: An Analysis of Causality. *Annals of the University Dunarea de Jos of Galati: Fascicle: I, Economics & Applied Informatics, 24*(1), 85–90.

Kaya, M. V., & Bozkurt, İ. (2011). İşsizlik, Kişi Başına Milli Gelir (Yoksulluk), Suç Oranı ve Yeşil Kart: 1993–2009 Türkiye Örneği. *Dumlupınar Üniversitesi Sosyal Bilimler Dergisi, 30*, 1333–140. (in Turkish).

Mert, M., & Çağlar, A. E. (2019). *Eviews ve Gauss Uygulamalı Zaman Serileri Analizi*. Ankara: Detay Yayıncılık. (in Turkish).

Öztürk, S., & Uçan, O. (2017). Türkiye'de Sağlık Harcamalarında Artış Nedenleri: Sağlık Harcamalarında Artış–Büyüme İlişkisi, *Süleyman Demirel*

Üniversitesi İktisadi ve İdari Bilimler Fakültesi Dergisi, 22(1), 139–152. (in Turkish).

Phillips, P. C. B., & Perron, P. (1988). Testing for a Unit Root in Time Series Regression. *Biometrika, 75*(2), 335–346.

Piabuo, S. M., & Tieguhong, J. C. (2017). Health Expenditure and Economic Growth a Review of the Literature and an Analysis of the Economic Community for Central African States (CEMAC) and Selected African Countries. *Health Economics Review (2017), 7*(23), 1–13.

Some, J., Pasali, S., & Kaboine, M. (2019). Exploring the Impact of Healthcare on Economic Growth in Africa. *Applied Economics and Finance, 6*(3), 45–57.

Suhrcke, M., McKee, M., Stuckler, D., Sauto Arce, R., Tsolova, S., & Mortensen, J. (2006). The Contribution of Health to the Economy in the European Union. *Public Health, 2006*(120), 994–1001.

Swift, R. (2011). The Relationship Between Health and GDP in OECD Countries in the Very Long Run. *Health Economics, 20*, 306–322.

Taban, S. (2006). Türkiye'de Sağlık ve Ekonomik Büyüme Arasındaki Nedensellik İlişkisi. *Sosyoekonomi, 2006*(2), 31–46. (in Turkish).

Yenisu, E. (2018). Enerji Tüketimi, CO_2 Emisyonu ve Ekonomik Büyüme İlişkisi: Türkiye Örneği. *Van YYÜ İİBF Dergisi, 3*(5), 9–29. (in Turkish). https://www.tuik.gov.tr/ (Date of Access: 09.02.2022).

Ozkan Zulfuoglu

A Fiscal Policy Proposal on the Relationship Between Indirect Taxes and Inflation in Türkiye

1. Introduction

Inflation is a problem that Türkiye has had to endure for a long time. Especially in many developing countries, the cause of inflation seems to be directly related to structural reasons. Structural reasons such as lack of raw materials, shortage of qualified personnel and insufficient supply can be determinants in inflation. However, the problems caused by long-term inflation in the economy can reach very serious dimensions. First of all, due to inflation, income distribution deteriorates to the detriment of wage earners. Consumption patterns in the economy are changing due to price increases, which leads to a deterioration in the supply and demand structure. Due to the rising interest rates, investments are decreasing and the tendency to short-term speculative investments is increasing. The rate of accumulation of the economy slows down, and the distribution of resources deteriorates to the detriment of future generations. In addition to all these, the real values of tax revenues can be eroded due to the Olivera-Tanzi effect, which may lead to a vicious circle in the relationship between budget deficit and inflation. The serious economic and social costs of these problems raise the issue of tight fiscal policy practices that will be implemented with determination in the fight against inflation.

There are many factors that determine the success of the fiscal policy in the fight against inflation. In order to be successful in the fight against inflation, first of all, the cause of inflation must be correctly identified. For example, the solution of demand inflation and cost inflation will require different fiscal policies. If the inflation experienced is demand inflation, total demand will decrease in the short run. However, if inflation arises from cost as seen in Türkiye, demand-reducing policies will not be sufficient for its solution. In order to determine a successful anti-inflation policy, the relationship between tax and public expenditures and inflation should be analyzed correctly. The policy of reducing demand through tax increases, which is frequently brought to the agenda for the solution of inflation, cannot be easily implemented when cost inflation is concerned. The most important reason for this is the complex causality relationship between indirect taxes and inflation. Although inflation brings a raise in indirect tax rates to the agenda, the increase in indirect taxes can also lead to inflation by increasing the costs themselves. Considering that tax revenues in Türkiye mainly consist of indirect taxes, the relationship between indirect taxes and inflation should be examined in detail in order to establish an effective fiscal policy. In this direction, the relationship between indirect taxes and inflation in Türkiye will be analyzed empirically and suggestions on fiscal policy will be made with the help of the findings.

2. Tax Revenues Inflation Relationship and Türkiye

Between 1920 and 1939, the fight against recession was seen as the most important issue of economic policy. However, in the following period, economic development and the fight against inflation became the main areas of economic policy. It has been frequently discussed in the post-World War II period whether economic development will be possible, especially with inflation. Inflation is the continuous increase in the general level of prices, and as a result, the purchasing power of money decreases (Türk, 1959, p. 1). The idea of interventionist state, which emerged with Keynes after World War II, was founded on the idea of intervening economic problems with public expenditures, taxes and borrowing, which are fiscal policy tools. At this point, taxes are seen as one of the important tools of intervention.

Taxes are the most important source of revenue for the state. Classical economists, in accordance with the neutral state understanding, stated that taxes should only have a fiscal purpose, that is, taxes should only be used to finance public expenditures. The neutral state understanding of classical economists started to be discussed with the 1929 Depression and as a result, the Keynesian view came to the fore. The understanding of the state of this view is formulated as an interventionist state that takes an active role in the economic and social field. In the interventionist state idea, one of the most important tools that the state can use to intervene in the economy is taxes. Thus, taxes not only finance public expenditures but also started to be used as a means of intervention in the economic and social sphere when necessary. In Türkiye, it is seen that taxes are frequently used as a tool to intervene in both the economic and social fields in accordance with the modern fiscal understanding. As a matter of fact, in the Constitution of the Republic of Türkiye, it is stated that "fair and balanced distribution of the tax burden is the social purpose of fiscal policy", and an approach in line with the modern fiscal understanding has been adopted (Constitution of the Rebuplic of Türkiye, article 73).

Examining Türkiye in particular, it is seen that fiscal objectives come to the forefront in tax policies followed especially during crisis periods, and tax measures are applied to reduce the budget deficit. For example, after the crisis in 1994, the priority arrangements made in the 5 April Stabilization measures were to make adjustments to the taxes on crude oil and petroleum products and to introduce additional taxes (Yıldırım ve Yıldırım, 2001, p. 14). It is seen that a similar process continued throughout the 1990s. While the ratio of tax burden to national income was 11.4 % in 1990, it increased to 17.2 % in 1998, 18.9 % in 1999, and 21 % in 2000. Between 1990 and 2000, the share of tax revenues in national income increased by 84 % (Terzi, 2001, p. 149). It is seen that the similar process was emphasized in the letter of intent sent to the IMF on 18 December 2000, after the turbulence of November 2000. In this letter of intent:

> *"Regarding direct taxes, the system of quarterly advance payment of income and corporate taxes will be extended to 2001 by increasing the advance corporate tax rate from 20% to 25%; withholding tax rates on deposit, repo and investment appropriations will be increased; indexing of income tax brackets to targeted inflation will continue advance income tax will be re-applied (based on living standards). Taking into account the end of tax deferral in earthquake zones, these measures are expected to yield 1.2% of GNP. As for indirect taxes, the duration of special communication and special transaction taxes will be extended to cover 2001–2002 by doubling the rate of special transaction tax; VAT rates on telephone services and natural gas will be increased; tax rates and levels on motor vehicles will be increased, and taxes on vehicles using LPG will be increased, along with other fees. These measures are expected to generate revenues of 1.2% of GNP. In addition, the monthly increase in fuel consumption tax will be determined to be at least equal to the targeted CPI inflation."*

statements are included (Türkiye Letter of Intent dated 18.12.2000). From this, it is understood that the increase in tax rates is not used for the implementation of a fiscal policy, but for the target of income increase.

In the light of these evaluations, it is seen that the tax increases applied during the increasing inflation process in Türkiye and other developing countries are mostly made with the aim of increasing public revenues. It is understood that tax increases do not come to the forefront as the main objective of fighting inflation. In the early 2000s, this situation in developing countries was followed under the name of indirect tax reform, and within the scope of the reform, an increase in value added tax and a decrease in trade taxes came to the fore in order to increase budget revenues. However, it is seen that informality in developing countries is ignored during the monitoring of these policies. The theoretical conclusions on indirect tax reforms are derived from partial models that ignore the existence of an informal economy. Since the value added tax base will not be fully taken into account, especially in developing countries where the informal economy is high, the policies implemented may reduce welfare (Emran & Stiglitz, 2005 p. 599).

3. Indirect Taxes in Combating Inflation: Theoretical Framework

The question of how taxes can be used in the fight against inflation leads us to the indirect-direct tax distinction, which is one of the oldest distinctions in taxation. In fact, the origin of this distinction goes back to the Middle Ages. Direct and indirect tax separation was also made by Smith, the founder of classical economic thought, and Mill, one of the important names (Tuncer, 1972, p. 211). First of all, it is thought that indirect taxes may be better in cyclical fluctuations in the economy, because indirect taxes are more sensitive to price movements than direct taxes. In addition, the efficiency of ad valorem indirect taxes increases during the recovery periods of the conjuncture. Conversely, the efficiency of indirect taxes decreases rapidly during the conjuncture contraction periods (Nadaroğlu, 1998, p. 331). With the prevalence of Keynes's interventionist state idea, the importance of changes in taxes and public expenditures in the short term has increased. As a matter of fact, Keynes also emphasized the importance of what measures should be taken against instability in the economy. The relationship between taxation and inflation gains importance at this point (Keynes, 1924, p. 41, 42). In this respect, intervention through changes in indirect taxes in inflationary and deflationary processes is frequently on the agenda.

It is accepted that tax collection will be basically deflationary, leaving the assumption that the collected taxes will turn into expenditures again. In this respect, as the fiscal policy to be implemented in the fight against inflation, it has been accepted as an increase in taxes while the expenditures are fixed or increasing the taxes more than the expenditures (Uluatam, 1990, p. 9) In the fight against inflation, it is aimed to reduce the income of taxpayers, that is, to reduce their liquidity, by increasing taxes or introducing new taxes. Thus, it is assumed that taxpayers will spend less. At this point, it is accepted that indirect taxes are more effective than direct taxes. Because indirect taxes have a more demand-absorbing feature, they show their effects in a short time, they are easy to apply and they attract less reaction from taxpayers (Edizdoğan, Çetinkaya, Gümüş, 2018, p. 524). Among the reasons listed in the fight against inflation, the most emphasized one in the literature is the idea that these taxes will decrease the demand while increasing the general price level. However, instead of evaluating indirect taxes as a whole, it would be beneficial to consider certain characteristics of each indirect tax in the formation of an effective anti-inflation strategy.

For example, indirect taxes such as value added tax, which has an increasing proportionality, are paid more by the people with a high propensity to consume than by the people with a high propensity to save. Therefore, depending on the demand structures, it is possible to increase the taxes on different goods groups. In addition, taxes on these goods can be increased in order to prevent those with a high propensity to save from turning to imported or luxury goods as a result of the relative reduction in tax burdens (Pınar, 2006, p. 84, 85). It should not be forgotten that fiscal policy can be implemented more effectively with such differentiations.

The opinions in the literature stating that indirect taxes are advantageous in the fight against inflation highlight the following issues (Türk, 1959, p. 15–16):

- If indirect taxes are used in the fight against inflation, as a result of the rise in prices, especially low-wage workers will work harder to maintain their living standards, and this situation may lead to the emergence of the "income effect" in taxation.
- In the inflationary period, when the income tax rates are increased, the workers will press for the payment of the tax by the employer. This may lead employers to avoid increasing employment volumes and reduce the productivity of enterprises. Indirect taxes, on the other hand, can be more advantageous at this point because they are easy to reflect.
- Although a synthetic inflation may occur during the reflection of indirect taxes, this inflation will be minimum if indirect taxes are collected during the transfer from the retailer to the consumer.
- Finally, it is faster and easier for indirect taxes to pass through parliaments. This situation creates a more advantageous situation than direct taxes in terms of delays in fiscal policy.

The type of tax policy to be followed in the fight against inflation also changes according to the type of inflation. For example, tax policies to be applied in case of demand inflation and cost inflation will also differ. The stagflation experienced in the 1970s brought the problem of cost inflation to the fore. The need to reduce aggregate demand in the fight against inflation and the view that the unemployment to be experienced as a result will prevent wage and price increases are advocated by both monetarists and economists advocating fiscal policy. With the 1970s, it was understood that it would not be possible to reach the full employment level without creating an inflation caused by excess demand, due to the indirect pressure of traditional demand-restrictive policies on wages and prices. On the contrary, it is stated that it is possible to approach the full employment level without causing inflation by directly suppressing wages and prices through incomes policy (Yamak, 1995, p. 88). For example, Cartenberry (1983) predicted that value added tax would be successful as an indirect tax at this point (p. 439). In this respect, it is important to implement a tax policy that differs according to the type of inflation instead of a uniform tax policy in the fight against inflation.

While discussing the tax policies to be applied in the fight against inflation in this study, another issue that should not be forgotten is that inflation itself causes many effects on taxation. These effects cause a decrease in the effectiveness of taxes in the fight against inflation. In this respect, these effects should be taken into account when discussing the success of a tax policy to be implemented in the fight against inflation. The effects of inflation on taxation can be listed as follows (Öncel, 1995, p. 492–498):

- With inflation, the tax burden is reduced in specific-based taxes applied per unit on criteria such as weight, length and volume. Since the tax base determinations are made for 3–4 years or longer in taxes collected on buildings and land, the tax burden decreases as the determined value is eroded due to inflation. In this case, it can be said that the tax revenues of the state decrease.
- Inflation exacerbates the proportionality of the income tax, leading to a continuous increase in the real tax burden. Even if their real incomes do not increase, taxpayers' move to higher tiers causes the tax burden to increase in real terms. In this case, the progressive tax tariff applied to distribute the tax burden more equitably creates the opposite results with inflation.
- Another problem is experienced in the interest earnings in income tax. In an environment where money is constantly depreciating, unless interest income rises above inflation, it does not create a real income flow. Taxation under these conditions can have negative consequences on savings.

Another issue that should be taken into account in the tax policy applied in the fight against inflation is the concept of "excessive tax burden". When the rate of consumption tax (which can be sales tax or value added tax) on any service or good is increased, the tax causes the relative price structure to change. Due to this feature, consumption taxes are not neutral in terms of resource distribution. When a high rate of consumption taxation is applied, the goods or services whose prices increase will not be obtained by the individuals forming the society as before, and this will lead to a loss of welfare for the people. This loss of welfare that people will suffer is called "excessive tax burden" (Şener, 1996, p. 280). In this respect, it is inevitable that such side effects will arise in the fight against inflation through tax policy. Therefore, the social costs of tax increases to be implemented in the fight against inflation should also be taken into account. Otherwise, tax avoidance may occur through behavioral change of taxpayers, which is called the diversion effect (Stiglitz, 2000, p. 462). Changes in tax rates are often not only evaluated in terms of fiscal policy but also the efficiency losses in taxation and the situations to be experienced in terms of optimal taxation are highlighted.

How optimal taxation should be and how direct and indirect taxes should be applied in the context of fiscal policy in the economy has always been a subject of discussion. Diamond and Mirless (1971) emphasized that the government should optimize production decisions using market prices and not resort to tariffs, production taxes or subsidies as they create inefficiency in production. Atkinson and Stiglitz (1976) stated that especially a direct income tax is the most effective tool in terms of redistribution in the economy. Optimal tax theory has shown that, under simple assumptions, indirect taxation such as production subsidies, tariffs or differentiated commodity taxation is sub-optimal and that redistribution should be effected only by direct income tax. For this reason, it is suggested that in the long run, direct taxes are more successful than indirect taxes in increasing income and redistributing resources (Saez, 2004, p. 503). While this situation highlights direct taxes in terms of resource and income distribution, indirect taxes are brought to the agenda in the fight against inflation due to their demand-restrictive effects.

4. Literature

Although it is seen that the indirect tax-inflation relationship is examined with different models for each country in the literature, there is no consensus on the direction of the effect. The difference between the models is mainly due to three reasons: (i) differences in the aggregate level of prices, (ii) differences in the way in which price formation equations are set, and (iii) differences in the inclusion of indirect tax rates and the definition of these rates in the price equations (Choudhry, 1977, p. 451, 452). Due to these differences, it is seen that the assumptions and measurements of the studies vary.

First of all, although it is accepted that changes in indirect tax rates may have a significant effect on inflation, the direction and magnitude of the effect are uncertain. This is because it depends on firms' decisions about how much of the tax increase they can pass on to consumers or how much they want to pass on. For example, since 2004 Eurostat has been preparing a harmonized consumer price index (HICP) at flat tax rates and assumes full and immediate pass-through of changes in indirect taxes to consumer prices. By this measure, the contribution of changes in indirect taxes to HICP inflation in the euro area was 0.2 percentage points on average. In addition, the effect was more pronounced in periods when tax rates increased, such as 2007, 2011 and 2014 (Koester, Dreher, Vlad, 2020).

Koutsouvelis and Papastathopoulos (2013) examined the relationship between inflation and indirect taxes with a linear regression model for Greece. As a result of the study, it was found that the contribution of indirect taxes to inflation was at least 82 % in 2010 and 60.7 % in 2011.

Akıncı and Özçelik (2018) examined the relationship between indirect taxes and inflation in Türkiye for the period 2006–2018 with the help of ARDL model. As a result of the study, a long-term cointegration relationship was determined between indirect taxes and inflation.

Çakmaklı, Demiralp, Yeşiltaş, and Yıldırım (2018) examined the effect of indirect taxes applied to tobacco products on inflation in Türkiye during the 2005–2017 period. As a result of the study, they found that an increase in indirect taxes applied to tobacco products increases inflation in the short run.

Arısoy and Ünlükaplan (2011) analyzed the relations between value added tax rate, value added tax revenue, public expenditures and inflation rate in Türkiye for the period 1994–2010, and emphasized that value added tax revenues have an inflationary effect.

Güvenek, Alptekin, and Çetinkaya (2010) examined the relationship between inflation and indirect taxes for the period 1980–2008 in Türkiye using the VAR model. They concluded that there is a bidirectional causality between the consumer price index and indirect tax revenues.

Karadağ and Westaway (1999), in their study on value added tax in Türkiye, concluded that an increase in value added tax rates increases consumer prices in many sectors.

Akdoğan (2020) examined the relationship between indirect tax and inflation with the Toda-Yamamoto causality test, using monthly data for the period of 2004–2019 for Türkiye. As a result of the study, while no causality relationship could be found between producer price index and indirect taxes, a one-way causality relationship was found from consumer price index to indirect tax revenues. However, ARDL-boundary test findings indicated a long-term negative relationship between consumer price index and indirect tax revenues.

5. Econometric Model

Two different methods, Least Squares (OLS) and Vector Autoregressive Model (VAR), were used in the empirical analysis of the study. The data set consists of the monthly collections of indirect taxes collected in Türkiye from January 2006 to May 2021 and the CPI values of the same period. Indirect tax collections were obtained from the Ministry of Treasury and Finance, and CPI data were obtained from the Central Bank of the Republic of Türkiye.

Tab. 1: Variables used in models

<table>
<tr><th colspan="2">Value Added Tax</th><th colspan="6">Special Consumption Tax (SCT)</th></tr>
<tr><td>Domestic VAT</td><td>VAT on Import</td><td>Petroleum and Natural Gas Products</td><td>Motor Vehicles</td><td>Spirits</td><td>Tobacco Products</td><td>Cola Sodas</td><td>Durable Goods</td></tr>
<tr><th colspan="8">Other Indirect Taxes</th></tr>
<tr><td colspan="2">Banking and Insurance Transactions Tax</td><td>Gambling Tax</td><td colspan="2">Special Communication Tax</td><td colspan="2">Customs Duty</td><td>Stamp Tax</td></tr>
</table>

The main purpose of the analysis is to examine the relationship between inflation and indirect taxes. If this relationship is known, it will be possible to make comments on how a tight fiscal policy should be applied in inflation. In this context, firstly, a regression model was established in which CPI is the independent variable and indirect tax collections are the dependent variable. Model results are given below.

Tab. 2: CPI-indirect tax collections relationship (OLS model results)

MODEL	*Coefficients-Standard Error*	*Possibility*
Constant	1.474 (3.74)	p<0.001
Domestic VAT	7.34e-08 (2.30)	p<0.05
VAT on Import	0.000000184 (2.08)	p<0.05
Petroleum and Natural Gas Products (SCT)	-0.000000532 (-3.37)	p<0.001
Motor Vehicles (SCT)	-0.000000337 (-2.81)	p<0.01
Spirits (SCT)	-0.000000410 (-0.96)	0.0000
Tobacco Products (SCT)	9.26e-08 (1.20)	0.0000
Cola Sodas (SCT)	0.00000618 (2.36)	p<0.05
Durable Goods (SCT)	-0.000000318 (-0.42)	0.0000

(Continued)

Tab. 2: Continued

MODEL	*Coefficients-Standard Error*	*Possibility*
Banking and Insurance Transactions Tax	0.000000477 (1.47)	0.0000
Gambling Tax	0.00000326 (1.22)	0.0000
Special Communication Tax	-0.00000259 (-2.33)	$p<0.05$
Customs Duty	-0.000000124 (-0.26)	0.0000
Stamp Tax	8.33e-08 (0.15)	0.0000
R^2	0.2587	
Adjusted R^2	0.2020	
F statistics	4.56	

* Values in parentheses indicate standard errors.

Unit root was found in the variables of: VAT on imports, SCT on petroleum and natural gas products, SCT on motor vehicles, SCT on alcoholic beverages, SCT on tobacco products, SCT on cola soda, SCT on durable goods, banking and insurance transactions tax, gambling tax, customs duty and stamp tax. In this respect, these variables were made stationary by taking their first difference and their stationary state was used in the model.

According to the model results, there is a statistically significant negative relationship between SCT on petroleum and natural gas products, SCT on motor vehicles and special communication taxes and CPI. It has been concluded that there is a statistically significant positive relationship between the domestic VAT on import and SCT on cola sodas and CPI. The results highlight that the relationship between inflation and indirect tax collections shows a complex structure without uniformity. In this respect, the results of the regression analysis show that this relationship should be considered separately for each tax type, where indirect tax increases alone cannot be very determinative in terms of inflation.

As the results of the model showed and emphasized earlier, the 1970 stagflation experience showed that the choice of the tax policy to be applied in inflation was not easy. Therefore, the effect of changes in tax rates on cost and demand should be considered separately. If tax rates are to be increased, those with less impact on costs should be preferred. For example, when there is no wage increase, the net effect of indirect taxes applied at the sales stage is deflationary. However, if demand increases despite the after-tax price increase, the process may not be deflationary. At this point, the wage-price spiral triggered by the cost, together with the increase in wages, may lead to a stronger inflationary effect. In such a situation, stagflation may become more pronounced. Likewise, the cost-cutting effects of the tax cut may more than offset the inflationary worsening effects of the resulting increase in demand. At the very least, the situation could be improved by combining a cost-cutting tax reduction at one point in the system with a non-cost-increasing tax increase elsewhere (Musgrave and Musgrave, 1984, p. 635).

In order to expand the model results, as a second method, the causality relationship between the CPI and tax collections was also examined with the VAR model. For this purpose, impulse-response functions were created between CPI and taxes. The results are presented in Tab. 3. The variables in the graphs are listed in the order given in Tabs. 1 and 2.

Tab. 3: CPI-indirect tax collections impulse response functions (VAR)

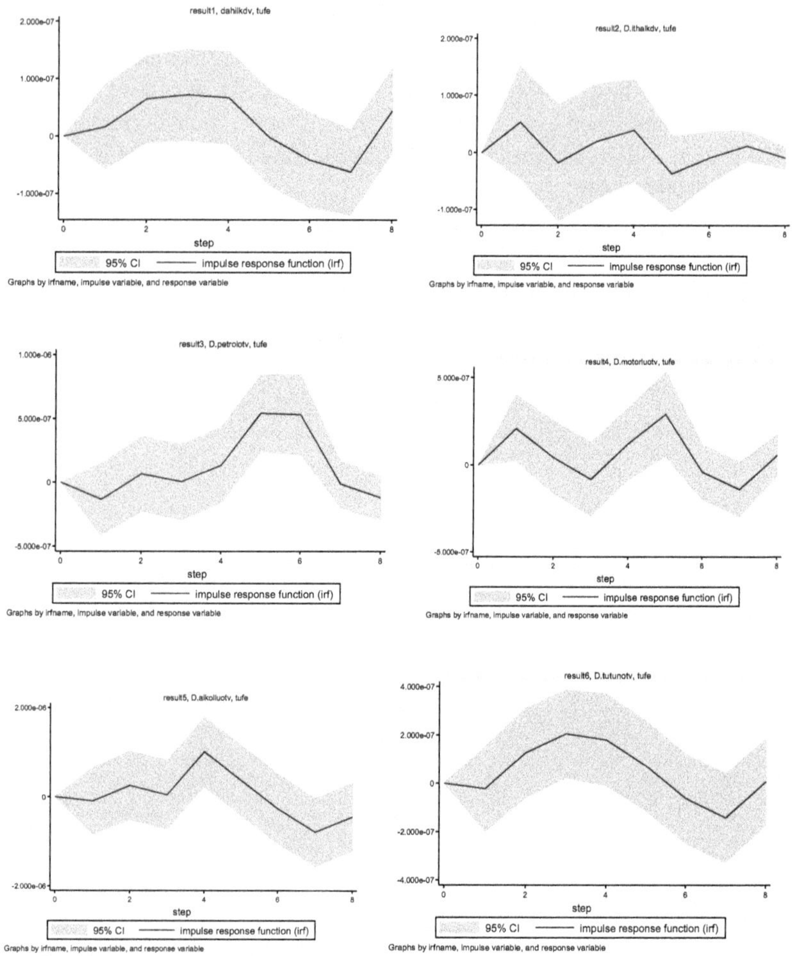

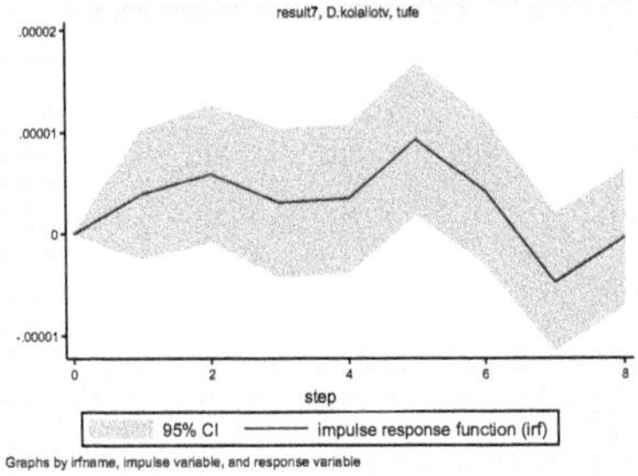
result7, D.kolaliotv, tufe
.00002
.00001
0
-.00001
0
2
4
6
8
step
95% CI
impulse response function (irf)
Graphs by irfname, impulse variable, and response variable

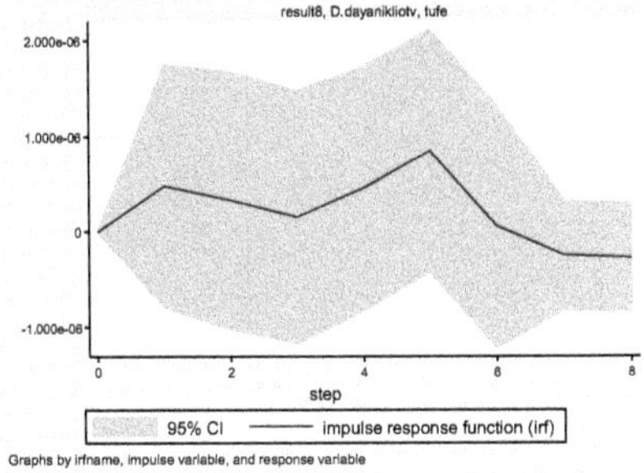
result8, D.dayanikliotv, tufe
2.000e-06
1.000e-06
0
-1.000e-06
0
2
4
6
8
step
95% CI
impulse response function (irf)
Graphs by irfname, impulse variable, and response variable

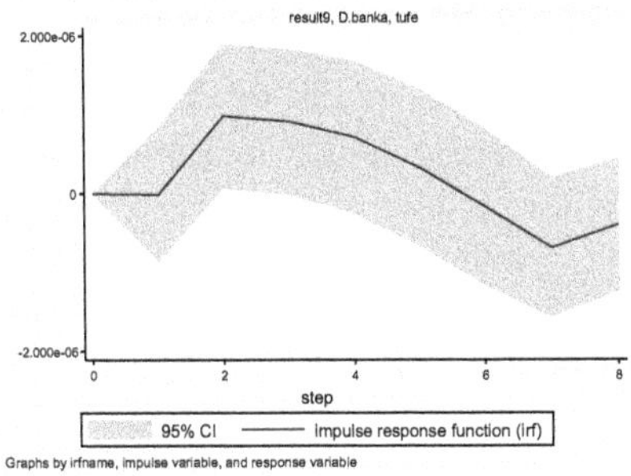
result9, D.banka, tufe
2.000e-06
0
-2.000e-06
0
2
4
6
8
step
95% CI
impulse response function (irf)
Graphs by irfname, impulse variable, and response variable

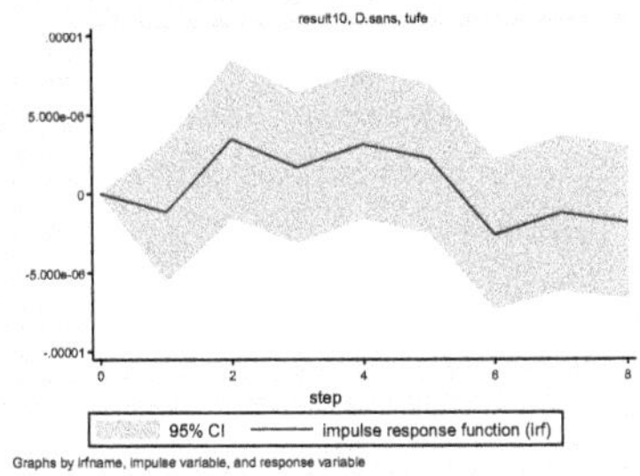
result10, D.sans, tufe
.00001
5.000e-06
0
-5.000e-06
-.00001
0
2
4
6
8
step
95% CI
impulse response function (irf)
Graphs by irfname, impulse variable, and response variable

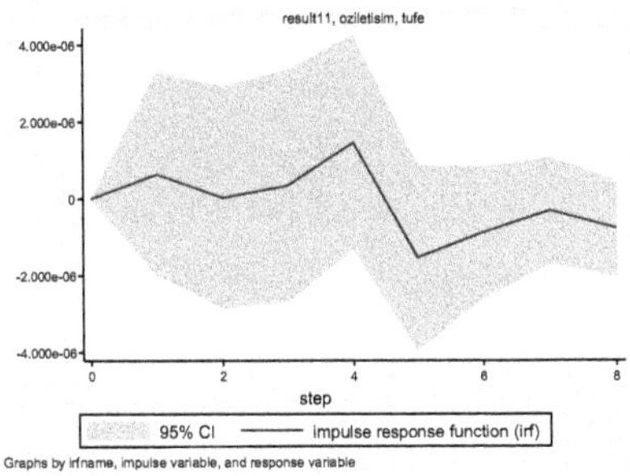
result11, oziletisim, tufe
4.000e-06
2.000e-06
0
-2.000e-06
-4.000e-06
0
2
4
6
8
step
95% CI
impulse response function (irf)
Graphs by irfname, impulse variable, and response variable

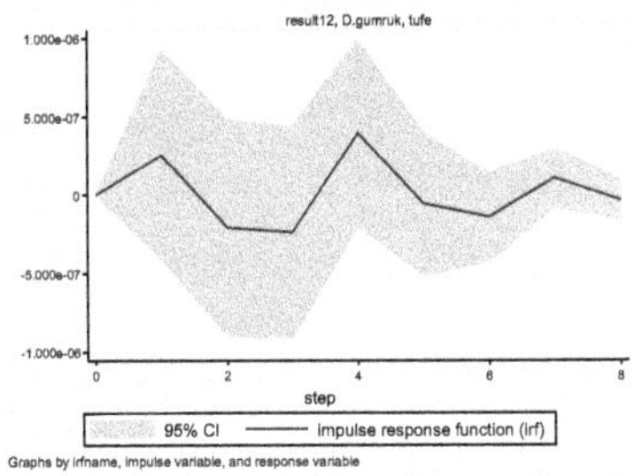
result12, D.gumruk, tufe
1.000e-06
5.000e-07
0
-5.000e-07
-1.000e-06
0
2
4
6
8
step
95% CI
impulse response function (irf)
Graphs by irfname, impulse variable, and response variable

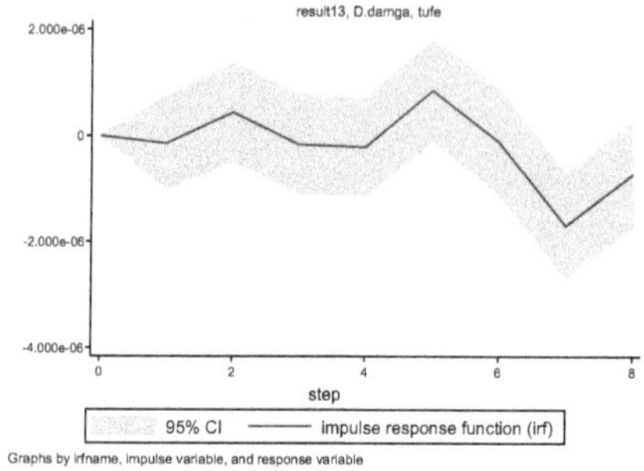

An eight-month period was used in the analysis, and as can be seen from the impulse-response function graphs, when there is an increase (shock) in any tax type, there is no decrease in the CPI in the medium or long term. Although the initial response of CPI to the increase in indirect taxes may be a decrease, this decrease does not turn into a trend (trend) in the medium and long term. CPI generally shows a fluctuating relationship with every tax type. Therefore, the results of the VAR analysis show that tax increases can only be effective in the short term in the fight against inflation in Türkiye. In the long run, tax increases trigger inflation as a cost factor. In this respect, the findings of the analysis support the finding that policies that reduce public expenditures rather than increase in tax rates may be more effective in the fight against inflation in Türkiye.

6. Conclusion

In many developing countries, indirect tax collections are above the direct tax collections. Since indirect taxes are taxes suitable for fiscal anesthesia, they can be hidden in the price and their collection costs are low. In addition, due to the idea that indirect taxes have a restrictive effect on total demand, it is thought to be an effective tool in the fight against inflation. As a country that has been struggling with inflation for a long time, Türkiye strives to establish and maintain fiscal discipline. In the fight against inflation, it is recommended that a tight fiscal policy be implemented, reducing public expenditures and reducing total demand through taxes. At this point, the complex structure of indirect taxes in Türkiye, the differences in the elasticity of demand for goods and services to which taxes are applied, the share of indirectly taxed products in the consumer budget complicates the question of how the effect of tax increases can be. Under these constraints, it is aimed to examine the relationship between indirect tax collections and CPI for the period of January 2006–May 2021. If this relationship can be revealed, it is possible to make inferences about how indirect taxes can be used in the fight against inflation.

In this direction, two different methods, OLS and VAR, were used in the study. The OLS model has shown that revenue increases in SCT on petroleum and natural gas products; SCT on motor vehicles and special communication taxes may have a reducing effect on CPI. On the other hand, the results of the VAR model show that although the increase in indirect tax revenues has a reducing effect on the CPI in the short term, the relationship has a fluctuating structure in the medium and long term. At this point, it can be said that many different factors such as consumer reactions to indirect taxes and price elasticity of goods and services come into play. For example, the after-tax price increase in cigarettes and alcohol often does not reduce demand and revenue. The price and income elasticity of cigarettes is very close to zero, and that of alcohol is very low. Therefore, price increases in cigarettes do not reduce tax revenues even in recession. In addition, gasoline can support price increases in the long run as a cost factor in production. Therefore, it can be concluded that a policy based on cutting public expenditures in the fight against inflation may have a higher chance of success. Finally, the fact that many different studies have reached different results in the literature shows that there is no consensus on this issue yet. In future studies for the Turkish economy, instead of using indirect taxes as a whole, examining the relationship of one of the sub-products from which VAT or SCT is charged one by one with inflation may be beneficial in terms of obtaining more specific results.

References

Akduğan, U. (2020). "Enflasyon ve Dolaylı Vergiler Arasındaki Bağlantı: Türkiye Örneği", *Manas Sosyal Araştırmalar Dergisi*, 9(4), 2248–2262.

Akıncı, A., & Özçelik, Ö. (2018). "Türkiye"de Dolaylı Vergilerin Enflasyon Üzerindeki Etkisi", *Maliye ve Finans Yazıları*, 110, 9–20.

Arisoy, İ., & Ünlükaplan, İ. (2011). "Katma Değer Vergisi, Enflasyon Oranı ve Kamu Harcamaları Arasındaki İlişkilerin Dinamik Analizi", *Sosyoekonomi*, 16(16), 93–112.

Atkinson, A. B., & Stiglitz, J. E. (1976). "The Design of Tax Structure: Direct Versus Indirect Taxation", *Journal of Public Economics*, 6, 55–75.

Çakmaklı, C., Demiralp, S., Yeşiltaş, S., & Yıldırım, M. A. (2018). "Tütün Ürünlerine Uygulanan Dolaylı Vergilerin Enflasyona Etkileri", *Koç University-Tüsiad Economic Research Forum Working Paper Series*, No: 1811.

Canterbery, E. R. (1983). "Tax Reform and Ineames Policy: A VATIP Proposal", *Journal of Post Keynesian Economics*, Spring, 430–439.

Choudhry, N. N. (1977). "The Treatment of Indirect Taxation in Econometric Models: An Analytical Survey", *IMF Staff Papers*, 1977(002), A007. Retrieved Aug 2, 2021, from https://www.elibrary.imf.org/view/journals/024/1977/002/article-A007-en.xml.

Constitution of the Republic of Türkiye.

Diamond, P. A., & Mirrlees, J. A. (1971). "Optimal Taxation and Public Production", *American Economic Review*, 61 8–27.

Edizdoğan, N., Çetinkaya, Ö., & Gümüş, E. (2018). Kamu Maliyesi, Bursa: Ekin Yayınevi, 9. Baskı.

Emran, M. S., & Stiglitz, J. E. (2005). "On Selective Indirect Tax Reform in Developing Countries", *Journal of Public Economics*, 89, 599–623.

Güvenek, B., Alptekin, V., & Çetinkaya, M. (2010). "Enflasyon ve Dolaylı Vergilerden Elde Edilen Gelirler Arasındaki İlişkinin Var Yöntemiyle Analizi", *Kamu-İş Dergisi*, 113), 1–28.

Karadağ, M., & Westaway, T. (1999). "The Impact on Consumer and Producer Prices in Turkey of VAT Changes Designed to Meet EU Membership Criteria: A Computable General Equilibrium Approach", *Economic Research Paper*, 99/19, Loughborough University Department of Economics.

Keynes, J. M. (1924). A Tract on Monetary Reform, Macmillan, https://delong.typepad.com/keynes-1923-a-tract-on-monetary-reform.pdf.

Koester, G., Dreher, F., & Vlad, A. (2020). "The Role of Indirect Taxes in Euro Area Inflation and its Outlook", ECB *Economic Bulletin*, Issue 6/2020.

Koutsouvelis, P., & Papastathopoulos, A. (2013). "The Effects of Indirect Taxes on Consumer Prices: Empirical Evidence for Greece", *Advances in Management and Applied Economics*, 3(1), 61–76.

Musgrave, R. A., & Musgrave, P. B. (1984). Public Finance in Theory and Practice, Fourth Edition, McGraw-Hill.

Nadaroğlu, H. (1998). *Kamu Maliyesi Teorisi*. İstanbul, Beta Yayınevi.

Öncel, M. (1995). "Enflasyon ve Vergilendirme", *Ankara Üniversitesi Hukuk Fakültesi Dergisi*, 44(1), 489–519. https://dergipark.org.tr/tr/download/article-file/629585.

Pınar, A. (2006). *Maliye Politikası*. Ankara, Naturel Yayıncılık.

Saez, E. (2004). "Direct or Indirect Tax Instruments for Redistribution: Short-Run Versus Long-Run", *Journal of Public Economics*, 88, 503–518.

Şener, O. (1996). *Kamu Ekonomisi*. İstanbul, Beta Basım Yayım Dağıtım.

Stiglitz, J. E. (2000). *Economics of the Public Sector.* W. W. Norton&Company, Üçüncü Baskı.

Terzi, C. (2001). "1980 Sonrası Vergi Politikaları", 16. Türkiye Mali Sempozyumu, Türkiye'de 1980 Sonrası Mali Politikalar, 28–31 Mayıs 2001/Antalya, Manisa: Emek Matbaacılık, 149–159.

Tuncer, S. (1972). Kamu Maliyesi. İstanbul, Üçüncü Baskı,Yalkın Ofset Matbaası.

Türk, İ. (1959). "Enflasyonla Mücadelede Maliye Politikası", *Ankara Üniversitesi SBF Dergisi*, 14(4), https://dergipark.org.tr/tr/download/article-file/37601.

Türkiye Letter of Intent dated 18.12.2000, https://www.tcmb.gov.tr/wps/wcm/connect/f5c83fd3-2a16-48ff-8fe9-0e0eed9b2fb3/18.pdf?MOD=AJPERES&CACHEID=ROOTWORKSPACE-f5c83fd3-2a16-48ff-8fe9-0e0eed9b2fb3-m3fB7yR, 26 March 2021.

Uluatam, Ö. (1990). "Enflasyon ve Vergileme", 6. Türkiye Maliye Sempozyumu, Çeşitli Açılardan Vergileme ve Sorunları, 21–23 Mayıs 1990/Antalya. http://www.maliyesempozyumu.org/wp-content/uploads/2017/10/Maliye-Sempozyumu_6_17_33.pdf.

Yamak, R. (1995). "Enflasyonla Mücadelede Vergi Esaslı Gelirler Politikası", *Ekonomik Yaklaşım*, 6(17), 85–92.

Yıldırım, E., & Yıldırım, R. (2001) "1980 Sonrası Uygulanan Maliye Politikaları ve Türkiye Ekonomisi Üzerindeki Etkileri" 16. Türkiye Maliye Sempozyumu,Türkiye'de 1980 Sonrası Mali Politikalar, 28–31 Mayıs 2001/Antalya, Manisa: Emek Matbaacılık, 7–24.

Piotr Jaworski

Stock Market Indexes: Are They Sensitive on the Ukrainian War?

1. Introduction

On 24 February 2022 the Ukrainian War started. It is the first war in Europe after the World War II. This event created a strong reaction on the stock exchanges, especially in the Russian and Ukrainian neighborhood. The direct effect of this military conflict between Russia and Ukraine are also sanctions given by the biggest countries. The European Union (EU) has adopted five packages of sanctions in response to Russia's military attack against Ukraine. The measures are designed to: weaken the Kremlin's ability to finance the war and impose clear economic and political costs on Russia's political elite responsible for the invasion. The mentioned sanctions that are taken by the EU can be divided into few groups: individual sanctions, economic sanctions, restrictions on media and diplomatic measures. The EU has also adopted sanctions against Belarus. The individual restrictive measures include assets freezes and travel restrictions for 1091 individuals (members of the Russian State Duma, members of the National Security Council, high-ranking officials, businesspeople and oligarchs) and 80 entities. The economic sanctions are aimed at financial sector. They relay on the restricted access to EU primary and secondary capital markets for certain Russian banks and companies. Transactions with the Russian Central Bank and the Central Bank of Belarus are also prohibited. The access to the SWIFT system is also limited to only several banks. Investments in Russia and Belarus and access to the primary and secondary capital market by Russian and Belarus investors are also prohibited. To the mentioned group of sanctions also belong the prohibition on the provision of euro-denominated banknotes to Russia and Belarus and investment in and contribution to projects co-financed by the Russian Direct Investment Fund. The strong restrictions also hit the energy sector. The coal import is also prohibited, similar to the export of goods and technologies to Russia in the oil refining sector and new investments in the Russian energy sector. In the transport sector the main restrictions are connected with the closure of EU airspace and ports to all Russian-owned and Russian-registered aircrafts. The road transport operators from entering the EU was also closed. The export of goods and technology to Russia in the aviation, maritime and space industry is also prohibited. Other sectors where limitations are presented are defense and raw materials and other goods. The export of dual-use goods and technology items to Russia that could contribute to its defense and security capabilities and trade in arms is also prohibited. The restrictions are also connected with the ban on imports of iron, steel, wood, cement, seafood, and liquor and luxury goods from Russia to the EU. In February 2022, the EU decided that Russian diplomats, other Russian officials and businesspeople may no longer benefit from visa facilitation provisions, which allow privileged access to the EU. This decision does not affect ordinary Russian citizens. Restrictions are also prepared on economic relations with Crimea and Sevastopol. The scale of sanctions is the biggest in history. Similar restrictions have been prepared by the United States. The US ban oil and gas imports. The UK will cut out Russian oil import by the end of 2022. The EU, which gets a quarter of its oil and 40 % of its gas from Russia, says it will switch to alternative supplies and make Europe independent from Russian energy "well before 2030". Germany has put on hold permission for the Nord Stream 2 gas pipeline from Russia to open.

As an effect the financial markets react strongly on the mentioned publications. Because of the scale of ban that has been put on the Russian economy, nearly every day sanctions by particular countries in all over the world have been published, beginning from Australia and ending in Canada. The presented paper takes a new scientific problem. It is lack of studies about the impact of the Ukrainian War on the stock indexes. The analysis in the next section, that is, the literature review about the impact of the military conflicts and the terrorist attacks on the stock markets suggest varied impact of the mentioned type of events on the stock prices. Next the presented paper will help to assess the scale of the reactions and differences between particular markets. Each market can react differently on the mentioned event. It can be connected with the geographical location, the closeness to the conflict or connection with Russian and Ukrainian economy. As a result, the aim of this chapter is to analyze the impact of the beginning of the Ukrainian War on the abnormal rates of returns on the main stock indexes. It has been put in the following hypothesis: it exists in the strong significant impact of the Ukrainian War beginning on the abnormal rates of return on the stock indexes by taking into account the geographical location, the connection with the Russian and Ukrainian economies. To the analysis the event study panel data models have been used. Data have been collected from the stock exchanges from 1 November 2021 to 25 April 2022. The analysis has been prepared by estimating three windows: pre-event window, event window and post-event window. As an event window has been used 24th February 2022, as a moment of beginning of the mentioned war.

The structure of the chapter proceeds as follows. In Section 2, the review of previous studies that investigate the impact of the military conflicts on the abnormal rates of return on the stock prices is presented. Section 3 reports the methodology by describing the features of data sample and model specification on which this study is based. Section 4 provides discussion of findings, and then Section 5 concludes by placing limitations of the current study and consequently suggesting future development.

2. Literature Review

The Ukrainian War is a new military situation; as a result, there are no noticed research about the impact of the mentioned phenomenon on the stock prices. It was published in only one study about the impact of this military conflict on the abnormal rates of return on the stock prices of the energy sector companies from all over the world (Chodnicka-Jaworska, 2022). The presented study does not take into consideration the particular sectors but the significance of the Ukrainian War as a predictor of the local crisis or the economic slowdown.

The prepared literature review suggests that the impact of the military conflicts or wars impact on the stock prices is due to the research problem poorly analyzed. Most of research takes into consideration the influence of the terrorist attacks on the financial markets. The most popular attacks that were studied are attacks in Basque country in Spain (Abadie & Gardeazabel, 2003 and 11 September attacks on New York in 2001 (Carter & Simkins, 2004; Chen & Siems, 2004). In most cases the negative impact of the mentioned situations are noticed on the stock prices market presented as abnormal rates of return. In the case of research prepared by Abadie and Gardeazabel (2003) the higher abnormal rates of return are noticed as an effect of the positive information than negative, that is opposite to the perspective theory. The hey compared the Basque portfolio outperformed the non-Basque portfolio after bad and good news. Also studies about the impact of the terrorist attacks on the stock prices have been prepared by taking into account the type of sector. Carter and Simkins (2004) found that as an effect of attacks from 11 September on New York in 2001, the most suffered stock prices were of the airfreight firms and international airlines. Similar results were received by Brounrn and Derwall (2010). They underlined that the effect was mildly negative which rebound within the first week of the aftermath, and the reactions are strongest for local markets and industries that are directly affected by the attack. This situation is rational because of the type of attack. The historical analysis of the terrorist attacks suggests that countries nowadays are coming out faster from crisis on the capital market caused by them, than earlier. It can be connected with the globalization of the financial market (Chen & Siems, 2004), but still the mentioned event has got the negative consequences on the stock prices. The negative relationship has been noticed also by Charles and Darné (2006). To the analysis they used ARIMA model. In their opinion the US market is less sensitive on the terrorist attack than other international markets. It can be connected with the liquidity and the size of the market. Not without significance is also the place where the attacks have been made. A similar research about the impact of the terrorist attacks on the index FTSE 100 has been prepared by Nikkinen and Vahamaa (2010). They found that these attacks caused three of the five largest daily increases in implied volatility from January 2000 through to December 2005.

The next group of studies analyzed the impact of the different wars on the stock prices. The studies have been prepared for different wars, i.e., World War II (Urquhart & Hudson, 2016), Iraq (Leigh et al., 2003; Rigobon & Sack, 2005), Israeli-Palestinian (Zussman et al., 2008) or some conflicts (Schneider &Troeger, 2006; Guidolin & La Ferrara, 2010; Hobbs et al., 2016).

The differences between the reaction of the stock prices on the war were observed by Schneider and Troeger (2006). They examined the effect of political developments within three war regions from 1990 to 2000 using data from the CAC, DJIA and FTSE, and they found reaction in the three markets, with the notable exception of the Gulf war on the DJIA.

In most studies the negative effects of the war events on the stock prices have been noticed. Kollias et al. (2010) and Dimic et al. (2015) indicate the presence of higher risk for stock exchanges in various countries during conflicts after 1990. Leigh et al. (2003) confirmed that because of the US commitment to the war in Iraq, the US equities fell down by around 15 %, especially in the consumer discretionary sector, airlines and IT, but sectors like gold and energy registered positive abnormal rates of return. The varied impact on the sectors has been noticed by Hobbs et al. (2016) and for Iraq by Rigobon and Sack (2005). The higher influence on the Türkiye, Israel and European economies is connected with the connection in the world economy or net oil importers (Leigh et al., 2003).

In some studies, like Urquhart and Hudson (2016), limited evidence of the strong links between war events and market returns has been noticed. Choudhry (2010) confirmed results received by Abadie and Gardeazabel (2003), and found by testing the DIJA that news seen as good by investors tends to increase the price the next day after the event and for the next five working days and leads to a fall in volatility. The similar results were received by Guidolin and La Ferrara (2010). Their study suggests that, on average, national stock markets are more likely to display positive than negative reactions to conflict onset, but the fraction of significant results is higher for international conflicts. The highest effect has been noticed in the case of Asia and the Middle regions. The abnormal returns would have accrued to investors systematically exploiting conflict onset to implement conflict-driven strategies. Results are robust to selecting a subset of high-intensity conflicts and to expanding the time window over which conflict events are defined. The positive effect of finishing war or positive news on the stock prices has been underlined by Zussman et al. (2008) and Franck and Krausz (2009).

Not without significance is the length of the war (Amihud & Wohl, 2004) or methods of financing war (Le Bris, 2012), which could lead to higher public expenditures, inflation and disruptions of the public services.

To the analysis of the impact of the Ukrainian War, the event study methodology to firm-level data like Abadie and Gardeazabal (2003) and Guidolinand La Ferrara (2007) will be taken.

3. Methodology

The research was conducted by using the panel data event study methodology. The data have been collected from the Refinitiv Eikon Database. The daily data of the stock indices from the world's major stock exchanges from 1 November 2021 to 25 April 2022 have been used to the analysis. The analyzed indices have been divided on two groups: countries which are direct neighbors of Russia and Ukraine that have longer distance to them. The other diversification that has been made is gathering group of European countries and non-European ones.

As the event date in all cases the date of starting the conflict, i.e. 24 February 2022 is taken. The analysis has been made for the event window (car_ret), that is the moment of publication of sanctions and one day after. The research has been also prepared for the pre-event window (car_retpre) starting five days before to one day before of the event date and two post-event window, first (car_retpost1) from second day to sixth day after the event, and the second (car_retpost2) from seventh day to day no. 26 after the event, as is mostly done with event study methodology. Logarithmized daily rates of return on the stock indices have been used to calculate the abnormal rates of return during the event window. The expected normal behavior of rates of return was calculated in two ways. First a normal moving average of previous 20 periods was employed. The second prediction method was using a basic market model described by the following equation:

$$R_{i,t} = \alpha_{i,t} + \beta_{i,t} RM_{i,t} + \varepsilon_{i,t}$$

where $R_{i,t}$ are the logarithmized rates of return on the analyzed index i in period t; $R_{i,t}$ are the logarithmized rates of return on the benchmark which is the Dow Jones Industrial Average in period t in all cases.

In the next steep there were defined the abnormal rates of return on the index prices as a difference between the real and the forecast value (limited by the information set in the estimating window Ω_{EW})

$$AR_{i,t} = R_{i,t} - E\left(R_{i,t} | \Omega_{EW}\right)$$

The average abnormal rates of return during t period is estimated according to:

$$\overline{AR_{i,t}} = \frac{\sum_{t=1}^{N} AR_{i,t}}{N}$$

where N is the size of the research sample. The standard deviation $\hat{\sigma}$ is estimated by:

$$\hat{\sigma}_{AR} = \sqrt{\frac{1}{N-1} \sum_{t=1}^{N} \left(\overline{AR_{i,t}} - \overline{\overline{AR_{i,t}}}\right)}$$

Next, in the pre-event window, event window and post-event window was tested the hypothesis. To verify the hypothesis has been used the t-Student test.

$$t_{STAT} = \frac{\frac{1}{N} \sum_{t=1}^{N} AR_{i,t}}{\breve{\sigma}_{AR}}$$

The use of a more advanced model, taking into account the heterogeneity of the variance of the random component and the autocorrelation, would require a longer estimation window.

4. Findings

The results of the impact of sanctions put on Russia against starting the conflict on the abnormal rates of return on the stock index price have been presented in Tab. 1. They are presented as _cons variables which are the average abnormal returns obtained above the predicted normal behavior from 20 period moving average or market model with DJIA benchmark (marked with "djia" postfix). Under the AAR the t-student statistic is presented, and below the N as the number of observations in current subsample.

The general picture shows that European Union sanctions have got the significant negative impact on the abnormal rates of return on the stock index prices for the whole period of the start of the conflict, in comparison to the expected returns based both on their historical behavior and global benchmark index taken as the Dow Jones Industrial Average. Almost all average abnormal returns are negative, which is marked as the _cons position in the below-listed table. As we can see the most statistically important impact can be found in the event windows, what was also expected to occur. The positive reaction has been noticed only for the post-event window 2, which is a week after the announcement of particular sanctions package.

The received results suggest few findings. First, it shows that some of the stock indices prices of the group of the entities react stronger than the benchmark. The abnormal returns on stock exchanges react more in countries near to Ukraine and Russia. The presented situation is connected with the direct neighborhood of the military conflict. Also neighbors placed in Europe react more, which can be explained because of the worries that this conflict can spoil on their territory as well. The impact of conflict on countries in the neighborhood confirms findings of Weber and Schneider (2022).

Second, the European countries also got stronger reactions than those from other continents. It is connected with more complex industrial and economic relationship with Russia, especially in the context of importing most of fossil fuels to other European countries. That kind of relationship was also shown by other authors in the context of the economic and political relationship (see Jing et al., 2003; Smeets, 2018).

Looking at the distribution of market reaction in time, we can observe that it is strongest in the direct moment of 24 February. Both abnormal returns calculated as the historical behavior and relative to the market benchmark are strongly negative and statistically significant there. It is in line with the economic intuition, because until this conflict began, most county leaders hoped that it won't be an open military confrontation. The pre-event window's AAR are also negative and significant, but not so strong as previous ones; this supports the thesis that the market did not price this crisis as definitely sure to be in the full scale.

Quite different situation can be observed in post-event window 2, which is a week after the conflict formally started. There we can see positive abnormal results with good statistical significance over historical rate of return. It brings us to a conclusion that the market reaction was very strong when the conflict began, and markets probably over reacted. After a week they tried to get back to their more natural levels, producing positive abnormal rates of return.

After the start of described conflict international community has put serious sanction over Russia. Their significance can be observed only in the long period. Assessing them in a short period bring us the information about the sensitiveness of stock exchanges to shock brought to them by military confrontation and assess the impact of the behavioral finance, but they do not give the final information about the effectiveness of capital markets on sanctions themselves.

Tab. 1: Impact of neighborhood and geographical location on the abnormal rates of return on the stock indices of analyzed countries

	All	Neighbor		Europe		Neighbor		Neighbor	
		0	1	0	1	0	0	1	1
						Europe		europe	
						0	1	0	1
car_retpre									
_cons	-0.0241***	-0.0179***	-0.0245*	-0.0103*	-0.0295***	-0.0109*	-0.0289**	-0.00638	-0.0306*
t-student	(-4.25)	(-4.69)	(-2.77)	(-2.64)	(-5.76)	(-2.66)	(-4.83)	(-0.38)	(-3.09)
N	32	23	8	16	15	14	9	2	6
car_ret									
_cons	-0.00936	-0.00991*	0.00454	-0.0128*	0.000858	-0.0139*	-0.00367	-0.00481	0.00765
t-student	(-1.91)	(-2.66)	-0.45	(-2.65)	-0.15	(-2.56)	(-0.95)	(-1.18)	-0.57
N	32	23	8	16	15	14	9	2	6
car_retpost1									
_cons	-0.00375	-0.0101	0.0104*	0.0134**	-0.0243*	0.0139*	-0.0475***	0.00977	0.0106
t-student	(-0.64)	(-1.32)	-2.72	-3.23	(-2.63)	-2.94	(-5.77)	-4.34	-2.04
N	32	23	8	16	15	14	9	2	6
car_retpost2									
_cons	0.0407***	0.0383***	0.0521*	0.0195*	0.0657***	0.0201**	0.0666***	0.015	0.0644**
t-student	-6.01	-5.54	-2.82	-2.47	-8.41	-3.22	-7.82	-0.24	-4.05
N	32	23	8	16	15	14	9	2	6
car_retpredjia									
_cons	-0.0111*	-0.00817	-0.00501	-0.00153	-0.0136*	-0.00222	-0.0174*	0.0033	-0.00779
t-student	(-2.11)	(-1.84)	(-0.64)	(-0.29)	(-2.61)	(-0.37)	(-3.08)	-0.33	(-0.77)

(Continued)

Tab. 1: Continued

	All	Neighbor		Europe		Neighbor		Neighbor	
N	32	23	8	16	15	14	9	2	6
car_retdjia									
_cons	-0.0238***	-0.0208***	-0.0148*	-0.0229***	-0.0153**	-0.0240***	-0.0157*	-0.015	-0.0147
t-student	(-4.27)	(-5.28)	(-2.54)	(-4.61)	(-3.70)	(-4.28)	(-3.21)	(-3.50)	(-1.86)
N	32	23	8	16	15	14	9	2	6
car_retpost1djia									
_cons	-0.00461	-0.011	0.0124**	0.0132*	-0.0244*	0.0136*	-0.0494***	0.0104	0.0131*
t-student	(-0.76)	(-1.38)	-3.58	-2.94	(-2.47)	-2.65	(-5.54)	-2.9	-2.84
N	32	23	8	16	15	14	9	2	6
car_retpost2djia									
_cons	0.000275	0.00362	0.0138	-0.006	0.0193*	-0.00495	0.017	-0.0134	0.0228
t-student	-0.03	-0.56	-1.01	(-0.71)	-2.73	(-0.59)	-1.82	(-0.29)	-1.95
N	32	23	8	16	15	14	9	2	6

Legend: neighbor: 0 – indices from countries that are not in the Russia and Ukraine neighborhoods, i.e. S&P Merval Index, S&P/NZX 50 Index, BIST 100 Index, IBEX 35 Index, Jakarta SE Composite Index, CAC 40 Index, Deutsche Boerse DAX Index, Hang Seng Index, TSX-Toronto Stock, Exchange 300 Composite Index, FTSE 100 Index, Tel Aviv Main 125 Index, Sao Paulo SE Bovespa Index, PX Prague SE Index, S&P BSE, Dollex 30 Index, OMX Stockholm 30 Index, FTSE Bursa Malaysia KLCI Index, FTSE MIB Index, Austrian Traded Index, Taiwan SE Weighted Index, Swiss Market Index, S&P/Bmv Ipc, ASX All Ordinaries Index, Korea SE Kospi Index; 1 – indices from countries in the direct Russia and Ukraine neighborhoods, i.e. Shanghai SE Composite Index, Tokyo SE JPX-Nikkei Index 400, S&P 500 Index, Warsaw SE WIG Poland Index, Oslo Exchange Benchmark Index_GI, Warsaw SE WIG-20 Single Market Index, Dow Jones Industrial Average Index, NASDAQ 100 Index.

Europe: 0 – indices from countries that are not European; 1 – indices from European countries.

Source: Own elaborations.

5. Conclusions

The aim of the chapter was to analyze the impact of the beginning of the Ukrainian War on the abnormal rates of returns on the main stock indexes. The hypothesis has been proposed as follows: the beginning of the conflict causes the negative abnormal rates return on the stock indices prices. The presented hypothesis has been partially fulfilled.

The markets, represented by world's stock indices, reacted strongly negative in comparison to their predicted behavior in the moment of the start of the conflict. They also produced negative abnormal returns in a week period before. The significance and strength of the reaction of the stock indices prices is also connected with the direct neighborhood of the described military conflict. Also European countries are exposed more because of their relations with Russia regarding trade of fossil fuels.

The received findings can be useful for regulatory bodies and governments because they show which countries are more exposed to the risk of capital outflow. This study can be also used by the investors, because it gives answer on which countries are less exposed to the risk and are potentially more stable to invest and generate abnormal rates of return on the stock prices than the global benchmark.

The presented study has also got some limitations. In future it should rebuild on the impact of sanctions that European Union and the international community have put on Russia. The interesting results will also give the comparison the rates of return on the stock prices effect between particular sectors of economy, and testing them against the local benchmark proper for each country.

References

Abadie, A., & Gardeazabal, J. (2003). The economics costs of conflict: A case study of the Basque country. *The American Economic Review*, 93(1), 113–132. http://www.jstor.org/stable/3132164.

Amihud, Y., & Wohl, A. (2004). Political news and stock prices: The case of Saddam Hussein contracts. *Journal of Banking and Finance*, 28(5), 1185–1200.

Brounen, D., & Derwall, J. (2010). The impact of terrorist attacks on international stock markets. *European Financial Management*, 16(4), 585–598.

Carter, D. A., & Simkins, B. J. (2004). The market's reaction to unexpected, catastrophic events: The case of airline stock returns and the September 11th attacks. *The Quarterly Review of Economics and Finance*, 44(4), 539–558.

Charles, A., & Darné, O. (2006). Large shocks and the September 11th terrorist attacks on international stock markets. *Economic Modelling*, 23(4), 683–698.

Chen, A. H., & Siems, T. F. (2004). The effects of terrorism on global capital markets. *European Journal of Political Economy*, 20, 349–366.

Chodnicka-Jaworska, P. (2022). Ukrainian War Impact on the Energy Sector Stock Prices Effect - are Distance and ESG Policy Important? „Review of Managerial Science" (in press) .

Choudhry, T. (2010). World War II events and the Dow Jones industrial index. *Journal of Banking & Finance*, 34(5), 1022–1031.

Dimic, N., Orlov, V., & Piljak, V. (2015). The political risk factor in emerging, frontier, and developed stock markets. *Finance Research Letters*, 15, 239–245.

Franck, R., & Krausz, M. (2009). Institutional changes, wars and stock market risk in an emerging economy: Evidence from the Israeli stock exchange, 1945–1960. *Cliometrica*, 3, 141–164.

Guidolin, M., & La Ferrara, E. (2007). Diamonds are forever, wars are not: Is conflict bad for private firms? *The American Economic Review*, 97(5), 1978–1993.

Guidolin, M., & La Ferrara, E. (2010). The economic effects of violent conflict: Evidence from asset market reactions. *Journal of Peace Research*, 47(6), 671–684. DOI: https://doi.org/10.1177/0022343310381853.

Hobbs, J., Schaupp, L. W., & Gingrich, J. (2016). Terrorism, militarism, and stock returns. *Journal of Financial Crime*, 23(1), 70–86.

Jing, C., Kaempfer, W. H., & Lowenberg, A. D. (2003). Instrument choice and the effectiveness of international sanctions: A simultaneous equations approach. *Journal of Peace Research*, 40(5), 519–535.

Kollias, C., Papadamou, S., & Stagiannis, A. (2010). Armed conflicts and capital markets: The caseof the Israeli military offensive in the Gaza strip. *Defence and Peace Economics*, 21, 357–365.

Le Bris, D. (2012). Wars, inflation and stock market returns in France, 1870–1945. *Financial HistoryReview*, 19(3), 337–361.

Leigh, A., Wolfers, J., & Zitzewitz, E. (2003). What Do Financial Markets Think of War in Iraq? *NBER Working Papers* 9587, National Bureau of Economic Research, Inc.

Nikkinen, J., & Vahamaa, S. (2010). Terrorism and stock market sentiment. *Financial Review*, 45(2), 263–275.

Rigobon, R., & Sack, B. (2005) The effects of war risk on U.S. financial markets. *Journal of Banking and Finance*, 29(7), 1769–89.

Schneider, G., & Troeger, V. E. (2006). War and the world economy: Stock market reactions to international conflicts. *The Journal of Conflict Resolution*, 50(5), 623–645.

Smeets, M. (2018). No ERSD-2018-03, WTO Staff Working Papers from World Trade Organization (WTO), Economic Research and Statistics Division.

Urquhart, A., & Hudson, R. (2016). Investor sentiment and local bias in extreme circumstances: The case of the Blitz. *Research in International Business and Finance, Elsevier*, 36(C), 340–350.

Weber, P., & Schneider, G. (2020). Post-cold war sanctioning by the EU, the UN, and the US: introducing the EUSANCT Dataset. *Conflict Management and Peace Science*. https://doi.org/10.1177/0738894220948729

Zussman, A., Zussman, N., & Nielsen, M. Ø. (2008). Asset market perspectives on the Israeli–Palestinian conflict. *Economica*, 75, 84–115.

Almiro de Oliveira, Pedro Fernandes da Anunciação

Information Systems Governance: Some Dimensions to Management

1. Introduction

Information and Information Systems (IS) are currently two vital resources in the context of the economy and society. Information emerges as a fundamental, differentiating factor and source of competitive advantage for, profit and non-profit, organizations that operate in a market where the norm is the globalization of the economy and society in general (Oliveira, 2019). Its relevance derives from the fact that it constitutes a raw material for the decision-making processes of managers and consumers, but also from the abundance associated with the "universe of economic data" that grows exponentially and represents an endless source of economic and competitive.

The economy has extremely short production and commercialization cycles, providing strategic "windows of opportunity" in increasingly shorter periods, which increases the difficulties of optimizing the management practices of Information Systems and Information and Communication Technologies (IS/ICT). The organizational environment, in this domain, is also prone to some difficulties and confusion, not only regarding the objectives to be achieved or the underestimation of the importance that IS/ICT has in profit and nonprofit organizations but even regarding the concepts of IS and ICT (Oliveira, 2019).

In general, all economic organizations have become increasingly Information-Based Organizations (Drucker, 1988; Oliveira, 1999). Most of its activities are focused on obtaining, producing, storing, consuming, and making information available. This centrality justifies a new configuration of organizations focused on information and new management skills in the IS domain. The IS cannot continue to be reduced to the technological aspect, framed only as a set of ICTs, however attractive they may be to economic agents. Management often looks at the various ICTs only as instruments and machines to "do what was done before and as it was done before", substantiating a rudimentary vision and knowledge of this problem, making the rational use of ICT impossible and not knowing how to take advantage of those excellent technologies to improve the quality of management (Oliveira, 2021).

IS constitutes key elements in supporting the organizational value chain, the development of the respective capabilities and processes, and the relationship with economic agents. These are, by integrating and incorporating the potential made available by technologies, present themselves as important strategic resources for obtaining competitive advantages in a relational economy, guided by the joint generation, and sharing of knowledge, participation in economic networks, by the integrated development of products and information services, among other aspects.

The competitive and pragmatic relevance of IS centrality emerges in the face of organizational and informational vulnerability related to difficulties in integrating different organizational information subsystems; the weakness of the architectures and the difficulties of implementing the IS, which constitute an obstacle to the respective management, operation, and organizational development; the advantages or disadvantages resulting from the timely sharing of information between the various stakeholders; the impossibility of extending the network to third parties, resulting from difficulties in extending organizational and technological protocols; or, the demand for higher levels of reliability, security, privacy, and integrity, superior to conventional internal IS, among other examples (Anunciação, 2014).

IS came to refocus economic activity on the adequacy of the functions of production, storage, and distribution of information. In this sense, as the context of the action of economic organizations is new, the context of management is also new, because the problems related to the quality of the main resource, Information, are new. The traditional concept of IS management must now be elevated to the level of Governance. Any economic organization needs purpose (mission), direction (strategy), organization (management), and monitoring (control). Corporate governance oversees how the organization creates value. If the generation of value depends on information and, consequently, on IS, the need for this new level in the general framework of Governance will be evident. Information and IS should be managed and developed if they can only be justified through criteria of practical and quantifiable utility. However, its value is no longer based only on its practical use or performance, but on the innovation and strategy that it brings to the market. And this is not just a management dimension.

If historically the two dimensions of Governance (Corporate and IT) sought to maximize economic value and minimize risks, through the definition of a set of policies, legislation, and regulations, always with a focus on sustainability, it is, therefore, natural that this requirement is now reflected at the level of information and IS.

The main objective initially envisaged through IT was to boost efficiency gains and, above all, productivity. However, the potential is currently significantly greater, as they provide new business paradigms and the dilution of competitive factors between companies. This reality gives rise to the need for two new dimensions of governance that, in conjunction with "traditional" governance, project the relevance of IS and Information.

This responsibility of Governance is not just business. It is a shared economic and social responsibility, as proposed by the Information Systems Governance European Club Manifesto (Anunciação, 2019). It is an instrument of reflection on the responsibility that, at different levels, the managers of economic organizations, profit or nonprofit, have in this new scenario of action:

- Top Management / Chief Executive Officer (CEO) must assume that IS and Information Management are critical areas in the life of economic organizations; that IS Governance constitutes a technical and management specialization, which should be the direct responsibility of top management; that Information should be viewed as one of the most valuable corporate resources; and that IS Governance encompasses new managerial and organizational processes and with new forms of business and professional performance.
- Chief Information Officer (CIO) must assume that Information (and not technologies) is the core business of their activity; that Information must be managed like a business; that all efforts and activities must be developed to qualitatively raise the level of information; and that there should be focus on the production and availability of Information in the Information Value Added.
- IT Director must frame and align their missions, objectives, actions, and responsibilities within the scope of the organization's IS; should be less concerned with physical technologies and more with the management of other resources that are part of the computer system; guide IT management to IT processes, maintenance, services, and operation and management of IT projects; and prepare and control the main indicators necessary for the management of the computer system.
- Stakeholders and users must promote IS Architecture from a client/server perspective within the organization; promote the design and implementation of IS, to provide the information that decision-makers need to support their activities; to stimulate and control the cost/benefit principle for the production and availability of Information; and differentiate Data, Information, and Knowledge.

- University professors should denounce the frequent identifications between the content of the courses taught and the marketing of IT product providers; develop studies and presentations in classes and courses, avoid the jargon of IT providers; scientifically separate the IT problem from the IS problem; denounce and characterize Information Systems Management, Information System for Management, Information Management, CIO and CITO, and Information Systems Governance; and differentiate the management job from the typewriter (with computer) job.
- Public administration policymakers and decision-makers must demystify the concept of the Information Society and the Knowledge Society; assume that technologies and technological structures can be used well or badly and that they were never the solution but are a resource; assume that many of the IT solutions constitute absurdities and utopias that reality has denied; and, to conclude that there is no scientific evidence that justifies a causal relationship between IT acquisitions and the productivity and competitiveness of economic organizations.

Excellence in coordinating information resources and the sustainability of their use will depend on IS Governance (Anunciação, Esteves & Santos, 2014; Anunciação & Esteves, 2012). The new technological and, consequently, economic, and social paradigms, such as Artificial Intelligence, the Internet of Things, Cloud computing, Blockchain, and Digital Transformation, among others, will tend to demand new instruments, policies, and commitments between economic agents, new Governance, where it is possible to create economic and social value based on technology.

2. The Different Governance Dimensions

The concept of Governance is not new and has not emerged within the scope of IS. This concept, which emerged in the context of business management, focused on protecting the interests of shareholders by the top management of business economic organizations (Kooper, Maes & Roos Lindgreen, 2011). This dimension of Governance, called Corporate Governance, was the first to emerge and emphasize the need for balance between stakeholders. Subsequently, another dimension associated with IT emerged. IT Governance sought, and still seeks, that the adoption of good practices in IT management in organizations (Mohamed & Kaur, 2012) provide an increase in organizational capabilities, the leverage of business strategies, and the contribution of IT to achieve organizational and economic objectives (Van Grembergen, 2004; Van Grembergen, 2000).

These two dimensions of governance represent two limits to the scope of the concept: corporate governance, upstream, as a guiding element; and IT governance, downstream, as support for the organizational activity. However, these two dimensions omit two others that are at the heart of the current designation of the economy and society, namely Information and IS. Note that Corporate Governance presupposes Information and Information presupposes the existence of IS, which integrates ICT. This finding makes it possible to identify the need to make a conceptual connection between the two dimensions initially presented. Now, assuming the dimensions of Corporate Governance and IT Governance as relevant, it seems to make perfect sense that, in terms of Information and IS, the dimension of Governance can also be adopted (ISGec, 2010). The core elements of the business are inseparable from business processes and the competitive differentiation factor depends on the ability to process, in increasingly shorter periods, massive amounts of data from not structured and often different sources (Gonçalves, Pimenta & Anunciação, 2019).

As early as 2003, Nicolas Carr stated that as the power and omnipresence of IT increased, its strategic importance decreased (Carr, 2003). The main IT functions (data storage, processing, and communication) became available to everyone, changing their relevance from potentially strategic resources to commodity-type production factors. They have become costs for the business, which must be paid by everyone, but which offer no distinction to anyone (Carr, 2003).

As we know, new factors of competitiveness emerged, more based on agility, with the prevalence of online and real-time business, which forced drastic reconversions of business processes, in an incessant search for competitive advantages, in the optimization and rationalization of value chains. These are aspects that are far from being commodities, and in the field of Information, systems are differentiating elements of organizations' strategy.

In general, there is a consensus that the relevant position of IS and ICT should no longer be the usual business support. The IS must be increasingly framed as an active element in the creation of value for organizations (Oliveira, 1996). This recognition is visible when we see the evolution of various terminologies, such as IT Governance (Weill & Ross, 2004) or Enterprise Governance of Information Technology (De Haes & Van Grembergen, 2015).

The IT Governance Institute reaffirms the responsibility of IT Governance as belonging to the Board of Directors, considering that it presupposes leadership capacity and the adequacy of organizational structures and processes so that IT supports and leverages the organization's strategy and objectives through the main economic resource, the information. Understanding the central role of Information (IT Governance Institute [ITGI], 2003), we can implicitly assume that the underlying principles must also apply to information governance and information systems governance.

Currently, IT Corporate Governance is considered to be part of corporate governance and that it necessarily affects the definition and implementation of processes, structures, and relational mechanisms in the organization, which allow the business areas and IT to perform their responsibilities in supporting the business/IT alignment, and in creating value for the business as a result of investments made in technologies (De Haes & Van Grembergen, 2015). However, it is possible to reflect on whether the strict scope of a technological nature present in the IT Governance concept cannot give too much focus to IT, considering that the focus of IS is centered on other resources, such as data/information, people, rules/procedures and the IT itself. It should be noted that the value generated by IT investments cannot be achieved only by technologies, as it is generated by the business areas.

In this context, we could assume, as referred to by Information Systems Governance European Club (ISGec), that IS Governance refers to the design and execution of specialized activities, related to Political and Strategic decision-making on IS and its compatibility with Corporate Governance. More specifically, it can be assumed that IS Governance comprises, primarily, the identification of objectives to be achieved in terms of IS investments, the definition of the IS Organization model and its insertion in the Institution's Macro Structure, and the characterization of the IS Management model and practices, namely, the Organizational Urbanism (Anunciação & Zorrinho, 2006), Architecture (Esteves & Anunciação, 2021) and Planning of the IS, the acquisition and implementation of the IS solutions, the economic and financial analysis of investments in the IS, the form of organization and the way of exploitation of the IS, and, also, the control of the performances of the IS.

Governance is, as mentioned, a challenge for all organizations. There are indeed differences between the different sectors, which can make its adoption not easy. Let's see, without claiming to be exhaustive and by way of example, some of the main differences between the public and private sectors (Luz & Fragoso, 2019; Campbell; McDonald & Sethib, 2009):

- Objectives are usually more concrete and measurable in the Private Sector and contain a relevant (sometimes dominant) component of a social and/or political nature in the case of the Public Sector.
- Products/Services provided are usually better defined and more focused in the Private Sector and are more difficult to make tangible in many cases in the Public Sector, at least in terms of the value delivered and its evaluation.

- Success Assessment, naturally well defined in most cases in the Private Sector and which implies various forms of assessment, explicit and implicit in many cases in the Public Sector.
- Organizational context, in general, in the Private Sector it is easier to define, implement, and manage components that are essential for the proper functioning of organizations: applicable legal contexts, procedural frameworks, evaluation, and motivation mechanisms are examples classics.
- Ownership or Control, in the Private Sector it is usually easier to implement combinations of internal/external solutions optimized for each type of challenge or stage of development of the organization.

3. Information Systems Governance Dimensions Proposal

The economic focus centered on technologies, investments, and associated costs, the required Payback, and IS security, among other aspects, raise some questions about the dimensions of IS Governance in economic organizations, the economic value gained, or even about the very competitiveness achieved with the use of information as an economic resource. The understanding of the relevance of information is, unfortunately, evidenced by the difficulties often felt in the absence of an architectural structure capable of making its usefulness as a management raw material "readable", and the system and IT associated with the respective "intelligible" treatment.

The functions traditionally associated with the IS area have not always been visible and assumed clearly and unequivocally among professionals who have authority and responsibility in this field. It is not always clear who is responsible for or who has authority over IS/ICT, who assumes power and dependence on ICT providers (often referred to as partners), or whether the objectives set for IS are clear and economically acceptable.

Similarly, we could also add that, often, the costs and benefits derived from the use of IS/ICT are not always evaluated, managing IT insertion projects in organizations with the same management rigor requirements that are so often applied to other investments, or are controlled in the fundamental performances associated with acquisitions and allocation of resources for the design and use of IS/ICT, disregarding the discipline of economic calculation and the rigor of investment analysis (Oliveira, 2004). The IS must capture and not belittle the interests, wishes, and objectives of the various organizational stakeholders and, in this sense, must be perfectly framed in the organizational vision and objectives, and must even be economically defensible.

Integrating the IS, a set of resources (people, data and information, hardware, and software) that, in an interrelated way (organization and rules), aim to reach a certain end (timely, quality information and in adequate quantities, in the first instance, to support the decision, in the second instance), the adoption of an IS Governance logic appears to be relevant in the field of economic organizations (ISGec, 2011).

Following the arguments presented above, it is considered that there is a need and it seems relevant to develop specific activities related to political and strategic decision-making in IS and, above all, regarding the vitality of their compatibility with Corporate Governance. It is in the alignment and coherence between the policies and strategies defined for the IS and the lines identified for the Corporate Governance that economic organizations should focus not only on their performance but above all on their development.

To this end, and not intending that the proposal presented below is exhaustive, four areas intrinsic to the IS Governance concept are proposed that may be adopted by managers in the analysis of existing Governance Practices in the respective organizations and that may allow, namely: IS Management, Organizational Model, IS investment Analysis and Decision, and Ethics.

The IS Management dimension reflects the fact that experience shows that having IT in organizational activity is not enough for the company to solve its information processing problems. Information, technologies, and activities must be conveniently integrated with other elements, such as human resources, procedures, and organizational objectives. This integration requires management skills in the architecture of the IS, and technologies, and technical and business knowledge are also included.

In this first field of study, it is proposed to specify the following aspects of analysis:

- the existence of a budget to assess the costs associated with the IS.
- the weight of these costs on the organization's total costs.
- the average evolution in the last three years.
- the nature of the associated costs.
- the existence of policies and practices for the internal allocation of IS costs for services provided to other departments.
- the nature of the value logic associated with the IS area (such as cost center or results center);
- the practice of a systematic evaluation of productivity, efficiency, and effectiveness of the IS and adopted indicators.
- the existence of quality assessment practices, variables used, and responsibility in the respective assessment.

- the existence of practices for the evaluation of the systematic control of the IS performance, as well as the identification of the responsibility for this evaluation.
- carrying out audits and their frequency.

The second study domain proposes the analysis of the existing organizational model. One of the central objectives of the IS consists of providing information to the various organizational areas on the activities carried out, analyzing the fulfillment of the company's objectives, as well as supporting the realization and coordination of the respective activities. These activities, carried out by the departments or services, presuppose specific information needs by the requirements underlying the specificity of the various tasks that comprise them.

The existence of an organizational function at the IS level derives, among other aspects, from:

- the importance of its role in the competitiveness of companies.
- its indispensability in the decision-making process by management.
- in the scope and coverage of all organizational areas.
- the integration, horizontally and vertically, of information flows in organizations.
- relevance as a factor of integration and functional cohesion in organizations.

The organizational function associated with the IS is responsible for promoting, coordinating, and collaborating and should aim at articulating activities and procedures aimed at optimizing the functioning of information systems and technologies, namely capture processes, architecture, validation, selection, manipulation, processing, conservation, storage, and communication of information. Furthermore, it also assumes responsibility for the acquisition and management of technologies, through the selection and availability of hardware and software suited to the needs of the users of the system, in supporting the formulation of policies and strategies, as well as in the planning, administration, and decision-making.

Its noblest function is thus associated with architecture, and it is responsible for ensuring the compatibility of the data format used by the various organizational departments and the suitability of technological resources in the face of identified treatment needs.

In this second field of study, the proposed dimensions of analysis associated with the organizational model are the following:

- the existence of a function for IS management in the organizational macrostructure, its level, functional content, and to whom the person in charge reports.

- the existence of an architectural model for the IS (objectives, morphology, functionalities, among others), what is the degree of intervention of the administration in this architecture, and what levels are covered.

The third study domain aimed at analyzing and deciding on investments in IS. The problem of inserting information and communication systems and technologies in the organizational context is reflected in the variety of resources to be used and in the complexity of tasks and specialized activities to be carried out, which cannot be left to the empiricism of performances or arbitrariness and voluntarism of the actors, not even to the will and interests of the suppliers of equipment or services (Oliveira, 2004). Such recognition raises the need to establish a critical path, a schedule of logical activities, rationally linked according to the investment objective, and, inexorably, the use of a methodology.

In this field of study, the proposed dimensions of analysis and assessment associated with the organizational model are the following:

- the existence of quantified and specific objectives associated with investments in IS, and the respective degree of achievement.
- the practice of economic and financial analysis associated with the investment, as well as the identification of the indicators adopted.

The last domain of analysis focused on ethics. The relevance of this theme derives from the fact that, particularly about the commercial relationships established between customers and suppliers, these may appear to be asymmetrical due to the specificity of the activities carried out, the nature and urgency of the need, and the different domain of knowledge and power held by the various parties. The lack of knowledge and technical experience to face the complexity and demands of economic and organizational challenges leads many organizations to look for a way to solve the problems they face in this domain in the subcontracting of activities associated with IS.

In this context, the proposed dimensions of analysis are the following:

- who clarifies information needs?
- who makes the explanation of the software and hardware needs?
- who provides training in the field of IS?
- what is the nature of the relationship between the supplier and the company?

4. Conclusions

There is a gap in the domain of management of economic organizations about IS, which results in the finding of a diversity of understandings and considerations of practices associated with IS. It is not always clear who is responsible for the IS. ICT providers (often called partners) capture the interests and desires of client companies' stakeholders. Nobody calculates the costs and benefits derived from the use of IS/ICT. No one manages ICT insertion projects in organizations with the same management rigor to which other areas of organizational life are subjected. The fundamental performances of the bulky acquisitions and other resources allocated to their design and use are not measured.

Assuming that organizations are increasingly based on information, it is up to Top Management to define policies for Information Systems because the management of Information Systems is, undoubtedly, a problem attributable to Top Management. However, IS Governance should not be confused with IT Governance.

In this sense, the present academic work leaves a set of proposals so that company managers can reflect on some of the central dimensions associated with IS. Only analysis and reflection consistent with the conceptual nature and importance of IS will allow an adequate evolution of organizational IS towards the relevance of information in the context of the economy.

IS Governance must be justified by the phenomenological complexity associated with Information Systems, which can be highlighted in the following aspects: company employees are both consumers and producers of information; there is a significant variety of resources (human resources, technologies, approaches, tools, etc)...involved in the solutions defined for the IS, and, not least, by the impact of Information Systems on the Competitiveness and Sustainability of companies.

Acknowledgments

The authors would like to thank the Instituto Politécnico de Setúbal (Portugal) for the support given to the publication of this research work.

References

Anunciação, P. F. (2014). *Ethics, Sustainability and the Information and Knowledge Society*, Chiado Publishing (*In Portuguese*).

Anunciação, P. F. (2019). *ceGSI Manifesto*, Information Systems Governance – Concepts, good practices, and case studies, *Information Systems Governance European Club* (ceGSI-Portugal), Chiado Publishing, 43–51 (in Portuguese).

Anunciação, P. F., & Esteves, F. M. (2012). Sustainability in the Information Society: A Proposal of Information System Requirements in View of the

DPOBE Model for Organizational Sustainability, *Procedia Technology Special Issue CENTERIS 2012/HCIST*, 5, October, 599–606.

Anunciação, P. F., Esteves, F. M., & Santos, J. R. (2014). Some Information Systems Requirements in View of Organizational Sustainability in an Information Society, *Information Resource Management Journal*, 27(1), 21–35.

Anunciação, P. F., & Zorrinho, C. (2006). *Organizational Urbanism – How Managing Technological Shock in Companies*, Lisbon, Sílabo Publishing (in Portuguese).

Campbell, J., McDonald, C., & Sethib, T. (2009). Public and Private Sector IT Governance: Identifying Contextual Differences, *Australasian Journal of Information Systems*, 16(2), 5–18.

Carr, N. G. (2003). IT Doesn't Matter, *Harvard Business Review*, 81(5), 41–49.

De Haes, S., & Van Grembergen, W. (2015). *Enterprise Governance of Information Technology: Achieving Alignment and Value*, Featuring COBIT 5, Second Edition, Boston MA: Springer US.

Drucker, P. (1988). The Coming of the New Organization, *Harvard Business Review*, Jan/Feb.

Esteves, F. J. M., & Anunciação, P. F. (2021). Architecture – Essential Dimension in Information Systems, *Information Systems – Paradigms and Solutions for Management*, Plátano Publishing (in Portuguese).

Gonçalves, F. M., Pimenta, J., & Anunciação, P. F. (2019). The Information Systems Governance and the New Paradigms in the Industry, *Information Systems Governance – Concepts, Good Practices, and Case Studies*, Information Systems Governance European Club (ceGSI-Portugal), Chiado Publishing, 117–133 (in Portuguese).

IT Governance Institute (ITGI). (2003). Board briefing on IT governance. IT Governance Institute.

ISGec – *Information System Governance European Club* (2010). *Why the Corporations are asking for an Information Systems Governance?*, Retrieved April 26, 2022, from http://www.cegsi.org/index.php/documents/telechargement-du-document-la-gouvernance-des-systemes-d-information-pourquoi/la-gouvernance-des-systemes-d-information-pourquoi (in French).

ISGec – *Information System Governance European Club* (2011). *The Importance of the Information Systems Approach in the Governance of Organizations*, Retrieved May 2, 2022, from http://www.cegsi.org/index.php/documents/l-importance-de-l-approche-par-les-systemes-d-information/the-importance-of-the-information-systems-approach-for-governance-organizations (in French).

Kooper, M. N., Maes, R., & Roos Lindgreen, E. E. O. (2011). On the Governance of Information: Introducing a New Concept of Governance to Support the Management of Information, *International Journal of Information Management*, 31, 195–200.

Luz, P. M., & Fragoso, A. (2019). *Information Systems Governance in Public Administration*, Information Systems Governance – Concepts, Good Practices, and Case Studies, Information Systems Governance European Club (ceGSI-Portugal), Chiado Publishing, 53–76 (in Portuguese).

Mohamed, N., & Kaur, J. (2012). A Conceptual Framework for Information Technology Governance Effectiveness in Private Organizations, *Information Management & Computer Security*, Bradford, 20(2), 88–106.

Oliveira, A. (1996). The Potential Value of Information Systems, *Management Studies*, III(1), 3–18 (in Portuguese).

Oliveira, A. (1999). The Role of Information Systems in the Context of Turbulence, *Galileu Journal*, IV(1) (in Portuguese).

Oliveira, A. (2004). *Analysis of the Investment in Systems and Technologies of the Information and the Communication*, Sílabo Publishing (in Portuguese).

Oliveira, A. (2019). IS Governance – Why?, *Information Systems Governance – Concepts, Good Practices and Case Studies*, Information Systems Governance European Club (ceGSI-Portugal), Chiado Publishing, 189–201 (in Portuguese).

Oliveira, A. (2021). *Information and Information Systems – Promises, Reality and Policies*, Sílabo Publishing (in Portuguese).

Van Grembergen, W. (2000). The Balanced Scorecard and IT Governance, *Information Systems Control Journal*, 2, 40–3

Van Greenbergen, W. (2004). *Strategies for Information Technology Governance*, Hersey: IDEA Group Publishing.

Weill, P., & Ross, J. W. (2004). *IT Governance-How Top Performers Manage IT Decision Rights for Superior Results*. Boston: Harvard Business School Pre.

Francisco Joaquim Madeira Esteves,
Pedro Fernandes da Anunciação

Information Governance: A Framework Proposal for Enterprise Managers

1. Introduction

Information and Governance are two central concepts in business and economic contexts. Information is a fundamental resource for economic activity because managers discovered that in the "economic data universe" there is huge economic value. But its configuration justifies the need to ensure the proper form of the system or systems required for its production, storage, and distribution. So, society and the economy demand adequate tools for the management of this vital organizational resource and economic asset. However, the different value chains, stakeholders, economic networks, etc., justify the management question: is the level of information management adequate for organizational necessities? Or does the economic context demand a new level of exigence? It`s time for Governance. Information Governance is the discipline of treating information as a strategic corporate asset (Anunciação, 2014; Hulme, 2012), from a long-term perspective. Information Governance is a subject of sustainability (Anunciação, Esteves & Santos, 2014; Anunciação & Esteves, 2012).

For management, Governance has focused on the role of boards of directors, representing and protecting the interests of shareholders (Kooper, Maes & Roos Lindgreen, 2011). A formal Corporate Governance system can help to ensure an effective division of authority among shareholders, the board of directors, and management (Bujaki & McConomy, 2002). Considering corporate governance as the first level of governance, we can consider that Information Technology (IT) Governance should be included in corporate governance and should ensure the respective performance and management of the associated risks (Van Greenbergen, 2004) (Weill& Ross, 2004). IT Governance involves discharging roles and responsibilities in assuring sound IT practices in organizations (Mohamed & Kaur, 2012). Van Grembergen (2000) refers to IT Governance that must ensure the ability to achieve the defined objectives and develop the desired organizational capabilities, at all management levels, with a view to the adequacy of IT strategies according to the business. In the information society, the fusion between business, companies, and technologies is evident and profound.

However, there seems to be a lack of a link between Corporate Governance and IT Governance. Recently, some authors have emphasized the relevance of the concept of Information Systems (IS) Governance. IS Governance doesn`t seem only a problem of technology. The concept of IS Governance establishes a link between Corporate Governance and IT Governance because IS integrates information and communication technologies to respond to the business. Thus, IS Governance should facilitate the clarification of the objectives that management seeks to achieve with IS investments (Oliveira 2010); the definition of an organization model for the IS; the definition of a model (operational, tactical and strategic) for IS management (Oliveira, 2009); the search for architectural and urbanism solutions suited to the complexity of the IS (Anunciação & Peñalver, 2017) (Anunciação & Zorrinho, 2006); and the adequate performance of IS (ISGec, 2010).

And how can we define the concept of Information Governance? Data is the DNA of a company, as it truly differentiates that company from any other and most often can provide a competitive edge if an Information Governance strategy is applied (Stout, 2015). It is evident that as an economic and management resource, information and information systems must, necessarily, be adequately governed (managed, optimized, and controlled). These resources, central to the development of economic and organizational activities, are of greater importance, more than any other traditional resource. For example, a lower level of information on operations and activities carried out in the products production or provision of services, as well as on complementary activities, creates management difficulties in the planning activities, in the allocation and control of different organizational resources, and compromise the definition of strategies for competitiveness, among others. So, information is essential not only to the present management activities but also to the organization's future as well as economic sustainability (Anunciação, Svirina & Santos, 2013).

The centrality of information in the development of organizational and economic activities can be highlighted, among others, by the following facts:

- the need to identify, understand, and characterize the facts and circumstances that limit organizational activities and management decisions, which must be known and controlled;
- the evidence that information allows an increase or change in the knowledge that managers hold at a given time;
- the lack of information corresponds to ignorance about a concrete situation;
- information is simultaneously raw material and finished product, that can incorporate multiple information systems and economic chain`s value;

- information management requires registration, classification, organization, and interpretation in a context that conveys meaning to it;
- currently relational society presents multiple contexts for information; and
- their relevance is linked to the impact and value of decisions.

However, because of technological innovation, information is often framed and managed in a contingency approach and according to the technology's attractiveness and the potential presented. Normally, the central focus of management is on technologies because they frame the functions of processing, storing, and distributing information. However, from a social and economic perspective, the central focus must be on information and its value.

Assuming the information as a set of data framed in a specific context presupposes that we must consider that its value is associated with the processing context. In this sense, its value depends on the ability to identify, in some way, meaning for someone, at a given moment or situation. This value of the information will only be evident if we can understand the respective architecture since it is the architecture that allows assigning meaning to the information through the framing of the treatments and the identification of the outputs considering the diversity of the decisions to be taken. Decision-making, which integrates complex processes of information transformation into actions, requires the existence of concrete and complete information on the various situations under analysis. This condition is critical to understanding the magnitude of existing situations and problems (basic or specific information), knowledge about the state of the environment that surrounds and the eventual occurrence of other associated events (complementary or surrounding information), and intervention in the system to guarantee its quality (production information or performance).

In this context and from a management perspective, the question that can be asked is: why Information Governance? Information Governance in economic organizations is closely associated with three different necessities: generate knowledge of the internal and external context of the organization, generate value through the achievement of objectives and results, and reduce risk in the decision-making process. So, it is important for managers and information systems managers to be able to select and provide relevant information. And this information must be consistent throughout the value chain as well as in the overall organizational domain (Anunciação et al., 2017; Denolf et al., 2015).

However, not all information is important. There is information that may not be of interest for management decision-making or may even have distortions or errors arising from gaps in the production or transmission processes, conditioning the decisions of managers. Thus, the aspect of information quality emerges. In this area, there are two key dimensions in assessing the quality of information: the temporal dimension, which is associated with opportunity (the information should be accessed at the time that is required) or actuality (the information should correspond to the facts more recent), and the dimension content, in which we can find the accuracy (the information must be free of errors) or the pertinence (the information must be related to the needs of the user and with the situation).

As evidenced earlier, several dimensions highlight the need for a broader perspective of information management (architecture, quality, and value, among others). So, at a corporate level, IS level or IT level, we consider that the issue of governance is a new challenge in information administration. Information Governance covers the same spectrum of dimensions as management, but at a higher level, that is, in the perspective of Top Management. Information Governance must assume the strategic dimension of this economic and organizational resource, present in the relationship of information with vision and business strategy. It must also support the intra-organizational structure and relationship of the strategy with the main organizational functions, framing the organizational activities, defining processes of planning, administration, and control of information infrastructure, applications, and information services themselves, among other dimensions. From a supply chain perspective, information sharing may result in concerns related to information security, information access privileges, and allocation of claimed benefits, among other factors. To mitigate such concerns to share information, relationships efficiently and effectively among the supply chain actors need to be managed and effective governance structures need to be chosen (Denolf et al., 2015).

The dimension of Information Governance is closely associated with the governance of information systems and information technologies themselves because there is a need to ensure:

- formats and timings appropriate to the viability of opportunities and the achievement of competitive advantages arising from the use of IS/IT;
- the interconnection between the objectives of the organization (business model) and the resources involved in obtaining information (IS/IT);
- understanding the nature of the activities, the limits of the various business areas, and the need for integration and sharing among the different organizational levels, enriching the information for the management, and adapting the organizational IS to the respective specificities;
- the adequacy of technological infrastructures and their performance (treatment and storage) to organizational requirements.

Governance, from an Information-Based Organization perspective, should provide a unique view of the organization and its activities.

2. Information Systems Governance and Information Governance

Information Governance constitutes a part of IS Governance and is integrated into IS Governance (ISGec, 2010). It is the assumption of information as a fundamental resource of economic activity and its configuration as a structuring element of management and organizational cohesion, which justifies the need to ensure proper form of the system or systems required for its production, storage, and distribution (Oliveira, 1996, 1999) insofar as its quality and availability depend on the effectiveness of Corporate Governance. Information Governance concerns the maximization of the business value of information and the total cost reduction of ownership of the information management landscape, whilst ensuring compliance, managing risk, and protecting the security (Hulme, 2012).

For all that has been exposed, it becomes evident of the need and relevance of the existence of specific activities related to making policy and strategic decisions about the IS and above all the vitality of its compliance with the Corporate Governance. It is the coherence between the policies and strategies defined in the IS and its compatibility with the lines identified for Corporate Governance that depends on performance and organizational development (ISGec, 2011).

Gartner (n.d.) considers that Information Governance should seek to develop a structure that guarantees accountability for activities associated with information management, namely creation, storage, use, evaluation, and deletion of information. This means that, within the scope of functions associated with Information Governance will be the definition of processes, functions, policies, standards, and metrics that guarantee the effective and efficient use of information to allow an organization to achieve its objectives. Governance also presupposes responsibility for the management of IS, insofar as the implementation of policies and strategies defined for information are also dependent on IS. The phenomenological complexity that traditionally characterizes the IS results, among other things, from the great variety and value of the resources involved (human, physical, logical, communications, consumables,…) and from the fact that any employee of the company is a consumer and producer of information, integrating and participating in a diversity of flows, emphasizes the central role that IS can have as dynamic or conditioning elements of competitiveness and organizational sustainability (Anunciação, Cavaco & Osmane, 2018). In this area, information and management correspond to two sides of the same coin, and therefore cannot be decoupled.

Due to the relevance of Information Governance in the context of IS Governance and Corporate Governance, it is important to define a framework that supports Information Governance in the different associated dimensions. Information Governance must constitute an instrument to promote IS effectiveness, organizational efficiency, and management performance through the enhancement of information. Some aspects of management that emphasize the relevance of Information Governance are associated with different types of needs, namely:

- understand information, as an organizational and economic resource, to identify the associated value (Anunciação, Fonseca & Rodello, 2017).
- structuring the information and means associated with its treatment, aiming to optimize its use.
- management of information sources, services, and systems according to organizational requirements and requirements.
- define an adequate degree of control over the information "environment".
- evaluation measures, by conducting investment assessment studies, cost-benefit analysis, performance appraisal, etc.

All these aspects underscore the importance of a top-level approach to the current information management dimension.

3. Methodology Approach to Information Governance

For any organizational problem, an approach is important to the adoption of a coherent methodology. In this case, the proposed objective of the research was the elaboration of a framework for Information Governance. So, the study was divided into four phases. The first phase corresponded to the validation through a focus group. The purpose of this validation is aimed to obtain a confirmation of real value for managers and generate knowledge about the potential of framework applicability in different organizations. The results obtained will be relevant to the relevance of this research work.

The methodology adopted sought to obtain objectivity in the analysis and understanding of the topic under study. The meeting of a group of specialists from various areas related to the subject allows a broader view of the subject and enhances the achievement of results in relation to the objectives of the study, through a more effective and pragmatic analysis of the subject. Through the focus group, it is expected to obtain a richer and more valuable knowledge generated through the sharing and integration of the different individual knowledge of the participating elements.

Furthermore, it is also sought with this methodological option to obtain information on the understanding, knowledge, and feeling about the relevance of the Governance issue as well as the central variables that must be considered in this context. The possibility of interaction and sharing of participants' views, knowledge, and experiences (Queirós & Lacerda, 2013; Berg, 2001; Morgan, 1996); the provision of psychological, social, and cultural characteristics (Berg, 2001); the generation of a consensus on ideas, issues, themes, and solutions due to the synergistic effect (Berg, 2001); and the generation of comparative data between experiences and points of view rather than individual data (Morgan, 1996) were some of the benefits sought with this methodology and that justified the adoption.

The constitution of the focus group considered the level of professional experience, responsibility assumed, and vision on the subject in areas related to information and information systems and technologies. Furthermore, an attempt was also made to create a diversified group in terms of economic sectors, insofar as there are sectors that are more information based than others. This focus group was attended by the heads of the following sectors: service providers in the information systems, health, industry, insurance, and financial institutions, as well as a member of a club dedicated to the study of Information Systems Governance in Europe.

Thus, the focus group consisted of the following elements: top manager of an information systems services company with responsibilities in software development and project management (Information Systems and Technologies); two professors in information systems and technologies area (Education); top manager, with responsibilities in quality, management performance indicators, audit, and clinical risk (Health); intermediate manager, with responsibilities in the information systems department of a district hospital (Health); top manager in a large company in the industry sector, with responsibility for information systems management (Industry); top manager of a large insurance company, with responsibility for information systems; top manager of a banking institution, with responsibility for the banking information systems (Banking and Insurance); and member of Information Systems Governance thinker club, with the responsibilities associated with general-secretary functions (ISGec).

The second phase of the study has, as the main objective, the assessment of each of the dimensions identified by the focus group. This assessment was made considering the sector of activity, the organizational reality, and the individual knowledge of each specialist.

Finally, in the last phase, it is the architecture of a framework proposal.

4. Information Governance Framework Proposal

Regarding the first phase of the study, the main dimension identification of the Information Governance framework identified the most relevant aspects: Business, Knowledge, Architecture, Channels, Technology, Content, Quality, and Security. The different nature of these dimensions justifies the necessity of systematization and specification. Thus, in Tab. 1 the different scopes or natures identified were the following: Strategic, Structural, Management, and Control.

Tab. 1: Most relevant dimensions of information governance

Strategic Scope	Structural Scope
Management Scope	Control Scope

In the second phase of the study, we sought to identify and specify the dimensions associated with each of the scopes, the synthesis of which is shown in Tab. 2.

Tab. 2: Relevant dimensions in the information governance

STRATEGIC SCOPE	STRUCTURAL SCOPE
• Key Business Drivers • Governance • Knowledge Management	• Enterprise Information Architecture • Metadata Management • Information Delivery Management • Information Technology Management
MANAGEMENT SCOPE	**CONTROL SCOPE**
• Reference and Master Data Management • Information Management • Enterprise Content Management • Organizational Accountability • Enterprise-Recorded Management	• Information Quality Management • Information Security and Privacy Management

In the Strategic scope, the dimensions were specified as follows:

- o Key Business Drivers – set of business drivers and associated information needs.
- o Governance – set of policies, strategies, principles, standards, and processes associated with information throughout the organization.

- o Knowledge Management – set of objective and coherent practices associated with obtaining, organizing, and disseminating the organization's intellectual capital.

In the Structural scope, the dimensions identified were specified as follows:

- o Enterprise Information Architecture – the model that supports the functions of ownership, administration, and management of information, providing instructions on treatment capacities and potential utilization to maximize the value of information throughout the organization.
- o Metadata Management – means facilitating a common understanding of organizational information using formal ontologies, taxonomic definitions, business rules, lineage identification, and usage documentation (dictionaries, catalogs, …).
- o Information Delivery Management – a common set of practices designed to provide/deliver, in an effective manner, the information to "knowledge workers" to enrich their perceptions ("insights") and provide timely actions to "drive" the growth of knowledge and business in the organization.
- o Information Technology Management – identification of hardware management capabilities, software applications, "tools", repositories, and "storage" that deliver efficiently the information through the organization.

In the Management scope, the identified dimensions have been specified as follows:

- o Reference and Master Data Management – ability to consistently manage "core" organizational information (the "master data" such as Customer, Employee, Product, Account, etc.) across the enterprise.
- o Information Management – set of processes, disciplines, and practices used to support the daily management of data and information across the organization, regardless of format or location.
- o Enterprise Content Management – set of business and technological skills for the management of unstructured or partially structured information (e.g. email, documents, Web content, and "social media", …) in the organization.
- o Organizational Accountability – an expression of appropriate business and IT responsibilities at the various levels of the organization to ensure that information can be effectively managed throughout its entire life cycle.
- o Enterprise-Records Management – supervision and administration of digital or paper records, regardless of their format, including activities relating to the creation, reception, maintenance, use, and disposal of records.

In the Control scope, the identified dimensions were specified as follows:

- o Information Quality Management – identification of the parameters of analysis and evaluation of the information regarding the needs, processes, and support practices, ensuring that a continuous effort to maintain an adequate level of quality instills confidence in the organizational integrity.
- o Information Security and Privacy Management – identification of the set of information system requirements necessary to safeguard the integrity and privacy of information, ensuring that it is properly protected by establishing access capabilities, classification, auditing, and storage.

In the third phase of the study, as previously mentioned in the methodology approach, a value assessment of each dimension's relevance in the economic domain of each participant was developed, as can be seen in Tab. 3.

Tab. 3: Results of the analysis of each of the dimensions in information governance

	1	2	3	4	Dnk /Dnr
STRATEGIC SCOPE					
Key Business Drivers	-	-	14 %	86 %	-
Governance	-	-	-	100 %	-
Knowledge Management	-	14 %	-	86 %	-
STRUCTURAL SCOPE					
Enterprise Information Architecture	-	14 %	14 %	72 %	-
Metadata Management	-	14 %	-	86 %	-
Information Delivery Management	-	-	14 %	86 %	-
Information Technology Management	-	14 %	29 %	57 %	-
MANAGEMENT SCOPE					
Reference and Master Data Management	-	-	14 %	86 %	-
Information Management	-	-	14 %	86 %	-
Enterprise Content Management	-	-	14 %	86 %	-
Organizational Accountability	-	-	29 %	71 %	-
Enterprise-Record Management	-	14 %	29 %	57 %	-
CONTROL SCOPE					
Information Quality Management	14 %	-	-	86 %	-
Information Security and Privacy Management	-	14 %	-	86 %	-

Generally, the results are expressed a significant relevance to the dimensions in the economic domain of each specialist. Unfortunately, some answers show differentiated perceptions of some dimensions and there wasn't an opportunity for a deepening of the non-standard attributions. However, we believe that the results are elucidating the dimensions that should be integrated into the framework. This clarification will certainly be an opportunity to develop future work.

5. Information Governance Framework

As a result of the previous analysis, we present, in Fig. 1, the proposed framework for Information Governance. In the presented proposal, several layers correspond to several segments of information governance. The first is the technology layer and this should frame the technological support of all activities associated with the treatment, storage, and availability of information. It should be considered elements such as hardware, software, applications, tools, repositories, storage, etc.

The second layer comprises security and privacy management. This should be framed based on the technological platform and, consequently, support various dimensions such as information quality, master data management, delivery, content management, or knowledge management. This layer must consider some elements like access, classification, auditing, and protection.

The third layer refers to the set of dimensions related to information as a product. It includes dimensions such as quality management, master data management, distribution management, content management, and knowledge management. This layer must support security and privacy and be framed by the layer of metadata.

The fourth layer, metadata, corresponds to information management. Information management must consider the ontologies, taxonomies, definitions, business rules, linage, and usage, and be framed by the enterprise information architecture. This enterprise information architecture, which constitutes the fifth layer, must be understood in the business drivers, integrating the latter layer at the top-down perspective corresponding to the analysis performed.

Although the key business drivers are the global layer and, therefore, should frame all others, the levels previously identified must also be framed by organizational accountability and governance, as shown in Fig. 1.

What stands out in the proposal presented is the centrality of key business drivers as central elements in Information Governance. It is a Corporate Governance dimension and, consequently, a level that must guide Information Governance. After these, the specific dimensions of governance, accountability, and information architecture should give meaning to the remaining dimensions.

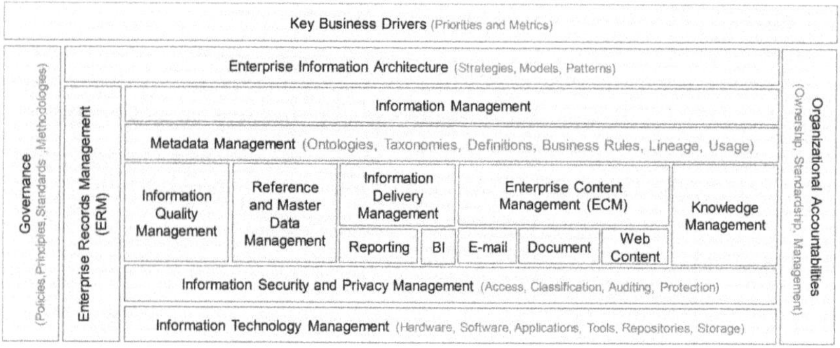

Fig. 1: Framework for Information Governance

We believe that this model covers the most significant dimensions of Information Governance. This model constitutes working in progress tool, in the field of organizational information systems, for support and validation of Information Governance practices.

6. Conclusions

The need for a governance framework is evident in the current context of society and the economy. The proposal of this framework presented here seeks to be a more concrete response addressed to the main output of the information system: information.

Given that information is constituted as the main economic resource, because it can integrate several economic chains simultaneously and because it is not generally owned by anyone, this individual asset and simultaneously collective must be well managed. This means that the focus should not only be on management, from the perspective of short-term management, of solving existing problems or meeting immediate needs. But, from a strategic perspective, information should be governed and should be framed by emerging problems and consider the orientation of economic and social activities within a framework of sustainability.

The only way to preserve the value of information will be to define an adequate framework for the respective governance, with the capacity to provide answers to management and managers in the various dimensions that affect the respective value. Managers must be aware of these dimensions and the relevance they assume in a global framework of corporate.

Acknowledgments

The authors would like to thank the Instituto Politécnico de Setúbal (Portugal) for the support given to the publication of this research work.

References

Anunciação, P. F. (2014). *Ética, Sustentabilidade e Sociedade de Informação e do Conhecimento*, Chiado Publishing (in Portuguese).

Anunciação, P. F., Cavaco, C. S., & Ossmane, S. R. M. (2018). Information Management and the Competitive Advantages: The "Ervas Lusas" Cooperative Case Study, Handbook of Research on Strategic Innovation Management for Improved Competitive Advantage. IGI-Global, Chapter 29, 565–582, DOI: 10.4018/978-1-5225-3012-1.ch029.

Anunciação, P. F., & Esteves, F. M. (2012). Sustainability in the Information Society: A Proposal of Information System Requirements in View of the DPOBE Model for Organizational Sustainability, *Procedia Technology Special Issue CENTERIS 2012/HCIST*, Vol. 5, October, 599–606.

Anunciação, P. F., Esteves, F. M., & Santos, J. R. (2014). Some Information Systems Requirements in View of Organizational Sustainability in an Information Society, *Information Resource Management Journal*, 27(1), 21–35, January-March.

Anunciação, P. F., Fonseca, G. L., & Rodello, I. A. (2017). Information Management and Enterprise Resource Planning: An analysis of the Medical Products Distribution Chain, *Handbook of Research on Information Management for Effective Logistics and Supply Chains*, Chapter 19, 334–349. https://www.igi-global.com/book/handbook-research-information-management-effective/154859.

Anunciação, P. F., & Peñalver, A. J. B. (2017). Information Urbanistic Perspective in the Context of Blue Economy: Analysis of Setúbal and Cartagena Tourism Offer, *International Journal of Sociotechnology and Knowledge Development (IJSKD)*, 9(3), 65–83.

Anunciação, P. F., Pereira, O., Lobo, M., & Mateus, G. (2017). The Importance of Perception and Appreciation of the Information Management for Effective Logistics and Supply Chain in Transport Sector, *Handbook of Research on Information Management for Effective Logistics and Supply Chains*. IGI-Global, Chapter 24, 453–468, DOI: 10.4018/978-1-5225-0973-8.ch024.

Anunciação, P. F., Svirina, A., & Santos, J. R. (2013). *A Tool to Measure Organizational Sustainability Strength*, *Journal of Business Management*, 7, December, 105–117.

Anunciação, P. F., & Zorrinho, C. (2006). *Organizational Urbanism - How Managing Technological Shock in Companies*, Lisbon, Sílabo Publishing (in Portuguese).

Berg, B. L. (2001). Focus Group Interviewing. In B. L. Berg (Ed.), *Qualitative Research Methods for the Social Sciences*, Vol. 4, 111–132, Needham Heights: Pearson.

Bujaki, M., & McConomy, B. J. (2002). Corporate Governance: Factors Influencing Voluntary Disclosure by Publicly Traded Canadian Firms, Canadian Accounting Perspectives, Toronto, 1(2), 105–139.

Denolf, J. M., Trienekens, J. H., Vorst, J. G. A. J., & Omta, S. F. (2015). The Role of Governance Structures in Supply Chain Information Sharing, Journal on Chain and Network Science, Wageningen, 15(1), 83–99.

Gartner (n.d.). *IT Glossary*, Retrieved September 11, 2018, from https://www.gartner.com/it-glossary/information-governance/.

Hulme, T. (2012). Information Governance: Sharing the IBM Approach, Business Information Review, Hartlepool, 29(2), 99.

ISGec – Information System Governance European Club (2010). *Why the Corporations Are Asking for an Information Systems Governance?*, Retrieved December 11, 2017, from http://www.cegsi.org/index.php/documents/telechargement-du-document-la-gouvernance-des-systemes-d-information-pourquoi/la-gouvernance-des-systemes-d-information-pourquoi.

ISGec – Information System Governance European Club (2011). *The Importance of the Information Systems Approach in the Governance of Organizations*, Retrieved December 11, 2017, from http://www.cegsi.org/index.php/documents/l-importance-de-l-approche-par-les-systemes-d-information/the-importance-of-the-information-systems-approach-for-governance-organizations (in French).

Kooper, M. N., Maes, R., & Roos Lindgreen, E. E. O. (2011). On the Governance of Information: Introducing a New Concept of Governance to Support the Management of Information, *International Journal of Information Management*, 31, 195–200 (in French).

Mohamed, N., & Kaur, J. (2012). A Conceptual Framework for Information Technology Governance Effectiveness in Private Organizations, *Information Management & Computer Security*, Bradford, 20(2), 88–106.

Morgan, D. L. (1996). Focus Groups, *Annual Review of Sociology*, 22. Retrieved June 21, 2018, from http://www.jstor.org/stable/2083427.

Oliveira, A. (1996). The Potential Value of Information Systems, *Management Studies*, III(1), 3–18 (in Portuguese).

Oliveira, A. (1999). The Importance of Information Systems for Industry, *Information Systems*, 11, 21–26 (in Portuguese).

Oliveira, A. (2009). *Information & Information Systems – Facts, Myths, Mitifications, Mystifications, Dangerous Half-truths & Lack of Common Sense*, Refertelecom Publishing (in Portuguese).

Oliveira, A. (2010). Governance of Information Systems – Why, *ISGec Conference*, Madrid.

Queirós, P., & Lacerda, T. (2013). *The Importance of Interview in Qualitative Research.* In I. Mesquita & A. Graça (Eds.), *Qualitative Research in Sport* (Vol. 2). Porto: Center for Innovation and Intervention Training in Sport, Faculty of Sport. Porto University (in Portuguese).

Stout, E. (2015). Passive Information Governance: A Cost-Effective Way to Protect Your Information Assets, *Database Trends, and Applications*, Chatham, 29(3), Jun/Jul, 43–44.

Van Grembergen, W. (2000). The Balanced Scorecard and IT Governance, *Information Systems Control Journal*, 2, 40–3.

Van Greenbergen, W. (2004). *Strategies for Information Technology Governance*, Hersey: IDEA Group Publishing.

Weill, P., & Ross, J. W. (2004). *IT Governance-How Top Performers Manage IT Decision Rights for Superior Results.* Boston: Harvard Business School Press.

Pedro Fernandes da Anunciação, António Juan Briones Peñalver, Francisco Joaquim Madeira Esteves

Smart Tourism: The Case of Setúbal and Cartagena

1. Introduction

The current context of tourist activity, post pandemic, is quite different from the traditional one we were used to. After the impacts associated with the pandemic, related to the strong limitations on tourist travel, we can assume that the hospitality and tourist industry had to reinvent itself (Chang, McAleer & Ramos, 2020; Kumar, 2020; Chandrasekaran & Dhanalakshmi, 2020) and have generated an unprecedented economic crisis in the different countries. From east to west, the pandemic affected the different economies and sectors, leaving markets, companies, workers, and consumers in future uncertainty and with real difficulties in sustainability. The variability of the pandemic evolution have made the identification of management scenarios and the definition of commercial strategies difficult.

Never have the world economy faced such an uncertain and unpredictable scenario of the global dimension. Economic and social issues such as Brexit or the trade conflict between the United States and China have lost relevance in comparison to the impact and magnitude of a pandemic situation that has affected everyone and everything. These impacts are significant in the various economic sectors, from industry to commerce, from tourism to health, and from sport to leisure, and they were reflected in the loss of income, bankruptcies, and unemployment, among others. These are some examples of real situations that gradually economic and tourism organizations try to find an answer.

Countries, cities, and local places whose economic activity depended heavily on tourism have to reinvent themselves now, seeking to minimize the impacts of this troubled period that still conditions tourist travels. Tourist operators must find new solutions though it is not possible to return to the normality before the pandemic. However, this presupposes an innovative effort to recreate the demand for the desired tourist destinations. It is in situations of crisis that normally economic agents stimulate innovation and entrepreneurship to minimize or overcome existing difficulties.

Information technologies provide a future anticipation of tourist options. This tool, through the most recent innovations, offers the possibility of a previous experience that can constitute a differentiating factor when deciding on the choice of a tourist destination (Graziano & Privitera, 2020). Virtual tours make it possible to optimize your options throughout the year, valuing the diversity of destinations and the respective differentiating factors.

Information technologies provide innovation in tourist activities and provide new ways of creating value in the tourism value chain (Buhalis, 2020). But, for that to happen, it is important to understand the potential of information technologies from the consumer's perspective. The customer can currently access more information, compare and select more tourist products, increase their level of knowledge about tourist offers, better support their decisions, or even benefit from virtual tourist experiences through technologies (Neuhofer, Buhalis & Ladkin, 2014).

The pandemic forced stakeholders to consider innovation in the sustainability equation, forcing them to reinvent the business and develop new strategies, often in partnership, for new solutions, benefiting from new technological solutions such as 5G (Khan, 2020). Some solutions to combat COVID-19 are technology-based; also, the reopening of tourism and the economy can be leveraged through information technologies. Technology offers some different solutions: apps for fast and real-time decisions, humanoid robots to meet and deliver materials, digital and contactless passports, and automatized measuring body temperature, among others are some examples of the role of technologies in tourism activity (Sigala, 2020).

To this end, it is necessary that tourist organizations adapt to this opportunity and adequately manage the implicit change (Kotsemir, Abroskin, & Meissner, 2013). In the information society, technologies represent critical success factors, but to achieve the associated competitive advantages, it is necessary to include them in the dynamics of the tourist business (Baggio, 2014; Lovelock e Wirtz, 2007) and improve the perception of better services (Grudzewski et al., 2018).

Technology is reshaping nature, objectives, and tourism experiences, and it is taking part in the customer journey when people travel (Huang et al., 2016). In this sense, the tourism context will tend to increase the level of associated technologies, allowing the evolution and convergence of Tourism 4.0 to intelligent tourism (Pencarelli, 2019).

The adoption of new technologies by operators and tourists is usually carried out with a perspective of value generation. This presupposes new business models supported by digital technologies. New technologies demand organizational flexibility and new paradigms of quality to information systems.

In the tourism case, the digitalization of product and services increase travel expectations and the desire to travel (Li, Robinson & Oriade, 2017; Um & Chung, 2019). This desire, which is reflected in the competitive potential, can be measured through the ease with which a tourist identifies, evaluates, and decides his commercial options regarding the desired tourist products and services (Prebensen et al., 2012).

To understand the digital competitiveness of the tourism sector, it is important to identify the levels of information technology adoption in each phase of the value chain. In the tourism scope, the generation of expectations started with information and images sharing about the main cultural or natural elements existing in the tourism destinations. The possibility of digital channels, proportionated by government agents or tourist agents, supports many travelers' preferences and constitutes the main interaction platform between tourism service providers and customers.

The dynamic proportionated by technologies allows a complementarity between images and sounds, highlighting the differentiating characteristics of tourist destinations. And if these image and sound characteristics are more attractive when videos are made available, when compared to traditional photographs, the possibility of adopting technologies associated with virtual reality or augmented reality opens new windows of opportunity and competitiveness in supporting the dynamization of the touristic offer. The presentation and sensorial stimulation of the relevant elements in the tourist destinations, through technological innovation, provides more relevant qualitative information and influences in the decision-making of tourists.

Virtual reality and augmented reality provide a higher level of knowledge and stimulate tourist interest (Moro et al., 2019), as they provide an almost real experience, allowing them to immerse themselves in a real-life environment. In this environment, the tourist will confirm his interest as he will have the opportunity to perceive the trip to the desired destination.

The virtual environment provides a digital interface that connects the user to reality, through a computerized system, allowing the construction of a realistic relationship with the element under analysis. This possibility provides, to the visitor, a real feeling about what is being seen as an approximation to the real context. Virtual reality allows a virtual mobility of the user to an environment that replaces the tourist destination through the provision of cultural and heritage content or other digital tourist scenarios, providing a simulation of what can be known through a computerized support.

Augmented reality incorporates the latest innovation in the field of information systems and technologies and allows virtual elements to be superimposed on our view of reality.

All these initiatives awaken tourists' knowledge of the set of differentiating aspects of tourist destinations. The peculiarity of the natural surroundings of a given place, the value of the cultural heritage, among other examples, can simultaneously awaken the residents of the region to the preservation of these elements and make them active participants in the conservation and improvement of the environment. This can be another benefit enhanced by disruptive technologies.

In this context, recent technological innovations in augmented reality have come to provide a new opportunity for innovation in tourism. It will be possible to reshape and redesign tourism information and above all generate knowledge about the presented realities. The augmented reality allows a combination of virtual reality and physical reality through the incorporation of digital images within the real scenario captured in the tourism area. Virtual reality or augmented reality allows the discovery of particularities of certain destinations providing sensory experiences that facilitate the immersion of a potential tourist in the desired environment (Tussyadiah, Jung & Dieck, 2018).

From the perspective of Culture and Tourism, the virtualization of tourist destinations will facilitate the increase in the value of the cultural product in historic centers and the consequent improvement of heritage resources. Likewise, in this area, cultural and heritage resources are combined with different points of interest, providing quality tourism, which contributes to the socio-economic development of all associated areas, and the strengthening of business dynamics in the provision of different services from a perspective of sustainability and respect for the environment.

2. The Role of Technological Innovation in the Stimulation of the Tourism Sector

With all the impacts resulting from the pandemic, which persist and will certainly continue, many people who traditionally took advantage of their vacation periods or weekends to travel to more distant or closer destinations, respectively, saw a requirement to postpone their travel plans. Many people have expressed on social networks their concern about travelling options in future when they consider the increased travel risks for certain countries with high incidence rates of the virus.

However, it is also evident that people who like to travel, even if they are unable to do so or are limited by the rules in different destinations, try to keep themselves updated or take advantage of these conditions to plan new adventures as soon as possible. Thus, these confinement periods are used by many tourists to digitally discover certain destinations to which they have a potential interest in moving in the future.

Digital tourism has enormous potential to stimulate the sector, although it does not represent immediate solutions. Digital experiences do not turn into financial income and do not allow to minimize the economic difficulties that tourist companies are experiencing. Digital tourism represents an opportunity to maintain the tourist desire and impulse by allowing people to travel virtually and travel without leaving home.

For example, the EarthCam and World Cams sites allow people to get to know places and sights around the world through a smartphone or computer or visit museums, such as the Louvre Museum in Paris, or the Frida Kahlo Museum in Mexico, which are available through multimedia platforms and can be visited, or even visit churches considered jewels of architecture like the church of the holy family in Barcelona. These are investments with a future.

Most tourist agents have expressed, through the media, that even after the reopening of borders and airports, tourism will go a long way towards achieving the desired rebalancing considering the pre-pandemic indicators. The pandemic has left marks that constitute economic and social wounds that will have to be gradually treated, and this will take time to heal.

Since the development indexes of the tourism sector reached worldwide in the pre-pandemic period, the forecasts will always be promising. People maintain the taste and desire to travel and meet. However, the resumption of activity will take place slowly and gradually, as the pandemic shows signs of being controlled and will gradually depend on the feeling of security that people may have.

It will therefore be natural that, in the first phase, travel takes place in domestic destinations, close to the areas of residence, limited to essential business, health, or family visits. And that, after a bigger control of the pandemic situation and bigger confidence in economic agents, leisure trips to external destinations will gradually resume.

It is also important to add, to these factors, that this recovery will also depend on the recovery of the economic power of families. Many have seen their income diminished or even lost with the pandemic. In Portugal, 55 % of families with children consider that their income has been reduced following the outbreak of COVID-19. In a broader scope, looking at a total of 24 European countries, the figure reaches 63 % in contrast to the 49 % of respondents without children, which shows that families are facing serious financial problems. Note that Portugal will not be the worst case. The special edition of "ECPR 2020 - European

Consumer Payment Report" shows that Italy and Greece are the countries where families with children face the greatest financial problems (74 %) (Intrum, 2020).

This means that the recovery of tourism indicators registered before the pandemic will take some years. It is also conditioned by the economic power of families. So, in this sense, we sought, with this work, to analyze the degree of adoption of smart technologies, as a driver to increase digital tourism, in the main monuments of two cities in different countries: Setúbal, in Portugal, and Cartagena, in Spain.

3. Objectives and Methodology

The presented study aimed to analyze and characterize the availability of digital alternatives to the physical limitations registered in tourist visits due to pandemic situations. As a presupposition for the development of the study carried out, it was considered that the desire associated with tourism can and should be stimulated in spite of the travel impossibility or constraints or physical visits to tourist destinations. It is true that information technologies, themselves, do not constitute competitive advantages. Competitive advantages result from the ability of managers, through technologies, to leverage business and economic activities.

As a case study, the city of Setúbal, in Portugal, and Cartagena, in Spain, was chosen. The choice of these two cities was due to the existence of a set of characteristics that make them similar, namely, they are both coastal cities, where various maritime activities are developed (fishing and ship repair), with strong potential for development in the tourist domain, with heritage and historical interest, and with a high natural beauty.

The research began with the identification and structuring of the tourist offer in main areas of tourism activity. Then, the analysis and typification of the technological characteristics associated with the tourist offer and dissemination were carried out. Considering the main tourist attractions in the cities and associated regions, there was an attempt to identify the potential of each city and region, by consulting the official tourist promotion website.

This analysis aimed to analyze the attractiveness potential offered, considering the potential for technological innovation (photography, video, and virtual reality), on the one hand, and, on the other, to identify the possibility of carrying out economic digital operations with the various agents (business-to-consumer – B2C).

Considering that the digital offer represents the first and most important opportunity to establish an emotional relationship associated with a tourist destination, the basic questions of the research were the following: is the offer of tourist information/products/services made available by official digital channels enhanced by technological innovation? Does the offer of information/products/services favor the relational economy?

As mentioned above and synthesizing the research carried out, the main objective of the first phase of the research was to analyze the offer made available to national and foreign tourists and the possibility of identifying and visualizing the main elements of tourist interest in each of the cities. In the second phase, it was to analyze and classify the potential for tourism promotion. This phase was subdivided into two sub-phases, the first corresponding to the identification of the technological means adopted for their dissemination (photo, video, or virtual/augmented reality), and the second corresponding to the analysis of the potential of relational economics, through the identification of the level of economic integration between the various stakeholders (general information, relational information, and economic intelligence).

Finally, we try to establish a comparative analysis between both cities analyzed in the two countries, presenting, for this purpose, a matrix with the various dimensions of analysis considered above.

4. The Case of the Digital Tourism Offers in Setúbal and Cartagena

The analysis began through the identification of similar dimensions in the tourist offer between both cities. To this end, we used the identification of official sites for the dissemination of tourist products/services, as well as the potential of the city/region. In the case of Setúbal, the analysis of the tourist offer was carried out through the official portal (https://visitsetubal.com) and the survey was carried out in the period between May and July 2021. In the case of Cartagena, the research and analysis were carried out on the Concejalía de Turismo website (https://turismo.cartagena.es/), with the research being carried out between November and December 2021.

Despite the fact that – with regard to the structure of the Setúbal-Portugal website – two different perspectives in information dissemination were found, a general perspective, which includes dimensions such as "nature", "flavors", "adventure", "culture" and "region"; and another perspective, with a more specific scope, which includes dimensions such as "where to sleep", "what to do", "what to eat", "script", and "map", it was possible to identify a set of common dimensions.

Regarding the first part of the research, the nature of the tourist offer was classified and identified. Given the different natures existing in the two case studies analyzed, the various dimensions of the tourism offer were defined considering: Accommodation, Occupational Activities (for example, birdwatching, dolphin watching, adventure sports, fishing activities, etc.), Culture, Gastronomy, Heritage/Monuments, Nature, Region, Other Tourist Offers (other economic activities, for example, wine tourism; or tourist suggestions, for example, itineraries proposals, among others). The results, shown in Tab. 1, show a similarity in the following dimensions between both the cities.

Tab. 1: Dimensions of the tourist offer in the city of Setúbal (Portugal) and Cartagena (Spain)

Nature of the Tourist Offer	Setúbal (Set)	Cartagena (Cart)
Accommodation (A)	Y	Y
Occupational Activities (OA)	Y	Y
Culture (C)	Y	Y
Gastronomy (G)	Y	Y
Heritage/Monuments (H/M)	Y	Y
Nature (N)	Y	Y
Region (R)	Y	Y
Other Tourist Offers (OTO)	N	Y

In this first level of analysis, it is possible to verify that the city of Cartagena provides information on all analyzed dimensions. The city of Setúbal does not provide information about other tourist offers that are not covered in the previous dimensions.

With regard to the second part of the study, which aimed to analyze and classify the potential for tourism promotion, a classification was carried out based on three types of possible and differentiating dynamics: the static (photos), in which the existence of photos that allowed identification and evaluation of the elements under analysis were considered; the dynamic (video), in which the availability of specific videos on the theme/offer made available was considered; and, finally, the interactive (virtual reality or augmented reality), corresponding to the possibility of conducting virtual visits associated with the topic under analysis.

Having identified similar dimensions and considering there is feasibility for the development of comparative analysis, then the study proceeded to the analysis and classification of the potential of tourism promotion and the potential relational competitiveness.

At this stage of the research, an attempt was made to identify the potential for the competitiveness of the tourist offer, considering three different levels of depth in the relational economy:

- the dissemination of general economic and commercial information, namely through the provision of, for example, contacts and location, but without linking to the operators' websites;
- relational information, with greater detail and level of knowledge about the researched topics, allowing, for example, the connection, through links, to tour operators, the configuration of commercial options referring to products or services; and,
- economic intelligence, associated with the possibility of direct execution of economic operations, such as, for example, tourist reserves, directly or indirectly (B2C) provided by official websites.

In the case study of Setúbal-Portugal, in both dimensions, general information is available, and in some cases, a link is provided to the respective operators, for example, in the case of "Accommodation" or in the "Occupational Activities" dimension, in which a variety of tourist stakeholders is available.

However, for example, in the case of "Gastronomy", in addition to general information, there is no indication of the main gastronomic stakeholders of a contact reference. Tab. 2 summarizes the main results of these dimensions of analysis for the city of Setúbal-Portugal.

Tab. 2 : Nature of the tourist offer in the city of Setúbal

	Potential for tourist promotion			**Potential of relational competitiveness**		
Nature of the Tourist Offer	**Photography**	**Video**	**Virtual/ Augmented Reality**	**General information**	**Relational information**	**Economic intelligence (B2C)**
Accommodation (A)	Y	N	N	Y	N	N
Occupational Activities (OA)	Y	N	N	Y	N	N
Culture (C)	Y	N	N	Y	Y	N
Gastronomy (G)	Y	N	N	Y	N	N
Heritage/ Monuments (H/M)	Y	N	N	Y	NA	N
Nature (N)	Y	N	N	Y	NA	NA
Region (R)	Y	Y	N	Y	N	N
Other Tourist Offers (OTO)	N	N	N	N	N	N

In the case of Cartagena-Spain, as shown in Tab. 3, a more targeted or orientated structure for tourist options is evident, available through options such as "Plan your trip" or "Itineraries". Generally, there is the availability of general information and photographs. However, it is noteworthy that, in the heritage area, there is the option to carry out virtual tours, although this option is not associated with the heritage but appears as an individualized option, which will only be performed if the user is attentive and looking for this functionality.

Tab. 3: Nature of the tourist offer in the city of Cartagena-Espanha

	Potential for tourist promotion			**Potential of relational competitiveness**		
Natureza da Oferta	**Photography**	**Video**	**Virtual/ Augmented Reality**	**General information**	**Relational information**	**Economic intelligence (B2C)**
Accommodation (A)	Y	N	N	Y	Y	Y
Occupational Activities (OA)	Y	N	N	Y	Y	N
Culture (C)	Y	N	N	Y	Y	NA
Gastronomy (G)	Y	N	N	Y	N	N
Heritage/ Monuments (H/ M)	Y	Y	Y	Y	NA	N
Nature (N)	Y	N	N	Y	NA	NA
Region (R)	Y	N	N	Y	Y	NA
Other Tourist Offers (OTO)	Y	N	N	Y	Y	Y

In the last phase of this study, we sought to highlight the positioning of the potential for tourism promotion and competitiveness through a framework that facilitates the definition of a roadmap for evolution towards digital innovation. Considering this framework, we proceeded to the positioning of each of the dimensions identified in each of the cases studied.

Tab. 4 : Potential for tourism promotion of Setúbal-Portugal and Cartagena-Espanha

Relational competitiveness potential	Economic intelligence		A (Cart) OTO(Cart)		
	Relational information	C(Set)	C(Cart)	OA(Cart)	
	General information	A (Set) OA(Set) G(Set) H/M(Set) N(Set) R(Set) OTO(Set)	G(Cart) P(Cart) N(Cart) R(Cart)		H/ M(Cart)
		Photography		Video	Virtual reality
		Technological competitiveness potential			

As we can see in Tab. 4, regarding the analyzed domains, the cities of Setúbal-Portugal and Cartagena-Spain are still positioned in the quadrant with the lowest potential for relational competitiveness and technological competitiveness, that is, they have a low degree of tourist promotion potential.

In the case of Setúbal-Portugal, only the Culture dimension stands out that goes beyond the basic quadrant, with a relational dimension in terms of the potential for relational competitiveness being noted. In the case of Cartagena-Spain, it is worth noting a more evident advance, especially in the dimensions of occupational activities, which is at an intermediate level of competitiveness, as it allows the sharing of relational information and the presentation of video as a means of dissemination. It is also worth mentioning the possibility of using virtual reality associated with general information made available to tourists.

Considering the tourist offer of each of the analyzed regions, it is possible to consider that there is still a long way to go in the adoption of the technological potential regarding the promotion of these two cities as destinations of interest for the generality of tourists.

5. Conclusion

The pandemic associated with Covid-19 had a very significant impact on the tourism sector worldwide. Statistical indicators in Portugal and Spain are evident and leave no doubt as to the direct impact on the activities of this sector. Although the direct impact on tourism has been analyzed, through the presentation of some indicators, we can consider a similar impact in several activities that are directly or indirectly related to this sector, such as restaurants or transport.

Information and communication technologies provide the possibility to find strategic alternatives that, not substituting the physical presence of tourists in the places of greatest interest, can enable the study and planning of future visits. Above all, the possibility of realizing virtual views or immersing yourself in tourist options in the context of augmented reality allows arousing interest in conducting face-to-face visits and increases levels of knowledge about the reality under analysis.

The results obtained through this study allow us to conclude that there is still a long way to go for the various tourist agents. Although these technological options are available, it is necessary that the entities responsible for tourism, in particular the Central and Regional Tourist Entities, have the sensitivity to their respective potential and develop projects with a view to evolving towards smart tourism. Smart tourism can be a long-term strategy for increasing the number of tourists as well as for retaining certain destinations.

As can be seen, there is little innovation in the promotion of the main tourist supply channels. On the websites of the various operators, both public and private, dissemination continues to focus on the use of images (photographs). The sharing of relational information associated with the various actors is very limited and the use of technological innovation (virtual reality) is practically non-existent. We can assume that digital tourism is still embryonic. In general, we can assume that there is no possibility of carrying out a previous virtual visit to encourage the desire to visit these two cities. About augmented reality, this possibility is even non-existent, with no reference to it being found on the websites visited.

In conclusion and as a balance, we can state that the city of Cartagena has a higher level of development than Setúbal, regarding the use of digital innovation in tourism. Thus, this constitutes a strategic challenge for both cities, not only for the entities responsible for the monuments or places of tourist interest but also for all the stakeholders that are directly or indirectly involved in the tourist sector.

The analysis was carried out in the public domain to provide a perspective funded by the principal public digital channels. However, it would be interesting to analyze the digital maturity of the various tourist stakeholders.

On the other hand, it would also be interesting to analyze the potential for tourism promotion and competitiveness between the different regions of Portugal and Spain to analyze whether there are more attractive regions in the tourism field at the national level.

Acknowledgment

The authors would like to thank the Instituto Politécnico de Setúbal (Portugal) for the support given to the publication of this research work. They also thank the Polytechnic University of Cartagena for their interest in the comparative analysis between the two cities, in the identification of strategic lines of development, carried out during the visit made to the IPS between May and August 2021.

References

Baggio, R. (2014). Technological Innovation in e-Tourism: The Role of Interoperability and Standards. In: Mariani, M. M., Baggio, R., Buhalis, D., Longhi, C. (eds) *Tourism Management, Marketing, and Development*. Palgrave Macmillan, New York. https://doi.org/10.1057/9781137354358_3.

Buhalis, D. (2020). Technology in tourism-from information communication technologies to eTourism and smart tourism towards ambient intelligence tourism: A perspective article. *Tourism Review*, 75(1), 267–272.

Chandrasekaran, K. S., & Dhanalakshmi, N. (2020). The pandemic effect on the tourism industry. *Strad Research*, 7(9), 33–39

Chang, C.-L., McAleer, M., & Ramos V. (2020). A charter for sustainable tourism after COVID19. *Sustainability*, 12(9:3671), 1–4.

Graziano, T., & Privitera, D. (2020). Cultural heritage, tourist, attractiveness and augmented reality: insights from Italy. *Journal of Heritage Tourism*, DOI: 10.1080/1743873X.2020.1719116.

Grudzewski, F., Awdziej, M., Mazurek, G., & Piotrowska, K. (2018). Virtual reality in marketing communication – the impact on the message, technology and offer perception – empirical study, *Economics and Business Review*, 4 (18), Nº. 3, 36–50, DOI: 10.18559/ebr.2018.3.4.

Huang, Y. C., Backman, K. F., Backman, S. J., & Chang, L. L. (2016). Exploring the implications of virtual reality technology in tourism marketing: An integrated research framework. *International Journal of Tourism Research*, 18(2), 116–128.

Intrum (2020). European Consumer Payment Report 2020, 8th Annual Edition. Retrieved February 17, https://www.intrum.com/media/10154/intrum-ecpr-2020.pdf

Khan, S. (2020). COVID-19: Tourism at Crossroads! Where Next? *Journal on Tourism & Sustainability*, 3, 32–40. ISSN: 2515-6780.

Kotsemir, M., Abroskin, A., & Meissner, D. (2013). Innovation Concepts and Typology – An Evolutionary Discussion. *University Higher School of Economics Research Paper Series*. https://doi.org/http://dx.doi.org/10.2139/ssrn.2221299.

Kumar, U. (2020). The Economic and Psychological Impact of SARS-Cov2 on Travel and Tourism Industry: With Special Reference to India. *Online International Interdisciplinary Conference on Our Earth Our Resources*, November 2020. Retrieved from https://www.researchgate.net/publication/341804662_Covid-[19]_and_Tourism_Industry?channel=doi&linkId=5ed579d7299bf1c67d326119&showFull615 text=true.

Li, S. C. H., Robinson, P., & Oriade, A. (2017). Destination marketing: The use of technology since the millennium. *Journal of Destination Marketing & Management*, 6(2), 95–102.

Lovelock, C. H., & Wirtz, J. (2007). *Services Marketing – People, Technology, Strategy*, Pearson.

Moro, S., Rita, P., Ramos, P., & Esmerado, J. (2019). Analysing recent augmented and virtual reality developments in tourism. *Journal of Hospitality and Tourism Technology*, https://doi.org/10.1108/JHTT-07-2018-0059.

Neuhofer, B., Buhalis, D., & Ladkin, A. (2014). A typology of technology-enhanced 636 tourism experiences. *International Journal of Tourism Research*, 16(4), 340–350.

Pencarelli, T. (2019). The digital revolution in the travel and tourism industry. *Information Technology & Tourism*. Retrieved from https://link.springer.com/article/10.1007%2Fs40558-019-00160-3.

Prebensen, N. K., Woo, E., Chen, J. S., & Uysal, M. (2012). Motivation and involvement as antecedents of the perceived value of the destination experience. *Journal of Travel Research, 52*(2), 253–264.

Sigala, M. (2020). Tourism and COVID-19: Impacts and implications for advancing and resetting industry and research. *Journal of Business Research*, 117, 312–321.

Tussyadiah, I. P., Jung, T. H., & tom Dieck, M. C. (2018). Embodiment of wearable augmented reality technology in tourism experiences. *Journal of Travel Research*, 57(5), 597–611.

Um, T., & Chung, N. (2019). Does smart tourism technology matter? Lessons from three smart tourism cities in South Korea. *Asia Pacific Journal of Tourism Research*, Published online. DOI: 10.1080/10941665.2019.1595691.

Victor Platon, Andreea Constantinescu, Daniela Antonescu, Simona Frone, Florina Popa

Influence of Eco-Investment and Innovation on Municipal Waste Recycling in EU

1. Introduction

In the last 30 years, EU has provided for a significant change in regard with managing municipal waste. From an approach that was focused mainly on disposal, EU countries have increasingly shifted their focus with regard to municipal waste towards methods for waste minimization and better recycling. The whole idea is to move the management of municipal waste higher on the "waste hierarchy" (Kemp, 2010). This is an essential step to obtain more value from the waste generated while reducing the burden on the environment. The main drivers of this new trend are eco-investment and eco-innovation. Both drivers are influential in providing raw materials and creating jobs.

This chapter is organized as follows: in the first part, in Introduction, we review the relevant literature regarding the relationship among municipal waste recycling, eco-innovation and eco-investment. In the second part, we present the date series, countries considered, time frame including data sources, the indicators used, etc. The next section includes the research methodology and the research hypotheses that were used in particularizing the panel data model used, followed by interpretation and discussions. Finally, we conclude regarding the findings.

While in the EU, the waste generated by municipalities is estimated only around 10 % of total waste generated, it is very noticeable, and slowdown of this waste type has the potential to decrease its environmental impact on the whole chain: generation, transport and disposal. The reality is that countries that have in place advanced and efficient municipal waste management systems generally perform better in overall waste management (Mazzanti et al., 2008). The preference for analyzing municipal waste is due to the fact that it allows broader comparability across EU countries, while industrial waste depends on the industrial structure of each country; so comparability is not easy.

Improving municipal waste management is discussed and analyzed in numerous studies. The main idea resulted from various articles and papers is that recycling is a serious and complicated business and should be dealt with appropriate tools. In the first place, municipal waste management has to protect human health and not harm the environment. Second, as the consumption of good and services increases day by day, simple elimination of the waste generated is no longer an acceptable solution (Gwarda, 2017; Horbach, 2020). In EU, the ultimate goal is to promote Circular Economy by decoupling of economic growth and welfare from resources extraction and waste generation. Recycling waste generated by humans is intended to reduce resource consumption, energy and waste generation by returning used resources and waste into the economy. All resources used into the economic cycle and waste generated have to be managed as permanent renewable resources (Platon et al., 2020).

In a recent study carried out for EU, DG Environment (Eunomia, COWI, 2019), it is estimated that the implementation of new waste legislation issued by EU in 2018 will require significant investment. It is important to mention that more stringent targets were introduced for municipal waste recycling (65 % for 2025 instead of a previous 55 % and 70 % for 2030 instead of 60 %). In these circumstances, the need for investment was estimated at EUR 16.4 billion euro. This amount takes into account only money that should be spent for building new capacities in member states without replacement of the old ones. If replacement cost is considered, then the total will be much higher. The additional new capacities for waste management would be 21.04 million tons for Municipal Solid Waste (dry and bio waste recycling), Biowaste (14.24 mil. tons), Recycling Preprocessors (10.3 mil. tons), Residual processing (2.74 mil. tons).

From the paper mentioned above, we may understand that the investment needs for waste management is huge. There are several solutions to reduce the amount of investment needed as: using eco-innovation, minimizing the waste at source, changing consumption patterns.

The importance of eco-innovation in recycling is highlighted by numerous studies. A recent one (Mele et al., 2022) brings some interesting thoughts. Recycling municipal waste brings new jobs, while simple landfilling and more complex incineration do not. Recycling is an activity that require labor, so the income becomes dependent on the volume of recycling, on the one hand, and on the eco-innovation and new technologies, on the other. The authors reported that could be identified the presence of a feedback linkage, indicating that municipal waste recycling can also result in income generation and jobs creation.

As human collectivities take steps towards better processing of municipal waste by collecting, treating and recycling in specialized facilities, the result is profit for the whole economy because it shares spillovers connections with innovation, jobs and income. Anyhow, this is not a valid assertion for any situation. As long as recycling costs are lower than the prices of recyclable sold, the virtuous cycle may continue (Wang et al., 2019). If the costs are higher than benefits, then a subsidy will be needed; so, we are going to face a vicious cycle.

2. Data and Methodology

In this section we are going to explore the influence by eco-investment (called Investment) and eco-innovation (called Innovation) on municipal waste recycling rate (MWRR). To do this, a panel regression model will be used in which the dependent variable will be MWRR and the regressors will be Investment and Innovation. The panel will include 24 countries for which Eurostat provides data.

2.1. Municipal Waste Recycling in EU

The data regarding municipal waste (MW) recycling are gathered and reported by all EU countries. This indicator measures the portion of recycled municipal waste in the total municipal waste generated in one year. Recycling activities contain several distinct actions as: collection, transport, solid waste recycling, composting of organic residuals and anaerobic digestion, landfilling, incineration. The indicator MWRR is expressed in percent (%) as both terms of the ratio (waste recycled/waste generated) are measured in the same unit (tons). There are data available for the period 2000–2020 and for 28 countries, members of the EU. In 2020 UK was technically still part of the EU, so it will be included in the analysis.

As we may notice from Fig. 1, the trend of recycling municipal waste is positive for all countries considered. Still, there are significant discrepancies among the 28 countries analyzed (Fig. 1). The most advanced countries (leaders) in MW recycling are Germany, Austria, Denmark and Netherland with recycling rate over 40 %. Other countries are in the middle range with recycling rate between 20 % and 40 % (France, Hungary, Ireland, Luxemburg, UK, etc.). We can notice a catching-up group of countries which recorded low values of recycling (less than 20 %). In this group there are some countries as: Bulgaria, Cyprus, Romania, Malta, etc.

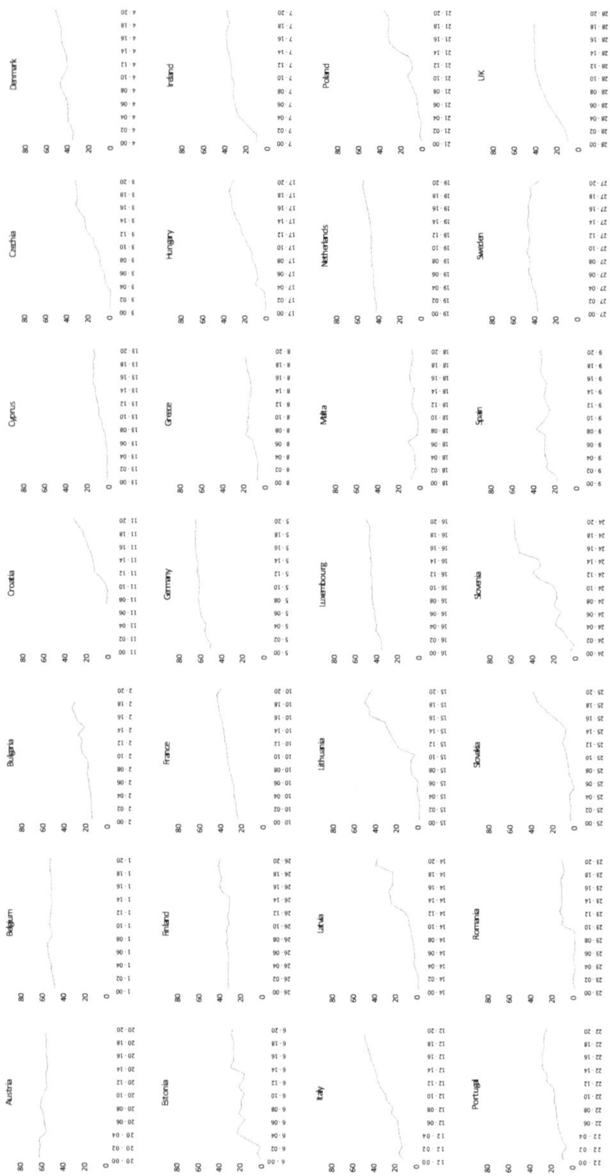

Fig. 1: Recycling rate for municipal waste, by country (2000–2020) (%)

Source: Processing data from https://ec.europa.eu/eurostat/data/database

2.2. Eco-Innovation

Eco-Innovation has a key role to play in the transition to a circular economy, in the development of new technologies, processes, services and business models. It is measured by the indicator *Number of patents*[1]. This indicator was designed to measure innovation in recycling and secondary raw materials processing (unit of measure – number) and is part of the Circular Economy indicator set. It is used to monitor progress towards a circular economy in the area of "competitiveness and innovation".

Patent statistics is part of the families of indicators widely used to assess technological progress in a particular industry, being accepted as innovation-oriented indicator. Recently, for example, the number of patent applications has been used as an indicator in the 2016 Raw Materials Scoreboard.

The development of innovative techniques for collecting, transporting, storing waste and especially for recycling materials will help reduce the EU's dependence on critical goods and improve the resilience to potential supply disruptions and support the competitiveness of domestic industries.

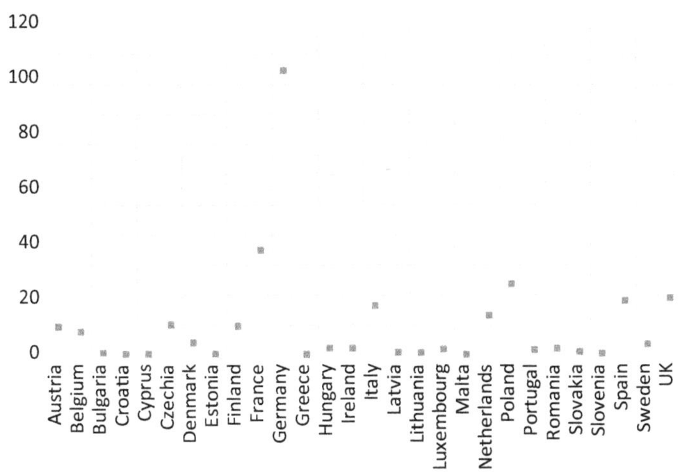

Fig. 2: Means of patents for recycling, by country (2000–2016) (no./ year)

Source: Processing data from https://ec.europa.eu/eurostat/data/database

1 Number of patents for climate change mitigation technologies related to wastewater treatment or waste management.

The indicator measures the number of patents related to recycling and secondary raw materials. The term "patents" refers to patent families, which include all documents relevant to a separate invention (for example, applications to several authorities), thus preventing multiple counting. The indicator is updated annually in Eurostat database. At present patent data for 28 EU countries are available for the period 2000–2016. These data are illustrated in the Fig. 2. We notice that most of the patents, in the period 2000–2016, are registered in Germany (average 103.2 patents/year). Some other EU countries have recorded lower values: France (38.11 patents/year), Poland (25.88 patents/year), UK (20.8 patents/year), etc. The big majority of EU countries have recorded lower values as can be seen in Fig. 2.

2.3. Eco-Investment

The indicator *Private investment, jobs and gross value added related to the circular economy sectors* – (unit of measure Value added at factor cost – million euros) is part of the set of indicators for Circular economy. It is used to monitor progress towards a circular economy in the area of "competitiveness and innovation". Job creation is a key priority for the EU, so the recycling, repair and reuse sectors are expected to make a significant contribution to this priority. Collection, transfer, sorting and recycling sectors are particularly labor-intensive, contributing to local employment.

The indicator includes "Gross investment in tangible assets", "Number of persons employed" and "Value added at factor cost" in the following two sectors: the recycling sector and the repair and reuse sector. Gross investment in tangible assets is defined as investment during the reference year in all tangible assets. New and existing tangible capital goods are included, whether purchased from third parties or produced for own use (i.e. capitalized production of tangible capital goods), with a useful life of more than one year, including non-produced tangible goods. Investments in intangible and financial assets are excluded.

Eurostat provides data for the period 2000–2018, for 24 countries: there are no data for Czech Rep., Ireland, Luxembourg and Malta. In the next figure (Figure 3) we could see the mean of Eco-Investment expressed as a ratio between total investment in recycling and population (€/inhabitant). This transformation was used in order to facilitate the comparability among countries.

As we could notice from Figure 3, the highest eco-investment was made in Sweden (414.4 €/inhabitant). Other countries with investment higher than 300 €/inhabitant are: UK, Austria, Denmark, Germany and Finland. Lowest investment, less than 100 €/inhabitant, is made in catching-up countries as Hungary, Bulgaria, Greece and Romania.

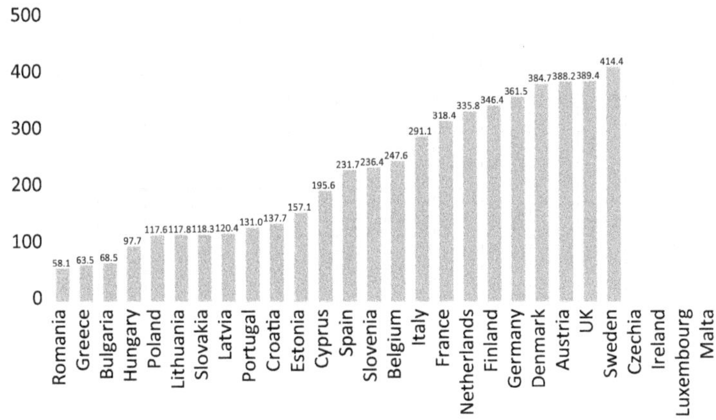

Fig. 3: Means of investment for recycling, by country (2008–2018) (€/inhabitant)
Source: Processing data from https://ec.europa.eu/eurostat/data/database

2.4. Methodology Used

Our goal is to identify the influence of independent variables Investment and Innovation on the dependent variable (MW recycling). As well we are going to investigate the heterogeneity existing among the 24 countries analyzed. To do this we have used two models for the panel regression (Baltagi, 2005; Wooldridge et al., 2002).

First model is of an OLS type, according with the Equation 1:

$$\text{OLS:} y_{it} = \beta_0 + \beta_i X_{it} + \epsilon_{it} \qquad \text{Eq. 1}$$

Y_{it} is the dependent variable, the matrix X_{it} includes the regressors (explanatory variables) and β_i are the respective coefficients. The cross-section (countries) dimension is represented by $\boldsymbol{i}$, the time dimension is represented by $\boldsymbol{t}$ and $\boldsymbol{\varepsilon}_{it}$ is the error term. In the OLS model the coefficients are specified as constant which is the usual hypothesis for cross-sectional analysis.

The OLS equation will be completed by adding several dummy variables ($D_1 \dots D_n$). Dummy variables denote the 24 countries. For example, the variable D_1 is set to take the value 1 for one country and the value 0 for the rest of the countries considered. In this way we obtain specific equations for all countries analyzed. So, the second model that will be used is called LSDV (Least square dummy variable) and is described in the Equation 2:

$$\text{LSDV}: y_{it} = \beta_0 + \beta_i X_{it} + \gamma_i D_i + \epsilon_{it} \qquad \text{Eq. 2}$$

We have used the notation presented in Tab. 1.

Tab. 1: Notations for LSDV model

Variables	Indicator	Notation used	UM	Variables in model
Y_{it}	Municipal waste recycled rate	MWRR	%	RECYCL_MUN_WASTE
X_{1t}	Eco-Innovation	PATENTS_RECYCL	No./mil. inhabitant	PATENTS_RECYCL(-1)/population
X_{2t}	Eco-Investment	INVESTMENT	€/inhabitant	INVESTMENT/population
D_i	Dummy variable	Country name	Binary (0/1)	Country name

Source: Own compilation.

We also mention that a gap of one year for the regressor PATENTS_RECYCL was introduced in the model due to the fact that patents do not show effects immediately after registration. Both regressors (Innovation and Investment) were introduced as relative indicators by dividing them with the number of populations.

3. Results

The results that were obtained by applying the methodology are mentioned in Tab. 2. We notice that both regressors (patents and investment) have positive and statistic significative coefficients ($p<0.05$). By comparing the two models, we consider that LSDV has better indicators (Tab. 2).

Tab. 2: Variables and coefficients of OLS and LSDV model

Variable	Model OLS (Eq. 1)	Model LSDV (Eq. 2)
Method	OLS	OLS
C	9.125***	6.290*
PATENTS_RECYCL(-1)/POPULATION	3.198**	2.925**
INVESTMENT/POPULATION	0.099***	0.090***
Root MSE	9.948	5.975
Akaike info criterion	7.46	6.657
R-squared	0.627	0.865
Prob (F-statistic)	0.000000	0.00000

Legend: *) p<0.1; **) p<0.05; ***) p<0.001
Source: Data from Annex 1 and Annex2.

The model LSVD has a higher R-squared (0.865 compared with 0.627), so it has a better explanatory power for the variation of the independent variable. Also, other indicators such as RMSE and AIC are smaller in the case of LSDV showing a better model despite the fact that AIC penalizes models that use more parameters. In these conditions, if two models explain the same amount of variation, the one with a lower AIC score is considered a better-fit model.

Within the *LSDV model*, the coefficient of the innovation regressor (*Patent_recycl*) has the value +2.925 and is higher than the unit and statistically significant for a probability of 5 %. In this case, the dependent variable (RECYCL_MUN_WASTE) may be considered elastic in relationship with the independent regressor. This means that the modification of the independent variable by 1 % has much more influence on the dependent variable (almost three times higher). Also, the fact that there is a lag between dependent variable and one regressor (*Patents_recycl*) means the variable Innovation practically influences the MWRR one year after a patent is registered. This lag accounts for all administrative and technical procedures that have to be in place before a patent could be effectively applied in economy. The practice confirm that a patent once registered has to proceed through various stages until it is finally applied.

The coefficient for Investment regressor is 0.09 and statistically significative (p<0.0000). This positive value reveals that an intensification of the investment activities contributes to an increase of the rate of the municipal waste recycling in a moderate way.

So, our LSDV model is as follows:

LSDV model with Substituted Coefficients: **Eq. 3**

==========================

RECYCL_MUN_WASTE = 6.29030513145 + 2.92569961256*PATENTS_RECYCL(-1)/POPULATION + 0.0901618332794*INVESTMENT_CIRC_EC/POPULATION + 22.8041313059*BELGIUM + 14.9056480715*AUSTRIA + 2.73810558029*DENMARK + 2.40144403334*FRANCE + 24.2601654475*GERMANY + 4.37891176116*ITALY + 12.1534481989*NETHERLANDS - 1.15457397816*ROMANIA + 10.5744678167*HUNGARY + 8.52219256369*LITHUANIA - 0.904048939486*LATVIA + 4.6023361941*GREECE + 3.88614668674*SPAIN - 3.52889544587*SLOVAKIA + 9.81698794486*SLOVENIA + 2.91048940074*SWEDEN + 6.29237803116*PORTUGAL + 1.11958614654*POLAND + 13.5848834991*BULGARIA - 3.21261909288*CROATIA - 12.2397782565*CYPRUS - 6.14914720473*FINLAND + 3.72126257626*ESTONIA

The model has the advantage to determine a specific equation for each country, allowing to highlight the heterogeneity among the 24 countries[2] that were analyzed. For instance, if we are looking to find out a specific relation for a country, the dummy variable would be one for that country and zero for the rest. As an example, for Belgium we have the next individual equation[3]:

RECYCL_MUN_WASTE (Belgium) = 29.09444 + 2.925699***PATENTS_RECYCL(-1)/POPULATION** + 0.090161***INVESTMENT/POPULATION** **Eq. 4**

All countries will have the same slopes (2.925 for patents and 0.0901 for investment) but intercept is different. The intercept shows the municipal waste recycled rate (%) if the regressors (patents_recycle and investment) would be zero. For the 24 countries analyzed, the intercept according to the Equation 3 is in Tab. 3. As the intercept is expressed in percentage, if the investment and innovation (patents) would be zero then, the MWRR would still be 9.12 % at the level of EU. For individual countries, the situation would be different according to the specific intercept that highlights the heterogeneity in recycling municipal waste among the 24 countries analyzed.

2 UK intercept is included in the coefficient C.

3 The intercept for individual equation is the result of the sum between coefficient C and each individual dummy coefficient.

Tab. 3: Intercepts of LSDV model, by country

Country	Intercept	Country	Intercept	Country	Intercept
GERMANY	30.6	GREECE	10.9	LATVIA	5.39
BELGIUM	29.1	ITALY	10.7	ROMANIA	5.14
AUSTRIA	21.2	SPAIN	10.2	CROATIA	3.08
BULGARIA	19.9	ESTONIA	10.0	SLOVAKIA	2.76
NETHERLANDS	18.4	SWEDEN	9.20	FINLAND	0.14
HUNGARY	16.9	DENMARK	9.03	CYPRUS	-5.90
SLOVENIA	16.1	FRANCE	8.69		
LITHUANIA	14.8	POLAND	7.41		
PORTUGAL	12.6	UK	6.29		

Source: Processing data from Annex 2.

As for example, Germany would still have 30.6 % recycling rate in the absence of investment and innovation. Similarly we may see some countries such as Belgium and Austria, identified earlier as recording higher rates in recycling municipal waste, which would also have higher intercepts. Only Cyprus displays a negative value for its intercept (-5.9) meaning that in absence of investment and innovation the municipal waste recycling will recede.

4. Conclusion

Findings – The article brings some new insights regarding the influence of eco-innovation and eco-investment on municipal waste recycling in EU. Analyzing the two series that were considered independent variables, we found an uneven distribution among member states and three groups of states: leaders, average performers and catching up. Regarding the dependent variable, municipal waste recycling, we highlighted a similar pattern. From the analysis made, we conclude that indicators selected as regressors have an asymmetric distribution across member states.

The model selected for analysis was that of a panel regression with two regressors (eco-investment and eco-innovation) and one dependent variable (municipal waste recycling rate), including 24 countries for a period of 10 years.

The second part of the chapter provides evidence of the influence exercised on municipal waste recycling by eco-innovation and investment. The model that resulted, carrying out a regression panel data, showed the linkage between the two regressors and the dependent variable selected. The linkage is significant from statistical point of view and after analyzing two variants of the model. Based on specific parameters we consider as optimal the LSDV model with 24 dummy variables. This model has the advantage of better goodness to fit indicators and allows identifying the heterogeneity existing among the 24 countries analyzed. From this model we could derive equations for each country. If we need to analyze the EU as a whole, we may use the OLS model.

This chapter demonstrates that the influence of the innovation on the municipal waste recycling is important. The innovation coefficient is almost 3.00, showing an elastic reliance of the dependent variable. Also, the coefficient for the investment regressor showed a positive value (0.09) meaning that an increase in investment will determine a rise of the rate of the municipal waste recycling in a moderate way. Another aspect highlighted is that the influence of innovation is not instantaneous, but there is a gap of one-year period between the moment of registration of the innovation and its implementation in practical activities.

Practical implications – From this chapter some practical implication could be derived. One direction is to make more efforts to enhance eco-innovation. As higher targets for waste recycling are declared by the EU, more investment in waste management will be needed. A better way to minimize the investment needed is to increase eco-innovation. Due to the fact that the coefficient for patents is higher than the unit (3.00), a 1 % increase in patents will induce a 3 % increase in municipal waste recycling (investment being constant). People who oversee innovative activities should also take notice that eco-innovation has a gap, between registering an innovative patent and the moment when it is operational, which is one year, on average.

Originality/value – This chapter has several originality aspects: it has taken into account two independent variables as drivers for municipal waste recycling and identified the heterogeneity present among member states. The model LSDV allow to identify a global equation from which equations for all countries analyzed could be derived in order to explore in more depth the influence of patents and investment on municipal waste recycling. Consequently, this chapter could give a better understanding regarding the drivers and barriers in the development of municipal waste recycling.

Further research – It is important to continue research studies to determine the drivers and barriers faced by eco-innovation and investment in improving municipal waste recycling. The main issue is that recycling alone cannot solve the issue caused by enormous waste generated by cities. Measures are needed to minimizing waste generation and maximizing reuse and recycling of materials.

References

Baltagi, B. H. (2005). *Econometric Analysis of Panel Data, Third Edition*, London, England: John Wiley & Sons.

Eunomia, COWI, European Commission, Directorate-General for Environment (2019). Study on investment needs in the waste sector and on the financing of municipal waste management in Member States, Publications Office, ISBN 978-92-76-09502-6, https://data.europa.eu/doi/10.2779/769124.

Gwarda, K. (2017). Eco-innovations in the sphere of municipal waste management in a Polish context. *17th International Scientific conference Business Logistics in Modem Management*, Osijek, Croatia, pp. 555–565.

Horbach, J., & Rammer, Ch. (2020) Circular economy innovations, growth and employment at the firm level: Empirical evidence from Germany. *Journal of Industrial Ecology*, 24(3), June 2020, 615–625, https://doi,org/10,1111/jiec,12977.

Kemp, R. (2010). Eco-innovations: Definition, measurement and open research issues. *Economia Politica*, XXVII (3), 398–401.

Mazzanti, M., Montini, A., & Zoboli, R. (2008). Municipal waste generation and socioeconomic drivers: Evidence from comparing Northern and Southern Italy. *Journal of Environment and Development*, 17(1), 51–69.

Mele, M.,·Magazzino, C., Schneider, N., Gurrieri, A.-R., & Golpira, H. (2022). Innovation, income, and waste disposal operations in Korea: Evidence from a spectral Granger causality analysis and artificial neural networks experiments. *Economia Politica*, https://doi.org/10.1007/s40888-022-00261-z.

Platon, V., Frone, D. F., Frone, S., & Constantinescu, A. (2020). Green economy prerequisites of waste management. *Scientific Papers Series Management, Economic Engineering in Agriculture and Rural Development*, 20(4), 211–218, PRINT ISSN 2284-7995, E-ISSN 2285-3952, http://managementjournal.usamv.ro/pdf/vol.20_4/Art27.pdf.

Wang, Q., & Wang, S. (2019). Decoupling economic growth from carbon emissions growth in the United States: The role of research and development. *Journal of Cleaner Production*, 234, 702–713, https://doi.org/10.1016/j.jclepro.2019.06.174.

Wooldridge, J. M. (2002). Econometric Analysis of Cross Section and Panel Data. Cambridge: The MIT Press.

Konrad Gunesch

Cultural and Art Economics and Administrative Assistance on Institutional Levels from Macroeconomic, Sociopolitical and Philosophical Aspects: Against the Motion

1. Introduction and Overview

1.1. Recent Interest in, and Future Relevance of Cultural and Art Economics

The literature points out a recent "steady expansion in the [...] interest in the economics of art and culture [with] suggestions for promising lines of future research [and] we are likely to see [its] expansion in the future" (Throsby, 2006, p. 21). At the same time, basic questions about art and cultural economics keep being asked for a long time now, exemplified by Blaug's 2019 book *The Economics of the Arts*: its sixteen chapters are all reprints of writings between 1956 and 1974. Several of these are cited in detail in this research, revealing their thoughts still valid in today's globalized and complex economic, artistic and cultural landscape(s).

One challenge of analyzing "economics" together with "arts" and "culture" is the reputation of economics as "the dismal science" (see the book titles of Levy, 2002; Marglin 2008; Rodrik, 2015), whereas art and culture, even when analyzed through an economic lens, are considered "sublime" human experiences (see the book and the chapter titles of Amariglio, Childers & Cullenberg, 2009), characterized by "the creative genius in literature, music, and the visual arts" (see the chapter title of Simonton, 2014), in which the perceived value of the "aesthetic experience" (see the chapter headings of Locher, 2014) contribute to "art's economic exceptionalism" (see the book title of Beech, 2015).

Another challenge is the state of flux in the field's most basic elements – starting with its very name. As Ginsburgh and Throsby maintain in the second volume of their *Handbook of the Economics of Arts and Culture* (2014), the "historical evolution" within the decade since the publication of the first volume (2006) allowed for "the discipline known as cultural economics [to be] more appropriately referred to as the economics of art and culture" (2014, p. 1; similarly Frey, 2019, p. 3). I use the short terms "art economics" and "cultural economics" for euphony and concision.

The field is divided into numerous economic investigations of art aspects and products: from paintings (Throsby & Zednik, 2014, pp. 81–100) over music (Levinson, 2014, pp. 101–117) and concerts (Courty & Pagliero, 2014, pp. 299–356) to festivals and cultural awards (English, 2014, pp. 119–143; Frey, 2019, pp. 63–70) and from cultural heritage and museums (Frey, 2019; pp. 77–88, 97–114; Willis, 2014, pp. 145–182) up to movies and books (Walls, 2014, pp. 185–214), or from organizational and technical aspects such as new technologies (Potts, 2014, pp. 215–232) over labor, property and investment (Whitaker, 2021, pp. 177–243) to international transactions and trade (Bisin & Verdier, 2014, pp. 439–484; Mandel, 2014, pp. 233–260; Platteau & Wahhaj, 2014, pp. 633–678), up to cultural organizations (Castañer, 2014, pp. 263–276), or from legal aspects such as digitization and copyright (Waldfogel, 2014, pp. 277–298) over media ownership (Doyle, 2014, pp. 357–378) up to cultural trading systems (Iapadre, 2014, pp. 381–410; Macmillan, 2014, pp. 411–438), or finally from considerations of cultural values over diversity up to open conflict (Aldashev & Platteau, 2014, pp. 587–632; Ginsburgh & Weber, 2014, pp. 507–544; Montalvo & Reynal-Querol, 2014, pp. 485–506; Schwartz, 2014, pp. 547–586).

Against this plethora of viewpoints, and integrating the most relevant recent literature (see Whitaker, 2021), we combine historical, macroeconomic and sociopolitical perspectives in favor of government support and subsidies in cultural and creative industries.

1.2. Origin, Terms and Relationship of Cultural and Art Economics

The birth of the field of Cultural Economics is acknowledged to be Baumol and Bowen's 1966 book *Performing Arts – The Economic Dilemma: A Study of Problems Common to Theater, Opera, Music and Dance*, in which the authors "demonstrate that straightforward economic analysis could illuminate [...] the role of the arts sector in the economy" (Throsby, 2006, p. 4). Yet only in the book's last part, "Sources of Financial Support", and in two of the last chapters do the authors deal with "Government Support in Practice" or the "Rationale of Public Support" (Baumol & Bowen, 1966, pp. 347 ff., 369 ff.).

The first journal in the field, *Journal of Cultural Economics*, was established in 1977, and only as of the end-1990s had the field gathered enough material to warrant an overview of it (Throsby, 2006, pp. 4–5). One of the first findings was that cultural economics was the wider area, embracing media, heritage and art studies, but also that it was not yet well defined, being concerned with multiple disciplines including art history, art philosophy, sociology, law, management and economics (Throsby, 2006, p. 5).

Only in the twenty-first century did scholarly confidence grow that "a sufficiently cohesive body of work has accumulated [...] to identify a field labeled 'cultural economics' or 'the economics of the arts and culture' [...] even though the outer boundaries [...] remain somewhat fuzzy", allowing the "assembling a purposeful collection of essays commissioned from researchers working at the theoretical and empirical frontiers of the field" (Throsby, 2006, p. 6).

I was immediately pointed out that "a basic issue [...] is that of defining whether and how cultural goods and services differ from other goods and services in the economy", and "whilst it is the mysterious and possible unfathomable nature of art in all its forms that ultimately must underlie much of the behavior of individuals, firms and markets in the arts, economics requires a more systematic basis on which its analysis can rest" (Throsby, 2006, p. 6).

1.3. Terminology and Differentiation

The terms "Cultural Economics" and "Art Economics" require definitions of "art" and "culture". For simplicity and inclusivity, I follow Throsby's broad definition of culture "comprising or being defined as a set of attitudes, beliefs or values common to a group that somehow identifies and binds the group together", which enables us "to speak of a national culture, a religious culture, a corporate culture and so on" (2006, p. 6).

Functionally, culture can also be defined as "the practices and products of cultural activity, including especially the arts", which are "sometimes divided into the performing arts (acting, dancing, singing, playing a musical instrument, etc.) and the initial creative arts (visual art, sculpture, craft, creative writing, musical composition, etc.) though there are obvious overlaps between these categories", all of which makes "the arts comprise a subset of culture more broadly defined" (Throsby, 2006, pp. 6–7).

Consequently, the concept of "cultural goods" includes overlapping elements of cultural, art and creative economics, in that "cultural goods have some public-good properties; in aggregate they yield positive externalities or diffused benefits that may be demanded in their own right" (Throsby, 2006, p. 7). On this basis, we follow the literature that defines "cultural industries" straightforward and "simply as those industries producing those good" (Throsby, 2006, p. 11).

2. Literature Review

2.1. Intersection of Cultural and Economic Policy

The literature reveals "four specific areas where cultural and economic policy intersect: support for the arts; trade in cultural goods, heritage; and urban and regional development issues" (Throsby, 2006, p. 19), and five areas of cultural policy that are especially well suited for economic analysis: "support for the creative arts; cultural goods in international trade; the management of cultural assets; industry and innovation; and foreign policy" (Throsby, 2012, p. 106). The first area, support for the (creative) arts, is the focus of this chapter.

This area is further defined in the literature as follows: "The intersections between cultural policy and economic policy are extensive, including [...] the appropriate level for government support for the arts and culture, and the balance between direct (grant-related) and indirect (tax-related) means of support", as well as "the role of the arts and culture in employment creation and income generation in towns and cities; especially those affected by industrial decline" (Throsby, 2006, p. 18).

2.2. Discussion of State Support for the Arts

The originators of the field of Cultural Economics, Baumol and Bowen, expressed their insecurity about "the long-run prospect for government support in the arts", while for the United States they merely and generally stated that it "seems favorable" (1966, p. 405), or that "future professional performance may well survive and prosper" (1966, p. 407). One can see conceptual similarities to recent literature that highlights the relationship between the arts and state support, reasoning that there is a longstanding yet conceptually and empirically unresolved practice, causing its proponents to call for more research (Throsby, 2006, p. 19):

> The rationale for state support for the arts has been one of the longest-running issues [...] in the literature of cultural economics over the last 40 years. [...] The empirical evidence is by no means extensive, and positive theories of assistance may be more useful in explaining levels and patterns of support actually observed in various democratic countries around the world [...] Why, at a time when the trend is towards privatization in many sectors of the economy, the provision of government grants, tax relief and regulatory protection continues in the arts and heritage industries. The answer [...] lies in government skepticism that consumers know what is best for them; in these circumstances producer interests can exert a strong influence on government policy, with consequent effects on both allocative and productive efficiency.

This justification of governmental support and related regulations is apparently rooted in a liberal economic and political tradition.

2.3. Reaches of Cultural Policies

The literature differentiates between "the broad reach of cultural policy in general terms" and the fact that "its coverage and its level of importance in national policy agendas vary considerably between countries" (Throsby, 2006, p. 18). A comparison is made between Europe and the United States of America, yet only at an unspecified "central government level":

> In Europe [...] there are substantial differences between countries in the volume of public resources they devote to the arts and culture in the ways those resources are deployed. Administrative structures also vary [...] ranging from arm-lengths arts councils to full-scale Ministries of Culture. There are also sub-regional and supra-regional interests in cultural policy in Europe; on the one hand sub-national regions with distinctive cultural identities promote their own artistic and cultural endeavors; on the other hand the European Union and the Council of Europe have interests in developing pan-European cultural policies in various fields (Throsby 2006, p. 18; similarly Baumol and Bowen, 1966, pp. 360–365 for Western Europe before the establishment of the European Union).

Throsby (2006, pp. 18–19) contrasts this with America:

> In the United States [...] there has never been a great deal of interest in the formulation of specific cultural policies at the central government level; rather the major players in the formation and execution of direct public expenditure programs in the arts and culture are located at sub-national levels of government. [...] The largest share of support for the arts and culture is provided indirectly, via tax concessions for gifts to not-for-profit arts organizations and also via tax concessions to private owners of cultural heritage buildings and sites. The role of tax incentives in stimulating cultural donations and the significance of philanthropy as a characteristic of American life are [part of] the peculiarly American tradition of individual and corporate giving that has sustained the growth of the arts in the United States for more than a century. Despite the emergence of what many see as a distinctive and successful 'American model' for cultural support [...] it may be difficult to replicate it in other countries where institutional structures, income levels and tax-price responsiveness may differ markedly from the US situation.

We thus ascertain (as do Ekelund, Jackson & Tollison, 2017) a European preference for more centralized state subsidies for the arts, contrasting with a more individualistic, indirect and administrative hands-off American understanding of official artistic and cultural support.

3. Research Methodology: Transdisciplinary Framework of Analysis

The literature stresses the need to apply multidisciplinary frameworks for cultural economics: "If we were to adopt a broad definition of cultural goods that embraced popular cultural forms such as sports, television programs, magazines, etc., we would open up an enormous field of interest in mass cultural consumption and production, a field that has been extensively explored within sociology, contemporary cultural studies, and media economics" (Throsby, 2006, p. 7).

Support for such a multitude of disciplines for art, culture and economics is found in the field's recent publications that describe it as having turned "from a sub-discipline of economics into a sub-discipline of anthropology" (Ginsburgh & Throsby, 2014, p. 1).

Hence our multidisciplinary approach combines a sociopolitical and socio-economic scope with a macroeconomic analytical focus. Going even further in disciplinary integration and related methodological benefits, and beyond the coexistence of approaches that could be described as multidisciplinary, I propose an explicitly "transdisciplinary enquiry" (see Martin, 2017, p. 130) as characterized by a mutual sharing and advancing of frameworks for fresh conceptual and/ or methodological insights.

4. Analysis and Discussion: Against Government Subsidies of the Arts and Culture

4.1. No Government Support for Commercially Viable Activities

Throsby (2007, p. 405) explains this argument as follows:

> Policy-makers have tended to be uneasy with a cultural policy whose primary focus is public assistance to the arts; typically they have believed that there is no special case for governments to support activities that should be commercially viable, and have probably been inclined to the view that existing arts funding is the outcome of regulatory capture, or of bureaucratic inertia where traditional modes of public assistance to culture are simply repeated year after year. These sceptics have remained unconvinced as to the existence of public-good benefits from the arts, and doubtful that the community would be willing to pay for them, even if they did exist; hence a market failure justification for public intervention does not impress them.

This opinion has neoliberal reasoning on its side; however, for some art branches, art works or artists, state support might be the only way to become commercially viable in the first place, and could then even benefit the state, with created revenues from tax incomes, workplaces earnings, and consumer interests. Our line of reasoning is akin to the "infant industry" argument in international business, where new companies request state subsidies in apparent contradiction to global free market rules, to let them enter the market at all (see Oqubay, 2015, pp. 25–26; Panagariya, 2019, appendix 2; Paul, 2019, p. 164; Yülek, 2018, pp. 47–48).

4.2. Tax Deductions as Governmental Loss of Control

Thus, Baumol and Bowen (1966, p. 356) state this train of thought:

> Tax deduction is a questionable way for the government to encourage philanthropy [as] a wealthy person is given a disproportionate degree of control over the disposition of government funds. If someone in the 20 per cent bracket makes a donation, the government, in effect, supports his gift by a rebate rate equal to 20 per cent of the total, while when a person in the 70 per cent bracket makes a donation, the government supplies 70 per cent of the total.

This questioning of philanthropy might not be against governmental influence, but against private power to decide what is fundable art. It could even be turned around: since private persons are the largest interest group by numbers of customers or consumers, they might as well indirectly influence who gets funded by the state, namely via their tax rebates for their philanthropic donations.

4.3. Poverty Stimulates Creativity

Baumol and Bowen relate the argument that "poverty is good and stimulates creativity", or that "only a hungry man feels compelled to say 'what's in him' " (1966, p. 371). Yet they concede that it is "an argument that most of us today would consider antediluvian" (1966, p. 371). One feels inclined to agree when thinking it through to its logical conclusion: the poorer the artists, the more worthy of funding their creations. Vincent van Gogh's example springs readily to mind, but mostly and compassionately for his troubled life, or for being able to sell only one painting in his lifetime (see Bailey, 2021, p. 13; Landau, 2016, p. 5; Swanson Sateren, 2002, p. 5).

4.4. Governments' Other Priorities

Baumol and Bowen relate the argument that "there are higher priorities, that poverty, disease, crime and ignorance have a stronger claim on government funds" (1966, p. 371), yet concede:

> While this alternative use of funds may be appealing [...] the money in question, if not used for the arts, may well not be employed to construct [housing for the poor] or for any other similar purpose. [...] Even if one believes that more money should be spent on the poor, it does not follow that less money should be spent on the arts. Perhaps economies should be affected instead in some other part of the government budget, or perhaps total outlays by the public sector should simply be increased. It is capricious and arbitrary to attack expenditures on the arts just because one believes some other projects have a higher priority. Such an argument is valid only if one can think of *no* better source of the

> requisite funds, and if one can be reasonably sure that the monies denied the arts would, in fact, be devoted to […] whatever else is deemed worthier (Original emphasis.)

We support this counter-argument all the more in the twenty-first century's benefit of hindsight of recent global reports of public misspending, economic mismanagement, and financial crises.

4.5. Government Support Displaces Private Funds

Baumol and Bowen relate the argument that "government support of the arts would serve mainly to displace private funds" (1966, p. 372), yet concede:

> There is little evidence on […] the effect of government grants on private contributions. […] In Western European countries there is little private giving to the arts; and […] governments do provide considerable direct support […] Government grants [might] have discouraged private giving, but it is at least equally plausible that causation has flowed in the opposite direction – that it is because of a lack of private support that continental governments have felt obliged to spent considerable sums on the arts. […] No strong tradition of private giving to the arts exist in any Western European country, and […] private contributions would be small even in the absence of government grants.

Hence private and public funding would not cancel each other out, and neither would increased public funding for the arts weaken private enthusiasm and donorship. One could even turn this argument around: the more a government demonstrates tangible interest in the arts, the more their citizens would follow suit, out of their own hearts – and pockets.

4.6. Public Support Leading to Public Control

Baumol and Bowen relate that "another argument against public support is the danger of public control", namely, as some maintain for the United States, that "the Federal Government eventually will do more harm in this field than good by overregulating it, by overcontrolling it" (1966, pp. 373–374). They, however, relativize this argument themselves as well:

> This objection, that public support implies public control […] has turned out to be one of the least valid in practice. There is ample evidence that government support in Western Europe has not meant public control […]We encountered no case of interference by state or local governments, even where the amount of assistance provided has been relatively large […] Indeed, one can make a strong case to the effect that interference by private patrons is far more frequent and imposes a far more imminent threat than does government control. It has been charged more than once that some performing organizations share the tribulations of the group 'controlled by a handful of people who consider the operation as their own private domain. They dictate not only

> administrative policy, labor policy, fund raising policy, but standards of public taste' [...] There is little factual basis for the fear that control would be an inevitable concomitant of government assistance.

This counter-argument links up with the previous one: public funding neither weakens private support nor does public support lead to overbearing control of artistic creation that would be fundamentally different from what private donors could restrictively exercise.

4.7. Government Subsidies Cause Creative Stagnation

Baumol and Bowen (1966, p. 375) relate:

> While government assistance may not circumscribe the freedom of the arts in any direct sense, it can effectively dampen their vitality. If support is channeled exclusively to old, established organizations, it can discourage experimentation and make for general stagnation [...] If, on the other hand, government support is spread thinly over a variety of enterprises of widely varying quality [...] to avoid 'favoritism', the inevitable result is a diffusion of mediocrity.

Yet they once more make room for opposite considerations (1966, p. 376):

> But these perils [...] seem unlikely to apply in [...] the United States [...]. No one is suggesting support [...] which would make government the exclusive source of funds for any activity, and a pluralistic arrangement in which private and public support both play a role automatically requires checks and balances. Such a mixed system has been highly successful in maintaining the vitality of our system of higher education, and [...] it should [...] work just as well in the arts.

In turn, to this argument in favor of support, they concede (1966, p. 376):

> There is, however, some danger that individual giving will follow patterns set by government grants. The psychological "seal of approval" conferred by government aid may supplement the effect of matching-funds requirements in diverting the flow of private funds toward the pattern adopted by public agencies.

This complex line of reasoning continues the previous two arguments, now for the creative-psychological realm: while neither public nor private support automatically dampens creative ardor, some imitative effect can be expected; but imitation is such a widespread human trait that it is hardly limited to private sponsors who monitor public interests and expenditures.

4.8. The "Market Test": Pay If You Want It to Stay

Baumol and Bowen (1966, p. 376) invoke the example of opera as an art form that is attended by few but funded by the taxpaying of many, and compare it with the automobile as an industry that would have received little public funds if manufacturers had not been successful:

> The most fundamental objection to public support [...] arises out of the application of the market test to the performing arts [...] If the arts provide so much to their audiences, why are the audiences not willing to bear their cost? [...] Those who want to see them ought to pay the price [...] This objection is not without merit. Insolvency *per se* does not constitute adequate grounds for public assistance [...] If audiences do not want [the performing arts] to cover their costs through admission charges, why should this [justify] public support? Might it not argue the contrary – that live performance is an obsolete vestige of a handicraft economy which deserves no public assistance precisely because effective demand for it is inadequate? (original emphases).

Yet again, they relativize and revert this argument, stating that improving on low public interest would be one of the roles and results of public support, thus linking it to the earlier argument of support for the arts contributing to national educational levels, and even considering it a macroeconomic boost (1966, p. 404):

> This socio-economic and geographic concentration of interest is not, however, necessarily a critical political disability if concern with the arts is indeed spreading along with the growth in the nation's educational level, its per capita income and the amount of available leisure time. [...] Given an influential and growing minority, one that strongly favors government support of the arts, the fact that not everyone attends live performance is not really critical. Indeed, it is hard to think of any type of government support, whether to the aviation industry or to agriculture, that goes directly to a majority of the nation's inhabitants.

Baumol and Bowen (1966, p. 405) conclude:

> The [...] prospect for government support of the arts [...] seems favorable. What form such support will eventually take is still unpredictable. But the nature of the forces that have aligned themselves behind it, and the pressures that will manifest themselves [...] portend an expansion of direct federal support for the performing arts.

They predict a related growth of artistic productions and support for microeconomic and macroeconomic reasons (1966, p. 407), before concluding:

> The cost of [preserving professional art performance] will be high and will rise inexorably. Fortunately, the very rise in productivity in other sectors of the economy [...] will also provide society with the wherewithal to pay the mounting bill if it is determined to do so.

5. Conclusion

We tried to argue "against the motion" of administrative and institutional assistance in cultural and art economics, when analyzed from macroeconomic, sociopolitical and philosophical aspects. Already in the literature, there seemed to be a reason for state support against every argument invoked against it. This lets us look forward to the second part of this research, to advocate "for the motion" of state support for the arts convincingly and comprehensively.

References

Aldashev, G., & Platteau, J. P. (2014). Religion, Culture, and Development. In V. A. Ginsburgh & D. Throsby (Eds.), *Handbook of the Economics of Art and Culture, Volume 2* (pp. 587–632). Amsterdam, Boston, New York and Oxford: Elsevier.

Amariglio, J., Childers, J. W., & Cullenberg, S. E. (Eds.) (2009). *Sublime Economy: On the Intersection of Art and Economics*. London and New York: Routledge.

Amariglio, J., Childers, J. W., & Cullenberg, S. E. (2009). Introduction: Sublime Economy: On the Intersection of Art and Economics. In J. Amariglio, J. W. Childers & S. E. Cullenberg (Eds.), *Sublime Economy: On the Intersection of Art and Economics* (pp. 1–26). London and New York: Routledge.

Bailey, M. (2021). *Van Gogh's Finale: Auvers and the Artist's Rise to Fame*. London: Frances Lincoln and Quarto Publishing.

Baumol, W. J., & Bowen, W. G. (1966). *Performing Arts – The Economic Dilemma: A Study of Problems Common to Theater, Opera, Music and Dance*. New York: Kraus Reprint.

Beech, D. (2015). *Art and Value: Art's Economic Exceptionalism in Classical, Neoclassical and Marxist Economies*. Leiden and Boston: Brill.

Bisin, A., & Verdier, T. (2014). Trade and Cultural Diversity. In V. A. Ginsburgh & D. Throsby (Eds.), *Handbook of the Economics of Art and Culture, Volume 2* (pp. 439–484). Amsterdam, Boston, New York and Oxford: Elsevier.

Blaug, M. (2019). *The Economics of the Arts*. New York and Oxon: Routledge.

Castañer, X. (2014). Cultural Innovation by Cultural Organizations. In V. A. Ginsburgh & D. Throsby (Eds.), *Handbook of the Economics of Art and Culture, Volume 2* (pp. 263–276). Amsterdam, Boston, New York and Oxford: Elsevier.

Courty, P., & Pagliero, M. (2014). The Pricing of Art and the Art of Pricing: Pricing Styles in the Concert Industry. In V. A. Ginsburgh & D. Throsby (Eds.), *Handbook of the Economics of Art and Culture, Volume 2* (pp. 299–356). Amsterdam, Boston, New York and Oxford: Elsevier.

Doyle, G. (2014). Media Ownership: Diversity Versus Efficiency in a Changing Technological Environment. In V. A. Ginsburgh & D. Throsby (Eds.), *Handbook of the Economics of Art and Culture, Volume 2* (pp. 357–378). Amsterdam, Boston, New York and Oxford: Elsevier.

Ekelund, R. B., Jackson, J. D., & Tollison, R. D. (2017). *The Economics of American Art: Issues, Artists and Market Institutions*. Oxford and New York: Oxford University Press.

English, J. F. (2014). The Economics of Cultural Awards. In V. A. Ginsburgh & D. Throsby (Eds.), *Handbook of the Economics of Art and Culture, Volume 2* (pp. 119–143). Amsterdam, Boston, New York and Oxford: Elsevier.

Frey, B. S. (2019). *Economics of Art and Culture*. Cham: Springer.

Ginsburgh, V., & Throsby, D. (2014). Introduction and Overview. In V. A. Ginsburgh & D. Throsby (Eds.), *Handbook of the Economics of Art and Culture, Volume 2* (pp. 1–12). Amsterdam, Boston, New York and Oxford: Elsevier.

Ginsburgh, V., & Weber, S. (2014). Culture, Linguistic Diversity, and Economics. In V. A. Ginsburgh & D. Throsby (Eds.), *Handbook of the Economics of Art and Culture, Volume 2* (pp. 507–544). Amsterdam, Boston, New York and Oxford: Elsevier.

Iapadre, P. L. (2014). Cultural Products in the International Trading System. In V. A. Ginsburgh & D. Throsby (Eds.), *Handbook of the Economics of Art and Culture, Volume 2* (pp. 381–410). Amsterdam, Boston, New York and Oxford: Elsevier.

Landau, J. (2016). *Vincent van Gogh: Master of Post-Impressionist Painting*. New York: Britannica Educational Publishing.

Levinson, J. (2014). Values of Music. In V. A. Ginsburgh & D. Throsby (Eds.), *Handbook of the Economics of Art and Culture, Volume 2* (pp. 101–117). Amsterdam, Boston, New York and Oxford: Elsevier.

Levy, D. M. (2002). *How the Dismal Science Got Its Name: Classical Economics and the Ur-Text of Racial Politics*. Ann Arbor: The University of Michigan Press.

Locher, P. J. (2014). Contemporary Experimental Aesthetics: Procedures and Findings. In V. A. Ginsburgh & D. Throsby (Eds.), *Handbook of the Economics of Art and Culture, Volume 2* (pp. 49–80). Amsterdam, Boston, New York and Oxford: Elsevier.

Macmillan, F. (2014). Cultural Diversity, Copyright, and International Trade. In V. A. Ginsburgh & D. Throsby (Eds.), *Handbook of the Economics of Art and Culture, Volume 2* (pp. 411–438). Amsterdam, Boston, New York and Oxford: Elsevier.

Mandel, B. R. (2014). Investment in Visual Art: Evidence from International Transactions. In V. A. Ginsburgh & D. Throsby (Eds.), *Handbook of the Economics of Art and Culture, Volume 2* (pp. 233–260). Amsterdam, Boston, New York and Oxford: Elsevier.

Marglin, S. A. (2008). *The Dismal Science: How Thinking Like an Economist Undermines Community*. Cambridge, Massachusetts and London, England: Harvard University Press.

Martin, V. (2017) *Transdisciplinarity Revealed: What Librarians Need to Know*. Santa Barbara and Denver: Libraries Unlimited and ABC-CLIO.

Montalvo, J. G., & Reynal-Querol, M. (2014). Cultural Diversity, Conflict, and Economic Development. In V. A. Ginsburgh & D. Throsby (Eds.), *Handbook of the Economics of Art and Culture, Volume 2* (pp. 485–506). Amsterdam, Boston, New York and Oxford: Elsevier.

Oqubay, A. (2015). *Made in Africa: Industrial Policies in Ethiopia*. Oxford and New York: Oxford University Press.

Panagariya, A. (2019). *Free Trade and Prosperity: How Openness Helps Developing Countries Grow Richer and Combat Poverty*. Oxford and New York: Oxford University Press.

Paul, A. (2019). Book Review: Arvind Panagariya, Free Trade & Prosperity: How Openness Helps Developing Countries Grow Richer and Combat Poverty. *South Asia Economic Journal, 20*(1), 164–166.

Platteau, J. P., & Wahhaj, Z. (2014). Strategic Interactions Between Modern Law and Custom. In V. A. Ginsburgh & D. Throsby (Eds.), *Handbook of the Economics of Art and Culture, Volume 2* (pp. 633–678). Amsterdam, Boston, New York and Oxford: Elsevier.

Potts, J. (2014). New Technologies and Cultural Consumption. In V. A. Ginsburgh & D. Throsby (Eds.), *Handbook of the Economics of Art and Culture, Volume 2* (pp. 215–232). Amsterdam, Boston, New York and Oxford: Elsevier.

Rodrik, D. (2015). *Economics Rules: The Rights and Wrongs of the Dismal Science*. New York and London: W. W. Norton.

Schwartz, S. H. (2014). National Culture as Value Orientations: Consequences of Value Differences and Cultural Distance. In V. A. Ginsburgh & D. Throsby (Eds.), *Handbook of the Economics of Art and Culture, Volume 2* (pp. 547–586). Amsterdam, Boston, New York and Oxford: Elsevier.

Simonton, D. K. (2014). Creative Genius in Literature, Music, and the Visual Arts. In V. A. Ginsburgh & D. Throsby (Eds.), *Handbook of the Economics of Art and Culture, Volume 2* (pp. 15–48). Amsterdam, Boston, New York and Oxford: Elsevier.

Swanson Sateren, S. (2002). *Masterpieces: Artists and their Works: Van Gogh*. Mankato, Minnesota: Bridgestone Books.

Throsby, D. (2006). Introduction and Overview. In V. A. Ginsburgh & D. Throsby (Eds.), *Handbook of the Economics of Art and Culture, Volume 1* (pp. 3–22). Amsterdam, Boston, New York and Oxford: Elsevier.

Throsby, D. (2007). Change and Challenge: Two Decades in the Economics of Art and Culture. *Economia Della Cultura, 17*(4), 399–408.

Throsby, D. (2012). Why Should Economists Be Interested in Cultural Policy? *Economic Record, 88*(1), 106–109.

Throsby, D., & Zednik, A. (2014). The Economic and Cultural Value of Paintings: Some Empirical Evidence. In V. A. Ginsburgh & D. Throsby (Eds.), *Handbook of the Economics of Art and Culture, Volume 2* (pp. 81–100). Amsterdam, Boston, New York and Oxford: Elsevier.

Waldfogel, J. (2014). Digitization, Copyright, and the Flow of New Music Products. In V. A. Ginsburgh & D. Throsby (Eds.), *Handbook of the Economics of Art and Culture, Volume 2* (pp. 277–298). Amsterdam, Boston, New York and Oxford: Elsevier.

Walls, W. D. (2014). Bestsellers and Blockbusters: Movies, Music, and Books. In V. A. Ginsburgh & D. Throsby (Eds.), *Handbook of the Economics of Art and Culture, Volume 2* (pp. 185–214). Amsterdam, Boston, New York and Oxford: Elsevier.

Whitaker, A. (2021). *Economics of Visual Art: Market Practice and Market Resistance*. Cambridge and New York: Cambridge University Press.

Willis, K. G. (2014). The Use of Stated Preference Methods to Value Cultural Heritage. In V. A. Ginsburgh & D. Throsby (Eds.), *Handbook of the Economics of Art and Culture, Volume 2* (pp. 145–182). Amsterdam, Boston, New York and Oxford: Elsevier.

Yülek, M. A. (2018). *How Nations Succeed: Manufacturing, Trade, Industrial Policy, and Economic Development*. London and Singapore: Palgrave Macmillan.

Alexandru Trifu

Workplace Environment/Culture and the Challenges of Our Days

1. Introduction

In this chapter, we intend to present the home environment of a firm/entity, that is the relationship between the main elements of the human factor of production: on the one hand, the entrepreneurs/owners and, on the other hand, the workers/employees. These two sides are responsible for the existence and well-functioning of the firm/organization. We used the qualitative research, that is the information and observation from media, from journals and books, from the experience of owners/CEOs, and, even, from our own experience in the higher education institutions considered as organizations – in which the human characteristic of the empathy is paramount. From all these updated sources, we can extract the trends in the interactions between entrepreneurs/CEOs and the employees in these new conditions and challenges.

The requirements of the firm/entity's functioning is represented by a flexible organization of the departments and of the work, taking into account the (online) work at home, the possibilities for telecommuting and the new methods introduced, such as kurzarbeit, but altogether in line with the owner/CEO's demands: resistance to stress; ability to perform multiple tasks; ability to work under pressure; willingness to work overtime. The Great Resignation phenomenon from the last year seems to continue this year, when employees will unleash their repressed desires accumulated during the last two years. They intend to make the desired changes in their careers, in opposition with the "classic" workplace culture of silence and obedience to managers' decisions. Therefore, we are interested to see, using tactics in the workplace culture, what is this year's trend , between a relative stable workforce and changing jobs which are no longer a constraint. In other words, an updated theory of the firm is needed, based on the new realities and the important challenges of these days. Understanding the present and the possible future trends within the human factor of production are determinant in drawing an applied Theory of the Firm.

2. Survey of the Topic Complexity

The culture and human relationships are the environment which surrounds us everywhere, at home, but definitely at the workplace.

The work relationships in a company influence all of the personal activities, including the relationships between CEOs/managers and the employees and usually significantly determine their efficiency and, finally, the firm's performance. The home environment of an entity, the relationships between the human factors of production involved in, is essential for the existence and development of the business. As it is presented and known in theory and practice, we speak about the *workplace culture* – culture which put the imprint of the business/firm/organization and present the personality of it. What interests in any survey is the *positive workplace culture*, with empathy, happiness, and no stress activities if it's possible – all these towards getting profit, of course, but also performance and motivation to innovate and to improve work tools and atmosphere (www.yourerc.com, 2019). In order to avoid some phenomena and actions disturbing this positive workplace culture, and which we shall see in the last part of the chapter, we have to highlight the importance of this way of being in business. Thus, a fruitful relationship between CEOs/managers and the employees/workers conceives to:

(a) The attraction of candidates eager to work and assert themselves, including the talented/gifted persons;
(b) The appropriate motivation and conditions for efficient work;
(c) The performance, satisfaction and, even, the happiness – those organizations ensure that these features outperform their competitors and develop a strong human background within the firm.

To complete the complexity image of the topic, and, at the same time, to highlight the role of skilled and performing people, eager to introduce new ideas and techniques, and improve the existent ones, two examples are eloquent:

1. First is the activity of Sir Thomas Wyatt (1503–1542), amongst others in different areas of science and culture, who asserted the necessity of self-confidence and boldness of each and every person in what he/she is doing[1] (Moser, 2010).

1 Sir Thomas Wyatt was known for marking new trends in English poetry, based on the novelties in this field coming from abroad (especially Italy).

2. The second one is represented by the demand that the base of entrepreneurship and, by consequence, the work into an organization/firm to be taught in educational institutes, especially in higher education.

As we detail this second example, we can say that the entrepreneurship pedagogy or teaching, according to academics and researchers, is critical to a nation's entrepreneurial activities because it influences the individuals' mindsets and behaviors, particularly when it comes to formulating new company ideas and taking risks (Castillo-Palacio et al., 2020). Entrepreneurship training encourages students to cultivate the qualities of a true entrepreneur, including the ability to envision, invent, and create, as well as to widen their horizons and take their ideas from concept to reality. The study reveals that entrepreneurs/CEOs, but people in general, are of competitive nature and have the propensity to take risks, with their final goal to boost the entrepreneurial activity.

Speaking from a developing country, a wealthy African country in natural resources, Nigeria, Agbai (2018) reiterates that early entrepreneurship preparation aids students in understanding the complexities of real-world challenges and experiencing great connection to learning objectives, which is likely to boost students' internal motivation and their experience of holistic acquisition of knowledge. According to the human capital theory in entrepreneurship, people have a range of entrepreneurial talents, attitudes, and behaviors that are aligned with an entrepreneurial intent. According to Becker (1994), training and education may enhance the ability of a person who already has a certain set of abilities. As students (aspiring entrepreneurs) build human capital via entrepreneurship education, their entrepreneurial intention should be strengthened as they demonstrate a willingness to take risks and develop new company concepts and innovativeness (Li & Wu, 2019). This study provides a better understanding of why and how entrepreneurial education increases the inclination to start-up, as we know these days, it is very important for the functioning of economies impacted by the pandemic and crisis. The study investigates the moderating role of team cooperation on the effect of entrepreneurial education, on entrepreneurial self-efficacy, and entrepreneurial passion. Thus, we arrive to a peak of this topic: the creation of a positive and efficient workplace culture, which leads to win-win benefits for the parts involved in, leads to profit and sustainability on the specific market. The straight and concise problem is to draw and realize the practical and mental connections between people involved in that business, in that economic enterprise.

We've selected from one of the examples in this respect (Agarwal, 2018); even this situation is presented before the pandemic started and also the crisis.

The elements counted now are represented by:

1. The open and honest communication and collaboration is vital for the unity of the team towards getting the desired goals. In this situation, it is not recommended to use work bullying/bossing for a positive and motivated collaborative environment;
2. Create clear goals and rewards for employees/workers. The ownership and general management are supposed to clearly affirm the strategy towards the proposed goals. It is not recommended to use misleading and hiding the real objectives pursued. The company success based on this situation substantially engages and motivates employees to support the ownership policy.
3. Even in our days' telecommuting and moving from one job or place to another, it is necessary to create a basic set of values and rules within the firm/organization, in order to show the responsibility of all parts involved in the functioning and "health" of the economic entity organism.

In the 3rd part of the chapter, we'll present positive and negative forms of human interactions at work, pros and cons instruments of the existing environment, with possibilities to reach the goals. It is important to create and maintain a positive culture and atmosphere at work, especially in our times, with psychological challenges. A positive workplace culture improves teamwork links, raises the moral, increases productivity and efficiency, and enhances the retention of the workforce. Job satisfaction, collaboration, and work performance are all enhanced. And, most importantly, a positive workplace environment reduces stress in employees.

3. Methodology

In this chapter, first we conducted a thorough review of the existing literature regarding the workplace culture and the human practices while also planning to conduct a qualitative analysis of working professionals about their actual experiences. Due to the literature review and the accumulated experiences, we provide a discussion of the positive and negative techniques in the workforce activity and their causes, the impact of workplace culture, and some good practices for human resources professionals and managers so that they can effectively prevent any negative incidents from taking place in their departments and organizations.

4. Features and Trends in the Functioning of Entities

The first negative practice in CEOs/managers–employees/workers relationships is that of *mobbing*. We consider that it has a long history, but now, in this kind of chaotic situation and within the *Brownian movement* of the employees, this psychological instrument is welcome and has given results in eliminating the undesirable persons. Workplace mobbing is the act of bullying/humiliating/pressurizing others in the work environment, in most situations with no real and obvious reasons, especially from owners and managers (Ågotnes et al., 2018). Mobbing at workplace can include professional, emotional, verbal, and physical abuses coming in downward, upward, inward, and horizontal forms. *Downward* mobbing or bullying is when powerful persons of authority, such as managers and supervisors, are using the power the organization has bestowed upon them, to exert their position power over their employees in a negative or intimidating manner (Vandekerckhove & Commers, 2003). Downward workplace mobbing is a pathology of current organizational shifts, resulting from not acting out the full ethical potential of the discourse of excellence, adventure, creativity, and responsibility, which characterizes these shifts. Foucault's power-knowledge rules are welcome in a survey like this. There are also situations where a group of employees band together to go against their boss or direct supervisor , and this is considered to be *upward* bullying. In certain industries, such as education or even healthcare, bullying can be *inward*, initiated by students, customers, clients, vendors, patients, or even the patient's families, as they develop a relationship over time and the employee may feel helpless as the patient exudes power over them. *Horizontal* bullying is when a group of employees working together harasses another co-worker, and neither has formal power over each other (De Cieri et al., 2019). Downward and horizontal bullying were the most prevalent forms. Workplace characteristics were more important predictors of bullying by different perpetrators than were demographic characteristics. These results are very important for understanding the topic and the realities within firms/entities. The particularization of this term which is more appropriate for the majority actions of this kind which came from superior managers, that are called *bossing* (Holatova & Březinova, 2021). Productivity of work, quality of products and willingness to innovate decrease, and the company image begins to be under threat.

Moreover, the negative effects are also manifested in the following directions:

- Increased absence and fluctuations of the employees;
- Decreased loyalty;
- Increased costs of hiring somebody else or qualifying another person;
- Potential increase in insurance costs;
- Potential fines or damages following lawsuits.

To continue, from the impact of these negative psychological instruments used in a company/firm's practice, we can, unquestionably, say that indirect facts like spreading lies about someone or about a situation, the attempt to please the boss or even bribe him, tolerance of inequalities are realities of daily activities.

From our own previous experiences, we can say that this kind of pressure, especially when other people were present, was a typical practice in order, either to block someone who aspires for higher positions and become a danger for the managers in function or to determine those persons to resign, that is, exit the system without being fired. Another of today's human relationships inside a firm/entity is the agreements between some important players from a specified field (IT & C, for example) not to solicit or compete for each other's employees (especially the performers). The agreements potentially restrict competition by preventing companies from recruiting or competing for employees by offering more competitive remuneration or employment terms. And thus, it appears a sort of monopoly situation on the market. The example of the Knorr-Bremse vs. USA process is iconic. The Knorr-Bremse settlement substantially advances our understanding of the Trump Antitrust Division's position on no-poaching agreements. It demonstrates the division's commitment to the Obama-era guidance on no-poaching agreements. It cements the line between pre-October 2016 conduct against which the DOJ (Department of Justice) will proceed civilly and post-October 2016 conduct, which will be subject to criminal prosecution. And it offers valuable guidance on the circumstances in which non-solicitation agreements will be analyzed under the rule of reason (Linehan, Aldrich, 2018). In Europe, several national competition authorities (including in Spain, the Netherlands and Croatia) have investigated no poach deals, including those made in the freight forwarding, hospitals, and IT employment sectors. While the European Commission hasn't previously looked at no poach agreements, there is clearly potential for them to fall foul of EU antitrust laws in the same way as other agreements that may be found to restrict competition (Tween, www.linlaters.com).

The type of agreements potentially restrict competition by preventing companies from recruiting or competing for employees by offering more competitive remuneration or employment terms. As another example in this respect is that one of Hong Kong experience in which, following several complaints received, the Competition Commission of Hong Kong has published a set of rules and norms in this matter. Indeed, in some industries, as we see IT & C, it's a practice in HR activities, but not considered as a standard method of workforce mobility. As positive methods, based on the pandemic realities, starting from Germany and spread into other states like Romania, we can speak in practice about *kurzarbeit* method/tool for working within the entities, but in the opposite meaning of the previous ones.

Kurzarbeit is, in many ways, an excellent crisis management tool. In a recession period, it protects workers' income and therefore supports aggregate demand. Since workers do not lose their jobs, they have less incentive to save on a precautionary basis. And companies retain firm-specific human capital, while avoiding the costly process of separation, re-hiring, and training (www.imf.org/en/news/, 2020). This method is a social insurance for the reduction in hours of work/day and implies the Government intervention to provide the income as a "replacement rate". A simple example is that of an employee loss in salary of 15 % for a reduction in hours of 30 %. In a word, *kurzarbeit* means the reduction of the norm per day for an employee/worker. We mention this tool ensuring the well-functioning of the firm is based on flexibility and the possibility of keeping workers in job with a reduced norm, but with the support of the Government. Generally speaking, the strong performance of employment during the global financial crisis bolstered domestic demand, with stable labor income supporting private consumption, and reducing the need for precautionary savings. This opened the way to a rapid recovery of the economy.

Kurzarbeit already seems to be playing an important role in preserving jobs during the current pandemic. Only in Germany, we are talking about more than 10 million people, or more than 20 % from the labor force, than during the previous economic crisis. This scheme of reducing daily working hours seems to be, in this specific case, more attractive to the workers.

In Romania, one of the most beneficial measures for employers during the pandemic, through which they can shorten the work schedule of employees, will be extended in the coming months (Herman, 2022). In the context of the uncertainty created by the pandemic, many employers have been in a position to reduce staff or reduce their work schedule. One of the measures that has been a real support for employers during this period, also known as kurzarbeit, is the one through which employers receive financial support from the state, in order for the companies to keep their employees and not make staff redundancies due to the decrease in turnover. The measure reduces the working hours of all or part of the employees. Kurzarbeit was one of the main types of government aid to companies last year; in fact, it was the only one to be granted throughout the year. The kurzarbeit settlement mechanism was regulated to apply for three months after the end of the alert state. We do not currently have any discussion on the part of the Government regarding its modification in the near future or the termination of its application. But, we are interested in the trends in the existence of workplace culture, in the activity/movement of the workforce, this year and in the years to come. The important phenomenon that happened last year and seeming to continue, not at the same level, this year, is "*the Great Resignation*". In November 2021, over 4.5 million workers in US left their jobs, but this work storm stun business leaders as turnover reaches new highs. Professor Anthony Klotz, also an organizational psychologist at Texas A & M University, coined this expression to characterize a kind a revolution within the human resources (Smith, 2022).

Indeed, what's happening now represents the re-examining of the role of work in our lives, but missing the broader consequences of this quitting wave, and what that means for the individual worker. It is the movement of the moment, dictated by the impulse of the worker to quit a job, for different reasons and no longer anticipate what's next, both for the employee and the firm.

Returning to Professor Klotz's predictions, *the first one is that the quitting movement will slow down*, corroborated with the turnover which will be not as high as in 2021. The process will continue, but not the same as it does in this moment. The reason for this movement is considered to be the better offers of the companies regarding higher salaries and benefits (as remote job), movement not so "rampant" as in the previous year.

This movement of changing workplaces/jobs could be moments of empowerment for workers, taking control of their work and even personal life, in opposition with the "classic" atmosphere of silence and obedience to the CEOs/managers' decisions.

On the one hand, *the organizational silence* refers to a collective-level phenomenon of saying or doing very little in response to significant problems that face an organization (Henriksen, 2006). The leaders, even the entrepreneurs and managers, must demonstrate a willingness to understand the complexity of the socio-technical systems of which they are a part and be prepared to break the silence. On the other hand, we deal with the problem of self-perception in leadership, either from entrepreneurs/owners, or CEOs and managers. For example, Sputtek R. (Kussin & Bundtzen, 2021) emphasizes the managers' (generally speaking) tendency to show little interest in subordinates/employees' feedback and desires/grievances which, by time, can hurt their employees' job satisfaction or motivation.

The second trend foresaw by Professor Klotz is that the flexible/telecommuting will be the norm not the exception in workforce activities. One expects that many firms, especially in the US, will embrace this tendency, in order to ensure more productivity and to attract and retain the gifted persons, as long as possible. Of course, the existence of relaxed, we may say, conditions at work and the possibility to do, house-holding activities also, became a psychological benefit for employees and improve their mental health. In opposition, entrepreneurs/CEOs who will refuse to do such flexible arrangements will lose talented personnel and the phenomenon of large-scale resignations will manifest itself (Smith, 2022).

The third prophecy of Professor Klotz is that the telecommuting will become more competitive by hiring international candidates and by introducing on a larger scale the digitalization and new technologies. As it is considered a remote organization, there is s an easier possibility to recruit workers from all over the world, who can do the same job at a cheaper rate. It is exactly the situation of today, when we are talking about the workforce migration from underdeveloped, or even emerging economies to the most developed/industrialized economies of the world.

All these aspects lead to the following pros and cons discussions and aspects. First of all, the positive methods presented are very efficient these days, with impact on the results, turnover, and profit. Furthermore, the working atmosphere is more relaxed; the communication with the general management is one click away, but it is through a "glass interface", not physically near you. Mentally, the worker/employee is not under such a pressure and he or she can think how to get more spiritual (as happiness, satisfaction) and material benefits (a better salary, a bigger and modern home, cars for him or her and the family).

On the other side, what about the entrepreneur/CEO's view on this situation? The workplace culture is the characteristic of the firm's environment. So, the general management follows personnel fluctuations (hiring, firing, resignations) that may occur not to significantly influence this amount established of values, beliefs, traditions, behaviors, and attitudes within the firm/company/organization. It is not beneficial for the entity that the general management has snapshots available for each period of stability regarding the staff.

A model, in 5 (five) steps proposed for eliminating possibly the stress, detente the work atmosphere and improve the work and general performance of the entity:

1. Presentation of the company's situation and opportunities based on SWOT Analysis
2. Thinking and crystallizing goals and focusing on these activities;
3. Organizing and using received or existing information;
4. Decision to select priorities and lines of action;
5. Monitoring, evaluating and making the necessary corrections, due to the challenges occurred.

We are talking about a favorable climate to the work and creation of each employee, to obtaining a job satisfaction, both for employees and for the entrepreneurs/ CEOs/ managers, in order to achieve all the proposed goals, at entity level and individually. As we can see, there are actions "in mirror" with those presented as threats for the well existence and functioning of the work culture and firm. The reality demonstrates that the entrepreneurship theory and, by consequence, the human interactions within a firm have developed somewhat independently of the rest of the fields concerning the company (Klein, 2016).

Thus, we believe that it is necessary to combine (like nowadays, after pandemic, but also during the crisis) all competitive findings regarding the Theory of the Firm as whole, to be a guide/handbook in order to see and understand, as a snapshot, what is the situation, how the entity manages the unexpected challenges, and what the solutions or line of actions can be to improve and to make it more flexible for the functioning of the economic systems.

5. Conclusions

Identifying and rewarding those who are actively striving towards creating a positive work culture, and supporting others around them, companies can encourage others to do the same. Positive attitudes and behavior in the workplace are the direct results of effective leadership and a positive management style. The error or mis-drawing of the work culture of an organization influences several areas which are critical to a corporate culture. Also, this indicates that an error prevention strategy can lead to the avoidance of a silence organization. At present, discouraging mobbing/bossing and other dysfunctional phenomena, or investing in people and in their professional development, remains an opportunity for the firm. But, above all, it remains the management's understanding and empathy, altogether with a fair and loyal feedback from employees, towards getting the desired results. The human resource professionals, in accordance with the structure of the firm and the general management strategies and tactics, must have policies in place for both managers and employees to train them in noticing any bullying, even bossing, behaviors. They should also have policies in place that require employees to uphold professionalism within the workplace to maintain a healthy office culture. We think that no entrepreneur or CEO would want staff fluctuations, which would jeopardize the firm/company operation and dismantle the workplace culture. Therefore, permanent and sound bi-univocal communication entrepreneurs/CEOs ↔ workers/employees is mandatory for a flexible and performing firm/company, based on its workplace culture.

References

Agarwal, P. (2018) *How to create a positive workplace culture*, www.forbes.com/sites/ retrieved April 11, 2022.

Agbai, E. P. (2018) *Pathways to entrepreneurship training towards addressing youth unemployment in Nigeria*. Walden University, www.scholarworks.waldenu.wdu/dissertetions/ retrieved April 6, 2022.

Ågotnes, K. W. et al. (2018) *The moderating effect of laissez-faire leadership on the relationship between co-worker conflicts and new cases of workplace bullying: A true prospective design*, Human Resource Management Journal, 28 (4), www.researchgate.net/publication retrieved April 5, 2022.

Becker, G. (1994) *Human capital: A theoretical and empirical analysis with special refrence to education*, www.econpapers.repec.org/bookchap/ retrieved April 8, 2022.

Castillo-Palacio, M., Batista-Canino, R., & Zuniga-Collazos, A. (2020) *The cultural practices that influence on the entrepreneurial activity: An empirical study from the globe project cultural dimensions*, www.saeb.feaa.uaic.ro/index.php/ retrieved April 6, 2022.

De Cieri, H., Sheehan, C., Donohue, R., Shea, T., & Cooper, B. (2019) *Workplace bullying: An examination of power and perpetratora*, www.psycnet.apa.org/record/ retrieved April 8, 2022.

Henriksen, D. (2006) *Organizational silence and hidden threats to pacient safety*, www.ncbi.nlm.nih.gov/pmc/articles/ retrieved April 18, 2022.

Herman, S. (2022) *Kurzarbeit 2022: State support for those who reduce working hours continues to apply*, www.ascentgroup.ro retrieved March 15, 2022.

Holátova, D., & Bŕezinova, M. (2021) *Impacts of mobbing and bossing in human resource management*, www.researchgate.net/publication/ retrieved April 2nd, 2022.

Klein, P. (2016) *Why entrepreneurs need firms and the theory of the firm needs entrepreneurship theory*, www.redalyc.org/journal/ retrieved March 31, 2022.

Kussin, L., & Bundtzen, H. (2021) *How error prevention and organizational silence influences managers' self-perception- a repertory grid study*, www.researchgate.net/publication/ retrieved April 18, 2022.

Li, L., & Wu, D. (2019) *Entrepreneurial education and students' entrepreneurial intention: Does team cooperation matter*, www.researchgate.net/publication/ retrieved April 11, 2022.

Linehan, P., & Aldrich, D. (2018) *No-poaching agreements and criminal antitrust enforcement: DOJ scrutiny ratchets up*, www.steptoe.com/en/ retrieved April 17, 2022.

Moser, J. (2010) *Creativity with purest energy-how Thomas Wyatt introduced modern English poetics*, the introduction, www.academia.edu retrieved April 10, 2022.

Smith, M. (2022) *Professor who predicted 'The Great Resignation' shares the 3 trends that will dominate work in 2022*, www.cnbc.com/2022 retrieved April 13, 2022.

Tween, D. (2022). *No poach agreements: What's the big deal?* www.linlaters.com/en/ retrieved April 9, 2022.

Vandekerckhove, W., & Commers, R. M. S. (2003) *Downward workplace mobbing: A sign of the times?* www.researchgate.net/publication/ retrieved April 14, 2022.

*** (2020) *Kurzarbeit: Germany's short-time work benefit*, www.imf.org/en/news/ retrieved March 12, 2022.

Sonata Staniuliene, Chrysi Miliordou

Managing Stress for Professional Athletes' in Sports Organizations

1. Introduction

Due to the transformation of society, work processes have become more complex and intensive, requiring more flexibility and mobility from individuals (Mack et al., 2015). Although, overall productivity increased, the prolonged work-related stress, exhaustion, burnout, and subsequent health disorders are also increasing (Quick & Henderson, 2016).

Professional athletes have long been thought to be immune to mental health issues. This has occurred partly since their pay is generally considered to be high, together with the perception that people who participate in professional competitive sports are "tough", meaning that they cannot suffer from stress, depression, or other related disorders. The pressure to perform in the game, together with their public lives, makes being an athlete incredibly challenging for a person's mental health. When an athlete faces a physical injury, they get the team and the medical assistance required in order to heal properly. However, when they face a mental health challenge, there is no guarantee that they will receive the needed support.

As professional athletes are considered organizations' employees, their occupational stress management strategies stem from the corporate world principles, with the required modifications, specific for the sport sector. Success in sports is not only reliant on physiological and bio-mechanical factors, but psychology as well. For these reasons, stress management interventions are of critical importance in facilitating athlete's performance in a range of sport-related settings.

Even though over the last years mental health in sports has received attention and research has been conducted, there is still lack of argumentation to the effectiveness of different stress management interventions in optimizing athletes' stress and performance. Few approaches have been adapted for coaches, athletes, and sports settings, but most of the techniques offered are monomodal, focusing on a specific approach or group of people. There is a need for further research in this issue and the development of more comprehensive interventions in the field of stress management in sports, which will include a combination of health science, psychology, and corporate management components.

Research problem addressed in this chapter is how stress of professional athletes is managed in sports organizations.

The object of the chapter is professional athletes' stress management in sports organizations, and the aim is to analyze stress management for professional athletes in sport organizations.

To reach the aim of this chapter, the following *objectives* were set: (1) to review scientific literature on stress management in professional sports, and (2) to analyze stress management of professional athletes in sports organizations.

Research methods are scientific literature review and survey of professional athletes in sports organizations.

2. Literature Review and Theoretical Framework

At its most basic level, stress could be considered as the body's reaction to pressures from a life event or a specific situation. Stress contributors can vary personally and could be related to their background, environment, and genetic predisposition. A new or unexpected experience, a potential threat or a perceived loss of control could trigger a reaction of stress. Adamo (2014) identifies this condition as chronic or long-term stress that can affect a person's physical and mental health (Glanz & Schwartz, 2008). According to Weber and Jaekel-Reinhard (2000), persistent or long-term exposure to or failure to deal with stressors is a precursor to burnout associated with a variety of symptoms, especially anxiety and depression and other physical disorders such as nausea, indigestion, headaches, muscle pain, cardiovascular disease, etc. (Niclas et al., 2020). Symptoms are often permanent and cause long-term absences. Burnout is most often caused by insufficient recovery after periods of stress and tension (Sonnentag et al., 2017). Melamed et al. (2006) explain how to recover from stress by recovering depleted resources. Stress management should be implemented to deal with stress problems in the workplace. It may be difficult to select the most effective stress management interventions because limited interrelationship research is currently available (Biron & Karanika-Murray, 2013).

Workplace stress can be a determinant to health and quality of life along with work-related performance. Work needs, lack of time, poor managerial support, customer aggression, non-standard working conditions, and unpredictable schedules have been shown to be associated with high stress in the workplace (Hinderer et al., 2014). Elstad and Vabo (2008) report lower work motivation, constant job dissatisfaction, higher job turnover, and absenteeism when employees experience stress-related symptoms in their workplace. Interestingly, workplace stress could both be a determinant and an outcome, which results to a dynamic feedback loop.

The dominant framework for measuring stress in the workplace is called the Job Demand-Control model (Karasek & Theorell, 1992), where stress is a function of an employee's perceived job needs and job control. The framework suggests the term "job strain", which increases the risk of health problems (Niedhammer et al., 2014), and defines the circumstances in which work-related stress can lead to physical and mental health problems. The model emphasizes two functions of work-related stress, which are the height of stress or needs and the breadth or control of the solution (Karasek & Theorell, 1992). Demands are the requirements of work, such as time pressure, availability, difficulty, remuneration, which are considered as psychological stressors. Control is the employee's perception on the level of workload and duties management. This perception involves both competence and decision-making authority. Job demands, job control, and workplace support as having a constant and additive effect on job strain and may not constitute its dynamic feedback relationship between influential variables (Jetha et al., 2016).

The goal of developing another framework – Sports Anxiety Scale-2 (SAS-2) was to offer a reliable multidimensional measure anxiety particularly in sports setting that would replicate the structure of the original SAS factors but more accurately measure its dimensions (Smith et al., 1990). SAS-2 is a tool to calculate individual differences in somatic anxiety and concentration disorders, to identify precursors and consequences of cognitive and somatic anxiety in sports setting.

One of the most studied and frequently cited areas within the field of applied sport psychology is that of competition stress and anxiety (Sheldon et al., 1997). This is indisputably linked to the stressful nature of sport, and the demands associated with the highly competitive environments that surround the modern-day athlete. Reviews demonstrate that elite athletes experience broadly comparable rates of mental ill-health relative to the general population in respect to anxiety, post-traumatic stress, depression, and sleep disorders (Rice et al., 2019).

There are several risk factors associated with the onset of mental health disorders in elite athletes. Athletic-specific risks are related to injury or concussion, overtraining, sport specific, with individual sports conferring a higher risk than team ones, and performance failure. In addition, general risk factors are the ones not directly related with sports like lack of sleep, reduced social support, and major life events. Athletes must deal with extended time away from friends and family, due to constant travel, a very competitive environment with increased demands and significant public exposure. Another critical period is the transition out of sport, involuntary or unplanned retirement and lack of a non-athletic identity (Knights et al., 2016).

Previous research concludes three types of stress sources which are competitive, organizational, and personal (Rumbold et al., 2012). Competitive stressors have already been mentioned as athletic risk factors, with the additional elements of pressure to perform before a big game and issues with form or technique. Athletes' responses to competitive stressors vary. Having a personalized approach and knowing when a competitive stressor is overwhelming an athlete, it can be an important preventative measure to avoid further issues. Organizational stressors are relevant to the relationship between the athlete and the organization: training set up, content and practicalities, interpersonal conflict with teammates, perceived lack of organizational support, and travel issues. Organizational stressors can be attributed to, and therefore solved by, the coaching and organizational set up surrounding a team (Rumbold et al., 2012). Personal stressors are the same as the general risk factors, with the addition of financial issues. This type of stressors is the most difficult to detect unless the athlete opens and talks about them. However, for openness to occur, the prerequisite is a trusting relationship between the athlete and the staff.

It is also important to consider the barriers that inhibit prompt and successful response to stressed athletes' needs. This stigma (Gulliver et al., 2012), reinforced by fear of consequences from seeking help, like being deselected and being considered weak, as these perceptions could still be prevalent in highly competitive sports. In addition, a tight schedule and lack of time could act as reasons for not asking for help. Creating an environment where help-seeking is normalized and de-stigmatized is not only important for the prevention and treatment of individual stress but also for the enhancement of team performance.

The significant role of leadership is clear in the creation or exacerbation of stress-related issues in the workplace. The abusive supervision and destructive leadership are linked to stress (Einarsen et al., 2007). Leadership behavior and managerial support are critical for the development and recovery of stress (Foels et al., 2000).

Stress management could be divided into different approaches on the management of symptoms (Wallenstein, 2003). Action-oriented approaches are individually based and could be introduced to employees via trainings. These approaches mostly refer to behavior and lifestyle change. Another approach in the category of action-oriented approaches is incentives and time management.

One more approach integrates the role of emotion regulation between the negative event and the reaction. The two prominent emotion regulation strategies applicable at the workplace are reappraisal and suppression (Jung et al., 2018).

These two regulatory strategies have been reported to have differing effects on stress, especially when stress is linked to mental resources (Schutte et al., 2009). As a result, it could eliminate stress and balance psychological wellbeing.

Sports organizations have identified a number of critical factors in supporting athlete wellbeing. A primary factor is the duty of care from employer to employee and the organization's responsibility to ensure staff's mental health. Furthermore, the need for regular screening to detect changes in athletes' behavior on mental health issues or offer the option of referral to external specialized professionals could ensure high levels of performance. Another crucial factor is the provision of confidentiality and support to athletes struggling with stress through an individualized approach.

Reduction approach is usually designed and offered by sport psychologists or other specially trained professionals and aims at teaching athletes' skills, such as physical relaxation or thought-controlling techniques. Compared to physical relaxation, mental relaxation techniques have been less studied and analyzed in the literature as treatments to reduce the symptoms of mental anxiety in athletes (Sheldon, Owen & Mellalieu, 2009). Specialists appear to have chosen to focus on alternative cognitive strategies that are not classified as relaxation to reduce the intensity of cognitive anxiety (Purcell et al., 2019). Research on mindfulness-based courses in the workplace is steadily increasing, including successful outcomes of stress, anxiety, and fear (Morgan et al., 2015).

Psychological strategies related to the restructuring approach are self-regulatory skills that give athletes a sense of perceived environmental control and allow them to maintain greater self-confidence, which protects from anxiety (Purcell et al., 2019). A useful strategy is self-talk in the form of cognitive restructuring and rationalization of stress symptoms, goal-setting principles, and visualization that emphasize emotional state control and strengthen their morale and self-confidence (Sheldon, Owen, & Mellalieu, 2009). One alternative approach of stress management that is gaining ground over the last decade is mindfulness. The positive effects of it have been witnessed in different mental health conditions (Hofmann et al., 2010). However, mindfulness is described as a no goal attitude, based on acceptance, and leading to the liberation of one's desire. On the other hand, competitive sports have a radical goal and outcome orientation in a fierce environment, where even the second place is a failure.

3. Data and Methodology

The quantitative approach applied was a questionnaire given to professional athletes. This method offers the opportunity to address a larger sample and get responses on specific questions that emerged from the analysis of previous literature.

The method for data collection was an online questionnaire addressed to professional athletes of any sports, who receive financial reimbursement and have signed a professional contract with terms and conditions of the employee and the employer. The questionnaire was forwarded via internet channels. The segmentation of the sample was mostly demographic, based on age, gender, location, sport activity aiming at getting enough representatives from each category. Questionnaire consisted of 28 questions, mostly multiple choice and was anonymous. To avoid bias multiple age ranges of 106 adults were included, from 18 to 40 years old. In addition, people from both genders were approached, even though the percentage of male respondents was eventually higher. With regards to sports performed, the majority of participants (64.15 %) were basketball players, which is a research limitation. Furthermore, tennis (9.43 %) players completed the questionnaire and a higher percentage (17 %) of athletes competing in athletics took part. Some smaller samples were collected from sailing, fencing, and volleyball professionals.

Professional athletes' questionnaire was a source of information about their views on stress and mental health. The questionnaire analyzed their familiarity with the term "stress", their ability to control their thoughts and emotions, and their body reactions when stressed. Furthermore, their ability to recover from failures together with their coping strategies were examined. From a corporate management point of view, the following relationships were studied: employee to employee, employer to employee, supervisor to subordinate. Attitudes on job demands and work-life balance were, also, investigated. The final part of the questionnaire is dedicated to the perceived importance of mental health in organizations and previous experience with support in the form of therapy. The questionnaire aimed at investigating the cognitive, somatic and acceptance implications of stress, their acquired coping strategies, the corporate environment and its effect on stress, and athletes' personal views on mental health, looking to achieve a holistic approach to stress management.

The questionnaire consisted of two parts: the first that describes personal experience on stress; and the second focuses on the employee–employer relationship as a determinant or effect of stress. The first part of the questionnaire focuses on concentration disruption, somatic anxiety, and worry, just as SAS-2. The Likert scale used was also taken from SAS-2. The second part of the questionnaire has elements of Job-Demand-Control Model and some questions on the role of leadership and the relationship between employer and employee, which, according to literature review, have a significant effect on workplace stress.

4. Results

A significantly high percentage of athletes (83.02 %) understand the stress when it arises from the symptoms (Graph 1). This confirms that stress is a widely known condition in sports. A significant finding is the lack of understanding of stress management techniques, as 43.44 % claimed that they are not acquainted with them and only 35.79 % feel confident to apply them. This comes in line with the previous finding of Graph 1, where only half of the participants could reduce their stress levels during competition time. Similar responses were given to the question about mindfulness as a stress reduction holistic practice, where a small percentage of 28.29 % are practicing it as a daily routine. Regardless of these, an encouraging discovery was the percentage of athletes understanding the connection between thoughts-feelings-behavior, as a promising finding in stress management awareness and application. Being familiar with their core theory of the connection between thoughts-feelings-behavior is a good starting point for the success of those interventions.

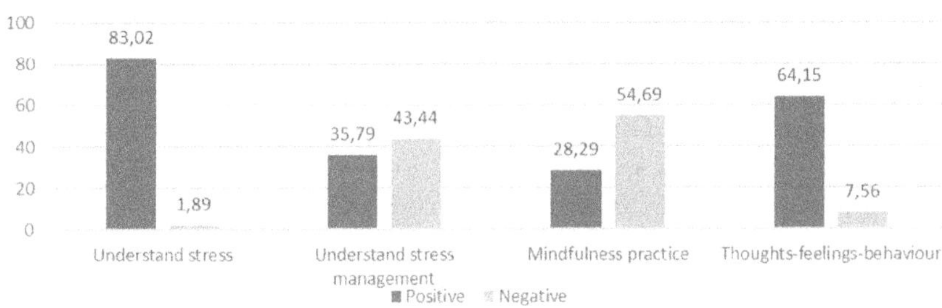

Graph 1: Athletes' familiarity with stress and stress management responses, %.

As discussed before, this might confirm the contradictory nature between mindfulness, as an acceptance approach and the extreme competition of professional sports. This could potentially explain why the previously mentioned mindfulness approaches have not been applied to a larger extent. Nonetheless, mindfulness has a range of benefits related to intrinsic motivation, and the state of "flow" during a game and those elements could be added to a comprehensive mental health framework for professional sports.

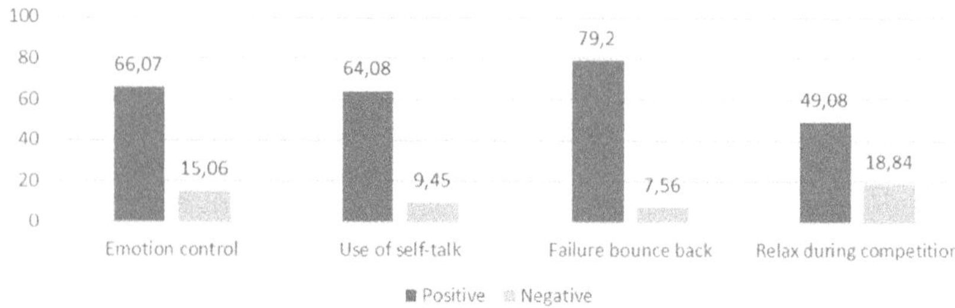

Graph 2: Athletes somatic and cognitive responses during stress, %.

Graph 2 explains athletes' cognitive responses during stress. According to the data produced, the majority of them (79.2 %) are able to bounce back from failure. A smaller, but still significant percentage (66.07 %), advised that they can control their emotions during a game, with only 15.06 % finding this difficult. Another coping strategy that they widely use is self-talk, with 64.08 % respondents agreeing that it helps them focus their attention to their performance. What seems to be harder for half of the participants is relaxation and reduction of arousal during a game, with 49.08 % claiming that they are capable of achieving this. Those findings suggest that even though athletes are familiar with their cognitive and somatic responses to stress and have developed some coping strategies, during the actual game/competition time, they don't always succeed in reducing their tension. This confirms the highly pressured nature of sports, but could, also, imply the lack of mastery of advanced stress management strategies. It might, also, be that knowledge is there, but practicing those skills is not yet adequate for encouraging results.

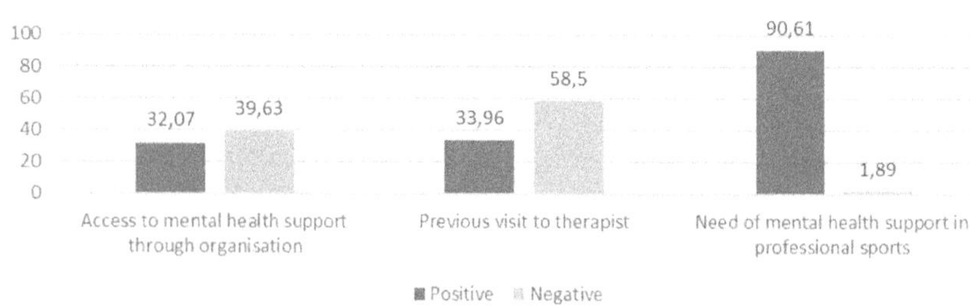

Graph 3: Professional athletes' views on mental health support in sports organizations, %.

Almost all (90.61 %) participants, regardless of sport and age group, need mental health support in professional sports. However, their current use of psychological support is significantly lower than that, with only 32.07 % having access through their organization and only 33.96 % having consulted someone privately. This could be linked to those in Graph 3, where 83.02 % of the participants understand the stress state but only 35.79 % develop effective stress management techniques. There seems to be a gap between stress awareness and stress management strategies, along with a realization of the necessity of mental health support.

The three sports with higher number of respondents were basketball, tennis, and athletics. For basketball the percentage of athletes' familiarity remains the same as that of the full sample. However, in tennis, which is an individual sport, stress management familiarity percentage drops to 20 %, while in athletics, which is again mostly individual it is a little bit higher – 50 %. The assumption that in team sports, colleague support could act as a source of information for stress relief techniques could not be validated, as both tennis and athletics are individual sports and do have different results.

Analyzing the familiarity with stress management approaches by gender, 35.3 % of women and 36.1 % of men agree that they are aware of stress management techniques, with the rest feeling either neutral or negative. The fact that both genders have similar, if not equal, scores means that stress management is not related to gender. The literature review did not specify intergender differences in corporate stress and classified risk factors according to organization, taking to account nature of sports and performance pressure as well.

Graph 4 exhibits views on the job itself and the relation with their colleagues of the same hierarchical level. The percentage of athletes understanding their role in the team, the role of others and how they all fit in the system is quite high (83.08 %). In general terms, relations with colleagues are shown as positive with 75.49 % relying on their colleagues for support and only a very small 2.8 % feeling unsupported. The two findings supplement each other, as having a sound understanding of your role in a group helps in having clearer communications with others, which, in turn, supports relationship building.

Views on work-life balance were expected to be mixed, as jobs in sports are known for their long hours and frequent travelling, as already discussed. As a result, 49.08 % confirmed that they could find balance between their professional and personal life, with 16.95 % being negative and 33.97 % feeling neutral about it. Regarding job control, respondents were asked whether they have the possibility to decide for themselves on how to carry out their work and if they could decide what should be done. Perceived control of job demands reached a percentage of 54.63 %, with 26.46 % feeling they cannot control their job demands and 18.91 % claiming to be neutral.

Graph 4: Athletes' perception on team role and job control, %.

The other aspects of the relationship between employee and leadership are highlighted in Graph 5. Responses here demonstrate potential issues, as only half of the athletes seem to be satisfied with the leadership of their organization. Specifically, 50.91 % claimed that their supervisors understand their needs, 13.2 % appeared negative, and 35.89 % were neutral. In addition, about half of them (54.69 %) trust the leadership of their organization. In most cases, the direct supervisor is their coach and team manager (in team sports) and the leadership are the owners of the team. Regarding compensation and remuneration, the majority of the athletes are not satisfied, as 32.1 % are not happy with their salary and 28.3 % are neutral. This goes in line with their responses on evaluation system and performance feedback, as only 52.08 % are happy about the appraisal process and content.

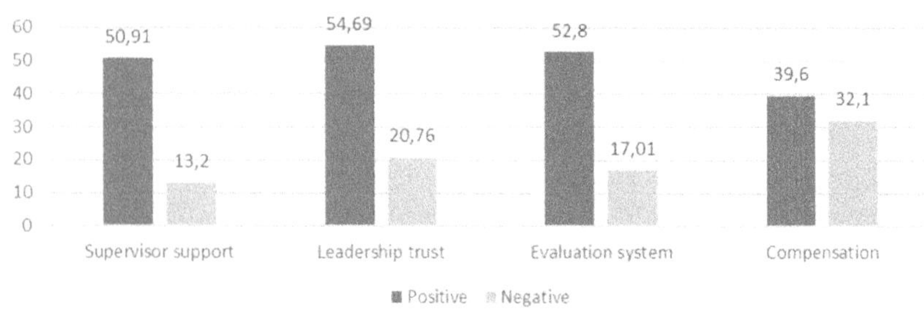

Graph 5: Employee–employer relationship in professional sports settings, %.

As shown in other corporate settings, the importance of feedback in the evaluation of performance is an important supervisory task, linked to job satisfaction and workplace stress.

5. Conclusion

Stress management programs in the workplace have common features regarding their intent and content. Their intent is to educate employees and teach them coping skills and to prevent future issues. The most popular stress management approaches are divided into three categories: action, emotion, and acceptance oriented. There are several work factors that have been concluded to affect corporate stress. These are job demands, time management, managerial support, colleague support, role of leadership, and working conditions. One of the most prevalent tools for the assessment of stress in workplace is the Job Demand-Control framework, where the interaction between job demands and sense of control defines stress levels, according to the given task.

Regarding sport organizations, one of the most studied subjects is competition stress, stemming from the nature of professional sports. The risk factors associated with the stress in sports are organizational, competitive, and personal, with the first two concentrating on the relationship between employer and employee and sport nature and the latter is about individual life challenges. Another distinction in stress management interventions is between cognitive and somatic issues.

Some facts that affect the sport sector but are not so recorded in other workplaces are the stigma associated with the stereotype that athletes are rich, perform an easy job, are strong, and cannot complain about their mental health. This is a significant barrier, as this stereotype is still prevalent. Another sport-specific problem is the risk of injury and its relationship with stress, either before or after the trauma. On the other hand, most stress management interventions in sports are intended for athletes only, without including the coach, coaching staff, and officials, who also face their own mental health challenges.

Quantitative method of athletes' questionnaire generated some important discoveries regarding stress prevalence and its management. Athletes use some action and emotion-oriented tools to relieve their stress, in the form of self-talk and emotion control and are generally able to recover under pressure. However, during competition or game time almost half of them are unable to relax and decrease their arousal levels. A large percentage recognize stress, but only a third are aware of stress management coping techniques. This highlights the importance of stress management programs in sports.

Regarding their role in the organization, athletes do understand their job and their tasks. They, also, demonstrate good working relationship with their colleagues. However, the same finding could not be confirmed for their rapport with their supervisors and leadership, with half of them complaining about evaluation, compensation, and support. Work-life balance seems to be another issue that needs attention, together with perception of job control.

Based on existing approaches and the needs of athletes and coaches, a recommendation of a comprehensive mental health solution could be made. This could be based on a 360 degree approach and the decision-making of the recruitment and appraisal process would be split between leadership, human resources, and coaches' feedback. The mental health specialist should deal with somatic, cognitive, and acceptance approaches in individual and group settings. However, as this would be applied to a workplace, personal athletes' struggles, that are not work-related, could be referred externally. The collaboration between the specialist and other departments of the sports organization could be suggested, together with their relationship with the coach and leadership.

It is important to draw limitations that it is outside the scope of this research to define which sports are more stressful or gender or other characteristic related, which could potentiality drive further, future, more specialized research. It could consider different cultures and attitudes to sport in different regions of the world as well.

A recommendation for further research refers to elite, leagues', clubs' athletes, coaching staff, officials of different sports in stress management field.

References

Adamo, S. A. (2014). The effects of stress hormones on immune function may be vital for the adaptive reconfiguration of the immune system during fight-or-flight behaviour. *Integrative and Comparative Biology*, 54, 419–426.

Biron, C., & Karanika-Murray, M. (2013). Process evaluation for organizational stress and well-being interventions: Implications for theory, method, and practice. *International Journal of Stress Management*, 21(10), 1037.

Einarsen, S., Aasland, M. S., & Skogstad, A. (2007). Destructive leadership behaviour: A definition and conceptual model. *The Leadership Quarterly*, 18(3), 207–216.

Elstad, J. I., & Vabø, M. (2008). Job stress, sickness absence and sickness presenteeism in Nordic elderly care. *Scandinavian Journal of Public Health*, 36(5), 467–74.

Foels, R., Driskell, J., Mullen, B., & Salas, E. (2000). The effects of democratic leadership on group member satisfaction: An integration. *Small Group Research*, 31(6), 676–701.

Glanz, K. and Schwartz, M. (2008). *Health behaviour and health education: Theory, research, and practice. Stress, coping, and health behaviour.* San Francisco: Wiley.

Gulliver, A., Griffiths, K. M., & Christensen, H. (2012). Barriers and facilitators to mental health help-seeking for young elite athletes: A qualitative study. *BMC Psychiatry*, 12(1), 157.

Hinderer, K. A., VonRueden, K. T., Friedmann, E., McQuillan, K. A., Gilmore, R., & Kramer B. (2014). Burnout, compassion fatigue, compassion satisfaction, and secondary traumatic stress in trauma nurses. *Journal of Trauma Nursing*, 21(4), 160–9.

Hofmann, S. G., Sawyer, A. T., Witt, A. A., & Oh, D. (2010). The effect of mindfulness-based therapy on anxiety and depression: A meta-analytic review. *Journal of Consulting and Clinical Psychology*, 78, 169–183.

Jetha, A., Pransky, G., & Hettinger, L. (2016). Capturing complexity in work disability research: Application of system dynamics modelling methodology. *Disability Rehabilitation*, 38 (2), 189–194.

Jung, Y., Sohn, Y. W., & Kim, M. Y. (2018. Emotion regulation and job stress: The mediating effect of relationship quality in the US and Korean samples. *Current Psychology* 39, 1106–1115. doi: 10.1007/s12144-018-9997-1.

Karasek, R. and Theorell, T. (1992). *Healthy work: Stress, productivity, and the reconstruction of working life*. New York: Basic books.

Knights, S., Sherry, E., & Ruddock-Hudson, M. (2016). Investigating elite end-of-athletic career transition: A systematic review. *Journal of Applied Sport Psychology*, 28(3), 291–308.

Mack, O., Khare, A., Krämer, A., & Burgartz, T. (2015). *Managing in a VUCA world*. Basel: Springer.

Melamed, S., Shirom, A., Toker, S., Berliner, S., & Shapira, I. (2006). Burnout and risk of cardiovascular disease: Evidence, possible causal paths, and promising research directions. *Psychological Bulletin*, 132, 327–353. http://dx.doi.org/10.1037/0033-2909.132.3.327.

Morgan, P., Simpson, J. and Smith, A. (2015). Health care workers' experiences of mindfulness training: a qualitative review. *Mindfulness (N Y)*, 6(4), 744–758.

Niedhammer, I., Sultan-Taïeb, H., Chastang, J., Vermeylen, G., & Parent-Thirion, A. (2014). Fractions of cardiovascular diseases and mental disorders attributable to psychosocial work factors in 31 countries in Europe. *International Archive of Occupational Environmental Health*, 87(4), 403–411.

Niclas, A., Jan, L., Lars-Göran, Ö., & Örjan, S. (2020). Behavioral stress recovery management intervention for people with high levels of perceived stress: A randomized controlled trial. *International Journal of Stress Management, 27*(2), 183–194.

Purcell, R., Gwyther, K., & Rice, S. M. (2019). Mental health in elite athletes: Increased awareness requires an early intervention framework to respond to athlete needs. *Sports Medicine – Open* 5, 46. https://doi-org.ezproxy.vdu.lt:2443/10.1186/s40798-019-0220-1.

Quick, J., & Henderson, D. (2016). Occupational stress: Preventing suffering, enhancing wellbeing. *International Journal of Environmental Research and Public Health*, 13(5), 459–470.

Rice, S. M., Gwyther, K., Santesteban-Echarri, O., Baron, D., Gorczynski, P., Gouttebarge, V. et al. (2019). Determinants of anxiety in elite athletes: A systematic review and meta-analysis. *British Journal of Sports Medicine,* 53(11), 722–30.

Rumbold, J., Fletcher, D., & Daniels, K. (2012). A systematic review of stress management interventions with sport performers. *Sport, Exercise, and Performance Psychology*, 1(3), 173–193.

Schutte, N. S., Manes, R. R., & Malouff, J. M. (2009). Antecedent focused emotion regulation, response modulation and well-being. *Current Psychology*, 28(1), 21–31. https://doi.org/10.1007/s12144-009-9044-3.

Sheldon, K. M., Ryan, R. M., Rawsthorne, L. J., & Ilardi, B. (1997). Trait self and true self: Cross-role variation in the big-five personality traits and its relations with psychological authenticity and subjective well-being. *Journal of Personality and Social Psychology*, 73(6), 1380–1393. https://doi.org/10.1037/0022-3514.73.6.1380.

Sheldon, Ph. D., Owen, T. and Mellalieu, S. (2009). Management of competitive stress in elite sport. In *Professional Practice in Sport Psychology* (pp. 30–42). Blackwell Publishing, UK.

Smith, R. E., Smoll, F. L., & Schutz, R. W. (1990). Measurement and correlates of sport-specific cognitive and somatic trait anxiety: The Sport Anxiety Scale. *Anxiety Research*, 2, 263–280.

Sonnentag, S., Venz, L., & Casper, A. (2017). Advances in recovery research: What have we learned? What should be done next? *Journal of Occupational Health Psychology*, 22, 365–380. http://dx.doi.org/10.1037/ocp0000079

Wallenstein, G. (2003). *Mind, Stress, and Emotion: The New Science of Mood.* Boston, MA: Commonwealth Press.

Weber, A., & Jaekel-Reinhard, A. (2000). Burnout syndrome: A disease of modern societies? *Occupational Medicine*, 50, 512–517. http://dx.doi.org/10.1093/occmed/50.7.512.

Kemal Cebeci

Reflections of 1929 Great Depression to the Cinema: Cinderella Man (2005) by Ron Howard

1. Introduction

There are economic, political and social turning points that bring along important transformations and breaking points in the historical process. While these events transform the life of the individual and society significantly, they also constitute a source for cinema, literature, music and many other branches of art. The cinema industry focuses on individual and social events and is an important branch of art that processes these milestones in several movies. Social, political and economic events such as: World Wars, revolutions, economic crisis, political instabilities, sport events, etc. constitute an important resource for the cinema industry. On the other hand, Hollywood cinema sometimes has focused on the effects of social, political and economic milestones on the lives of ordinary people rather than socio-political and economic events themselves – also addressing real human conflicts in a society as a result of socio-political breaking points (Escalonilla, 2016: 21).

The 1929 Great Depression, with its many dimensions, is an important historical event, sometimes as the main subject of movies that directly focused and sometimes as a background of the theme. Issues such as deep poverty, hunger, political problems, and reflections of the crisis on individual and social life, brought by the crisis of 1929, have been the core subjects that the cinema industry has focused.

Films on economic crisis have also been trying to humanize and sympathize with the situation of the victims of the conditions, those who lost their economic wealth such as real estates, jobs, earnings or personal savings (Pop & Sim, 2017: 682). At this point, the 1929 Great Depression is also important in terms of its effects on the personal and family life in micro sense, as well as its effects on a macro scale. However, its social and personal psychological effects are quite extensive. Considered from this point of view, the 1929 crisis has been an economic event that attracted the attention of the cinema industry both from a macro and micro perspective.

Cinderella Man (2005), movie examined in this study, is kind of biography movie that tells the story and life of a boxer named James J. Braddock.

Braddock – as a character, as a human, as a boxer, as a citizen – symbolized the hero's journey for a nation in an era of crisis (Wedding & Conner, 2006). James Braddock similarly and probably reflects the story of many Americans (Shipton et al., 2006: 6). However, on the life story of a boxer, it focuses on the problems and deep poverty created by the period from a micro perspective through a family life, and also has a macro perspective in terms of exhibiting the effects of the 1929 crisis on the whole of social life.

Rotella (2005), defines Braddock as: *"A boxer and stevedore laid low by the Great Depression and barely able to feed his kids, picks himself up, battles back, and eventually wins the heavyweight title"* (Rotella, 2005: 289). The film depicts the journey of a single person leading to the championship in the boxing ring, despite all kinds of difficulties and injuries. The movie discusses the negative effects of 1929 Depression in Braddock's life and its reflections on family life. The movie provides a parallel glance to Braddock's life adventure during the 1929 Depression and his journey in sports life. In this respect, Cinderella Man 2005 – as a unique movie – has a special place in the cinema history in terms of revealing many dimensions of the 1929 crisis personally, socially and economically based on the life of a boxer.

2. Method

In this study, first of all, the literature on the reflection of economic crises on the cinema was examined. In this context, a special focus was placed on the 1929 Great Depression, and the films that directly dealt with the 1929 Great Depression or periodically reflected the crisis period were discussed. The main focus of our study is the movie Cinderella Man (2005). Timing and background of the movie directly reflects 1929 Great Depression from the beginning till the end. So we had to focus on special scenes and tried to select the most impressive moments in the movie. In the Cinderella Man (2005), screenshots of scenes reflecting the effects of the 1929 crisis, particularly poverty, are shown in the tables. We selected 12 scenes directly or indirectly reflecting the 1929 Great Depression. In the headlines of the tables, the minute of the scene that took place in the movie was given. In the right side of the tables, the dialogs on the relevant scenes were included. And scenes have been analyzed together with the dialogs how and to what extent the 1929 crisis reflected on the relevant scene.

3. Literature

In the cinema history, it is possible to see numerous movies focused on economic crisis or use the crisis conditions as environment of the scenario. Recently in the last decade, it is possible to come across films mostly on the 2008 crisis, as it is a current issue. Cinema industry, especially Hollywood, is very successful in projecting economic events into films.

The 2008 crisis, which was the most important crisis after 2000, was covered in movies in the following years. Margin Call (2011), which tackled the 2008 crisis and sheds light on the functioning of financial markets, takes over the era through a money management firm. Another film that focuses on the 2008 crisis, Big Short (2015), clearly reveals the mechanism of operation of the mortgage-backed securities bubble that put financial markets in a difficult position. It is an adaptation movie from the book of Michael Lewis which explains the financial crisis called "Big Short: Inside the Doomsday Machine", announced by *New York Times* as one of the best books of the last two decades (Kakutani, 2010). Money for Nothing: Inside the Federal Reserve (2013), a documentary that can be associated with the 2008 crisis, both sheds light on the period and focuses on the careers of Alan Greenspan and Ben Bernanke and their shifting/changing views on the proper role of monetary policy on economy (Tucker, 2018).

The movies about 2008 crisis, also analyzed by researchers in the literature with the different points of views Feyel and Fourton (2019), brings together popular films, for analyzing the different aspects and cinematic representations of 2008 economic crisis. In addition to movies mentioned above: Too Big To Fail (2011), Inside Job (2010), Capitalism: A Love Story (2009) are listed as movies that focused on 2008 crises (Pop & Sim, 2017: 684–688).

4. Reflections of 1929 Great Depression in the Movies

In the movie industry, it is possible to come across many films about the Great Depression of 1929 or using the Great Depression as the habitat of the film. The Great Depression has become a very important resource for the cinema industry with its many aspects in terms of political, economical and social dimensions such as: poverty, unemployment problem, problems in family life, and psychological effects on individuals and society.

The Grapes of Wrath (1940)[1], directed by John Ford, is one of the most classical movie that tells the dramatic story of a poor Midwest family forced off their land during the 1929 Great Depression. The movie is based on John Steinbeck's novel about western migrants: "The Grapes of Wrath" (Baskind, 2004: 41). The story gives an idea about the hostility of Californians toward migrants and

1 IMDB, The Grapes of Wrath (1940).

illustrates the depth of this socio-economic concern (Boustan et al., 2010: 720–721). Another movie, Modern Times (1936) by Charlie Chaplin, expresses the economic and social conditions that deteriorated with the effect of Great Depression of 1929, and the problem of increasing unemployment. The film provides realistic interpretations of the social and economic conditions of Great Depression (IMDB[2]). Chaplin became the great cinema poet of the Depression with a trilogy: City Lights (1931), Modern Times (1936) and The Great Dictator (1940), by dramatizing the effects of Great Depression on the ordinary man of the global economic collapse (Mellen, 2006: 21). Sydney Pollack movie, They Shoot Horses, Don't They (1969), is also one of the other classical movies that underline the conditions of Great Depression era. Based on the novel by Horace McCoy, the film depicts a dancer named Gloria's adventure in a dance race for a cash prize that will keep her alive during the great depression (Hardwick, 2012). The film focuses on a disparate group of individuals and their story. The lives of a disparate group of contestants intertwine in an inhumanely grueling dance contest and painful competition[3].

Some other movies that directly or indirectly focus on Great Depression are: Some Like It Hot (1959), directed by Billy Wilder; To Kill A Mocking Bird (1962), directed by Robert Mulligan; Bonnie and Clyde (1967), directed by Arthur Penn; Once upon a Time in America (1984), directed by Sergio Leone; The Purple Rose of Cairo (1985), directed by Woody Allen; The Untouchables (1987), directed by Brian De Palma; Road to Perdition (2002), directed by Sam Mendes; Seabiscuit (2003), directed by Gary Ross; Lawless (2012), directed by John Hillcoat; Grapes of Wrath (1940) directed by John Ford[4].

Cinderella Man (2005), directed by Ron Howard, stands out as one of the most impressive films dealing with the 1929 crisis in terms of its story, acting and mirroring the period. The movie is based on the story of James J. Braddock, a supposedly washed-up boxer who has legendary return and came back to win the heavyweight title and an inspiration in the 1930s (IMDB, 2022d). The movie focuses on the comeback story of Jim Braddock and tells the story of Braddock and his family who were driven into poverty by the meltdown of the American economy and deeply faced with the difficult conditions of the depression (Llarena, 2018: 104).

---

2 IMDB, Modern Times (1936).

3 IMDB, They Shoot Horses, Don't They (1969).

4 Movies derived by the author from IMDB. www.imdb.com.

5. Causes and Consequences of the 1929 Great Depression

The crisis of 1929, which started in 1929 and affected many countries in the world until the end of the 1930s, is one of the most important depressions in history in terms of its scope, severity, length and depth. It was not easy to tell exactly when the depression began and when it would end. But it was clear that the roaring, turbulent, high-flying, buoyant era of the twenties came to a dead stop (Berton, 1990: 19). In the 1920s, America was the prominent leader of the world as an economic, financial, political and military power.

Changes in the pattern of consumer demand proved that, but at the same time, this fact is one of the important reasons of the depression in the following era. This change in patterns made it difficult for technology and workforce abilities to adapt to the new situation in the 1930s (Bernstein, 1987: 20). All these transformations as a whole in the economy cause imbalances at many sectors in the economy, and especially at total demand. The substantial decrease in total demand, problems and collapses in the banking sector, panic in the financial markets, wrong economic policies applied by government, and the bubble in the real estate sector caused the GDP to fall in the United States, resulting in the spread of the depression to other parts of the world in a short time[5].

The downturn began in 1929 and the Great Depression became markedly worse and severe until 1933. Both real GDP and price levels fell steeply. Enormous decline in industrial production was 47 % and combined with the 30 % fell of real gross domestic product. In addition, with the sharp decline in the total demand, the wholesale price index declined 33 %. When it is compared with the next worst crisis of America, Great Recession of 2007–2008, when the real GDP declined at 4.3 % and the unemployment rate peaked at less than 10 %, the severity of the Great Depression becomes especially clear and comprehensible (Pells & Romer, 2020). In 1933, the stock market lost 75 % of its value compared to 1929. National income fell to about half, and exports declined to its lowest level since 1904. More than a thousand properties, mostly owned by farmers, have been foreclosed (Alter, 2006: 148).

"The great depression is to economics what the Big Bang is to Physics. As an event, Depression is largely synonymous with the birth of modern macroeconomics, and it continues to haunt successive generations of economics. With respect to labor

5 *"While the gold standard, which linked nearly all the countries of the world in a network of fixed currency exchange rates, played a key role in transmitting the American downturn to other countries"* (Pells & Romer, 2020). And also enhanced the spillover effects of the crisis. For more info please: Duignan (2013).

and labor markets, these facts evidently include wage rigidity, persistently high unemployment rates, and long-term joblessness" (Margo, 1993: 41). Although there is no clear consensus on unemployment rates in the Great Depression, it widely argues that the level of unemployment exceeded 20 % and for some researches may reached over 25 % during the Depression era and its continuation (Lebergott, 1957: 215).

Under the difficult conditions of the Great Depression, Americans are hopeful to look to the future with hope. They keep this hope for their heirs, if not for themselves. Although Franklin D. Roosevelt's New Deal brought economic relief, Roosevelt knew that for their influence to be long-lasting, they had to be attached to a new American Dream[6] (Hanson & White, 2011, 3–4; Olson, 2001). The restructuring process of the US economy after Roosevelt's New Deal plan continued until the World War II, and it took a long time to overcome the negative effects of the crisis.

6. About Cinderella Man (2005) and the Story of James J. Braddock

Cinderella Man (2005), directed by Ron Howard, nominated for three Oscars (Best Performance by an Actor in a Supporting Role, Best Achievement in Film Editing, Best Achievement in Makeup) and also sixteen wins and forty-five nominations in several international cinema prizes. It is a film telling the journey of world heavyweight champion James J. Braddock in the content of America of the early 1990s.

6 For more details about American Dream and New American Dream, please look at: Hanson and White (2011).

k and Keeps Title — Giants S

PRINCIPALS IN TITLE BOUT AT STADIUM LAST NIGHT.

PIRATES SU
BY HUBB

LOSERS BLAN

Tommy Loughran.

James J. Braddock.

RAIN KEEPS YANKS

ATHLETICS TRIUMPH

Fig. 1: James J. Braddock vs. Tommy Loughran, 19 July 1929
Source: New York Times, July 19, 1929.

The life story of James J. Braddock, born in New York on December 6, 1905, draws attention with its similarity to the story of the average American of the time. The sports life of the boxer, who had a successful career until 1929, significantly declined simultaneously with the big problems that the American economy dragged along with the 1929 Great Depression (Schaap, 2005: 3). Braddock, like many Americans, lost all of his financial wealth in 1929, and he experienced ill fortune in his professional boxing career, a downturn in sport career when he began to lose fights (Shipton et al., 2006: 6). Like the economy that started to rise with Roosevelt's New Deal plan after 1934, Braddock's boxing career rose again in 1934 and became an adventure leading up to the world championship. Braddock's graph of life and the graph of the American economy are almost completely parallel. Braddock started boxing at the age of 21 and won 34 of 46 games by 1929. In 1929, he lost to Tommy Loughran in the title match, and like the crisis in the American economy, Braddock's career went into decline (Touchstone Pictures, 2005: 5).

American economy in the 1929 Great Depression has experienced a very difficult period with problems such as the collapse in the stock markets, problems with loans, poverty and unemployment (Rothbard, 1972: 13–14). Braddock's life also entered a period of great collapse, his boxing license was revoked, and he was trying to feed his family by working in daily jobs that he could find. He became unable to meet even the most basic food needs and had to apply to aid organizations. In fact, Braddock's life had the same poverty conditions as most Americans of the time (Touchstone Pictures, 2005: 5).

In 1934, the program called New Deal by Roosevelt aimed at reducing the negative effects of the economic crisis was put into practice (Schlesinger, 2003: 4). From this moment, Braddock's fortune began to turn like that of the American people. Surprisingly, he defeated the boxer John Griffin. He subsequently scored wins against John Henry Lewis and Art Lasky, who won a 15-game top. When he started earning money, he repaid all the debt he had received from charities and gained great respect for his behavior and became known as "Gentleman Jim". After his success, he had the opportunity to match for the title with Max Baer, that killed two people on the ring. Generally, the authorities agreed that this match would end in serious injury or death. Braddock's wife also wanted him not to play this match, scared of losing him on the ring. The Jim Braddock and Max Baer match was held in New York's Madison Square Garden in front of 35,000 spectators on June 13, 1935. Braddock won the match, which lasted 15 rounds, and won the championship and the title (Touchstone Pictures, 2005: 5–6).

In many regions of the country, ordinary people watched this match live. During the Great Depression, boxing gave an immediate sense of joy, pleasure and sense of belonging to the many Americans (Roşca, 2012: 127). This fight between Braddock and Baer showed that there is a way for people who seem desperate, and has been a beacon of hope for ordinary Americans. Sports writer Damon Runyon nicknamed him "Cinderella Man" because the story from poverty to richness so much resembled a classic fairy tale, and Braddock is now known by this nickname (Runyon, 1935). Braddock lost his heavyweight boxing title to Joe Louis in 1937. In 1938, after beating Tommy Farr, Braddock got the chance to play the title match but instead announced that he quit boxing and his retirement. He was admitted into the Ring Boxing Hall of Fame in 1964 and International Boxing Hall of Fame in 2001. He died on 29 November 1974 at the age of 68 (Touchstone Pictures, 2005: 7).

6.1 Reflections of 1929 Great Depression to the Movie: Cinderella Man (2005)

The Cinderella Man (2005) movie has many scenes that contain the reflections of the 1929 Great Depression, both in terms of the time it takes and the reflections in Braddock's life story. We found 17 scenes that reflected the Great Depression. We selected 12 of these scenes which can be accepted directly into the content of 1929 crisis and show them in Tabs. 1 and 2 along with the sample of dialogs in these scenes.

Tab. 1: Reflections of 1929 Great Depression to the scenes in Cinderella Man (2005)

Scene 1 (min: 8.35)	Not enough food for all
	*"- You know, Mae, I dreamed last night… that I was having dinner at The Ritz. With Mickey Rooney and George Raft. - Really! - Yeah. And I dreamed I had a steak. A thick, juicy steak. Like this, Rosy. And then I had a mountain of mashed potatoes…and I went back for ice cream three times. I'm stuffed."*
Scene 2 (min: 10.38)	Braddock seeking a job
	*"- I need nine men and only nine. One. Two. Three. Four. Five. Six. Seven. Eight. Nine. That's it! All right, let's get a move on! Go on, get going! Got a lot of work today!"*
Scene 3 (min: 11.48 and ongoing up to 12.42)	Braddock's son stole a salami
	*"- Hey, Rosy-cheeks. - How you doing? - Daddy, Jay stole! - What? - Jay stole. - What's all this about? - See? It's a salami."*
Scene 4 (min: 14.38)	Broken hand of Braddock
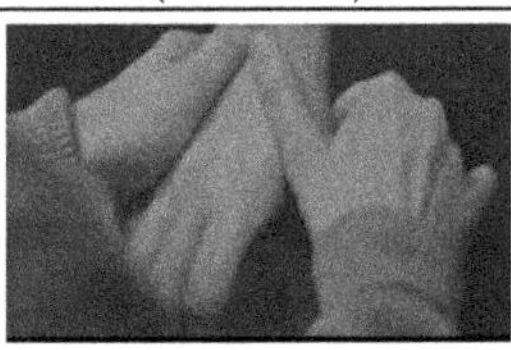	*"- Now, you see, that break's still a few weeks away. - I know. Yeah. - And you were gonna tell me about this when? - It's gonna be fine. - It's not fine."*
Scene 5 (min: 26.42)	Working with broken hand
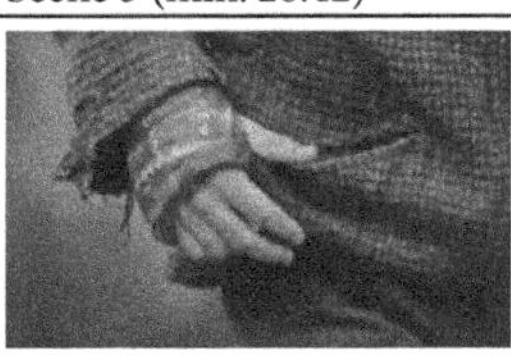	*"- I used to follow a pretty good fighter with that name. And there's some other guy going around using that name now. Can't fight for shit. Gambling man will löse a lot of money on him. Twice. That hand ain't gonna work. You can't slow me down. I need this job. - I need the job, too. - What's wrong with the goddamn hand? - You see us falling behind, Jake? He's all right."*

(Continued)

Tab. 1: Continued

Scene 6 (min: 30.22)	Cut the electricity because of debt
	*"- I'm sorry, lady, you're past due.* *- No, you can't. You can't. There's kids.* *- If I don't, they let me go. They already let two guys go.* *- Please. This apartment, It's what we got left that keeps us hanging on.* *- Lady, I got kids, too."*

Source: Cinderella Man 2005, Miramax Films, Imagine Entertainment, Parkway Productions. (Universal Pictures & Buena Vista International/Touchstone Pictures).

Note: Title of the scenes are given by the Author.

Scene 1 (min: 8.35, Not enough food for all): In this scene, Braddoc's daughter, Rosy, wants some more food. But since there is no food at home, Braddock offers his own food to his daughter Rosy. He explains that he is full by telling a small story and makes this a joyful game. This scene is one of the most striking moments in the movie in terms of telling about the 1929s period when serious problems were experienced in terms of nutrition.

Scene 2 (min: 10.38, Braddock seeking a job): In this scene, Braddock is seen amongst the people to be selected for a business looking for a daytime worker. The employer, who needs nine workers, makes his choice after many people waiting to be selected. Braddock cannot be chosen among these nine people and leaves the field in disillusionment.

Scene 3 (min: 11.48 and ongoing up to 12.42, Braddock's son stole a salami): It is one of the most important scenes of the film with its reflection of poverty and its social message dimension. Braddock's son Jay stole meat from the butcher. Braddock learns this and takes his child and goes to butcher. He asks Jay to return what he stole with apologizing from the butcher. At the end of the scene, he has an emotional conversation with his child, saying that theft is never a solution and is wrong no matter what. No matter how severe the conditions of the period are, it comes to the fore as a stage that tells about the virtues that make human beings human.

Scene 4 (min: 14.38, Broken hand of Braddock): In 1993, Braddock's right hand was broken in the fight with Abe Feldman. It was a dramatical moment in the career of Braddock. With his friend and manager Joe Gould's words "Jimmy . . . sometimes you just can't change things. I'm telling you . . . It's finished" (Shipton et al., 2006: 13–15). It is the scene where he states that he wants to have a boxing match because he needs money even though his hand is broken. In a conversation with his manager Joe, Joe reveals that he cannot fight with a broken hand. But Braddock reveals that he has no money left and no other choice. He made a very defense fight, and the match was very boring for the audience. After this fight, boxing authorities revoked Braddock's license. It is a very impressive scene about pushing a person's physical limits to meet their essential needs in terms of being survivor.

Scene 5 (min: 26.42, Working with broken hand): Braddock goes to the same place to find a daily job, this time being selected among five workers. His hand is bandaged while working. They have a conversation with the worker who is carrying a load together. The other worker says to Braddock that he makes him slow and he needs this job. Braddock also states that he needs this job. The employer notices that Braddock's hand is bandaged and asks. And at this moment, the other worker supports Braddock by saying that everything is fine and keeps his job. It is a very special scene depicting that poverty brings people closer to each other around a common goal.

Scene 6 (min: 30.22, Cut the electricity because of debt): In this scene, the officer comes to cut the electricity because of Braddock's debts. There is dialogue between Braddock's wife Mae and the officer. Mae says; "I have a child", and also the man says "I have a child", too. If I don't cut it, I will lose my job. It is one of the most dramatic scenes of the film that reflects the difficulties of the period and its destructive effects on the emotional world of people.

Tab. 2: Reflections of 1929 Great Depression to the scenes in Cinderella Man (2005)

Scene 7 (min: 32.40)	Street scent break up
	"- All right. Help me, pick up some of that wood."
Scene 8 (min: 36.55)	Braddock at Emergency Relief Administration of New Jersey
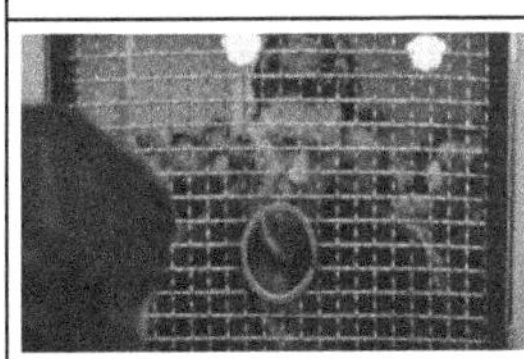	"- I never thought. I'd see you here, Jim."

(*Continued*)

Tab. 2: Continued

Scene 9 (min: 38.55)	Braddock seeks help
	*"- The thing is, I can't afford to…I can't afford to pay the heat. I've had to farm out my kids. You know, they keep cutting shifts down at the docks… and you just don't get picked every day. I sold everything I've got that anybody would buy. I went on public assistance. I signed on at the relief office……………… If you could help me through this time, I sure would be grateful."*
Scene 10 (min: 1.12.50)	Braddock, the rising star
	"-Jimmy Braddock just beat Lasky. They made him the number one contender."
Scene 11 (min: 1.27.15 and min: 1.28.15)	B. Johnson, "Boston Globe." and J. Greenblatt from "Chicago Trib
	*"- Jake Greenblatt from "Chicago trib."………… - Well, you know, the truth is, Jake… for a number of years there we was fighting injured. I broke my hand more than once. I got in a car accident one time, we was on the road… and I had to get that fixed. I had a run of bad luck. And, this time around, I know what I'm fighting for. - Yeah? What's that, Jimmy? - Milk."*
Scene 12 (min: 1.52.37)	Braddock wins the title and becomes the world champion
	*"- Ladies and gentlemen…we have your decision. It's unanimous! Winner, and the new worldnheavyweight champion… James J. Braddock!"*

Source: Cinderella Man 2005, Miramax Films, Imagine Entertainment, Parkway Productions. (Universal Pictures & Buena Vista International/Touchstone Pictures).

Scene 7 (min: 32.40, Street scent break up): A scene where the boards of a street scent break up to meet fuel needs. It is a landscape that reflects social poverty in harsh winter conditions. And it describes the absolute scarcity created by the 1929 crisis even at the point of basic needs.

Scene 8 (min: 36.55, Braddock at Emergency Relief Administration of New Jersey): Scene about the Braddock's application for help from the New Jersey charity and short sentence from the female officer. Braddock doesn't answer at all. A scene where silence reveals the reality of the 1929 crisis and the despair it created.

Scene 9 (min: 38.55, Braddock seeks help): As a last chance, Braddock goes to the club where the boxing organizers and managers are located, due to his difficulties with finding a job. He asks help from those out there. He makes a speech and reveals the difficulty he is in. It is one of the climax scenes of the movie in terms of drama dimension. It is also a scene where two different polar life models take place – wealth and poverty in the 1929 crisis environment.

Scene 10 (min: 1.12.50, Braddock, the rising star): On 16 November 1934, Braddock took to the Madison Square Garden and defeated Lewis and then defeated Lasky on March 22, 1935. With these victories, he now becomes the first candidate for the title match. In the cruel conditions of 1929, he has now reached the final stage of a fairy tale story.

Scene 11 (min: 1.27.15 and min: 1.28.15, B. Johnson, "Boston Globe." and J. Greenblatt from "Chicago Trib"): It is one of the most striking scenes in the movie – press conference for the world heavyweight championship/title match. Questions from two journalists from the Boston Globe and Chicago Trib come to the fore. At the end of the dialogue, Braddock's answer for the question of what are you fighting for is: "milk". Here the milk represents the "life of him and his family".

Scene 12 (min: 1.52.37, Braddock wins the title and becomes the world champion): On June 13, 1935, Braddock makes a title match against Max Baer at the Garden. It is the point of hope for Braddock, who spent his whole life in poverty and lived the conditions of the 1929 crisis with his family at the worst level. He becomes world champion by beating Baer.

7. Conclusions

In this study, the reflections of the 1929 Great Depression on the Cinderella Man (2005) movie are discussed. Selected 12 scenes are listed in Tabs. 1 and 2 with the dialogs in these scenes. Based on the screenshots and dialogs captured from the movie, it can be seen that there are very strong elements in the movie that reflect the 1929 crisis. It is seen that the movie Cinderella Man (2005) has a very important place in the history of cinema as it allows us to witness an important crisis in the history of the economy, within the framework of the life story of a boxer. Extreme poverty and cruel economic conditions in the circumstances of 1929 take the audience to that trial in the atmosphere created by the film and allow us to witness the life of ordinary people in America of that period.

References

Alter, J. (2006). *The Defining Moment: FDR's Hundred Days and the Triumph of Hope*. New York: Simon and Schuster.

Baskind, S. (2004). The "True" Story: LIFE Magazine, Horace Bristol, and John Steinbeck's The Grapes of Wrath. *Steinbeck Studies 15*(2), 39–74.

Bernstein, M. A. (1987). *The Great Depression: Delayed Recovery and Economic Change in America, 1929–1939*. United Kingdom: Cambridge University Press.

Berton, P. (1990). *The Great Depression: 1929–1939*. Canada: Anchor.

Boustan, L. P., Fishback, P. V., & Kantor, S. (2010). The Effect of Internal Migration on Local Labor Markets: American Cities during the Great Depression. *Journal of Labor Economics*, *28*(4), 719–746.

Duignan, B. (2013). *The Great Depression Economics: Taking the Mystery Out of Money*. New York: Britannica Educational Publishing.

Escalonilla, S. A. (2016). The Crisis of the American Dream in New Century Independent Cinema: Indiewood and the Recovery of the Ordinary Citizen (2002–2015). *Communication & Society, 29*(1), 21–34.

Feyel, J., & Fourton, C. (2019). Post-2008 Films: The Financial Crisis in Fictions and Documentaries, *Angles* [Online], (8), connection on 28 July 2020. http://journals.openedition.org/angles/640.

Hanson, S., & White, J. (Eds.). (2011). *The American Dream in the 21st Century*. Philadelphia: Temple University Press.

Hardwick, K. (2012). *They Shoot Horses Don't They?*. The Drama Studio, Wagga Wagga, Charles Sturt University Theatre Ensemble.

IMDB. (2022a). The Grapes of Wrath (1940), https://www.imdb.com/title/tt0032551/.

IMDB. (2022b). Modern Times (1936), https://www.imdb.com/title/tt0027977/.

IMDB. (2022c). They Shoot Horses, Don't They (1969). https://www.imdb.com/title/tt0065088/.

IMDB. (2022d). Cinderella Man (2005). https://www.imdb.com/title/tt0352248/.

Kakutani, M. (2010). Investors Who Foresaw the Meltdown. In *The New York Times*, March 14 2010.

Lebergott, S. (1957). Annual Estimates of Unemployment in the United States, 1900–1954. In Universities-National Bureau Volume Publisher (Eds.), *The Measurement and Behavior of Unemployment Volume* (pp. 211–242). NBER.

Llarena, F. O. (2018). Waitin' on the Ghost of Tom Joad: The Neoliberal Reconstruction of the Depression Years in Cinderella Man. *Miscelánea: A Journal of English and American Studies, 58*, 101–120.

Margo, R. A. (1993). Employment and Unemployment in the 1930s. *Journal of Economic Perspectives, 7*(2), 41–59.

Mellen, J. (2006). *Modern Times.* United Kingdom: London: *British Film Institute.*

New York Times, July 19, 1929. https://www.rarenewspapers.com/view/647403.

Olson, J. S. (2001). *Historical Dictionary of the Great Depression, 1929–1940.* United Kingdom: Greenwood Press.

Pells, R. H., & Romer, C. D. (2020). Great Depression. *Encyclopædia Britannica.* https://www.britannica.com/event/Great-Depression.

Pop, A. M., & Sim, M. A. (2017). Economic Crises Reflected in Films. *The Annals of the University of Oradea, Economic Sciences, XXVI*(1), 679–689.

Roşca, V. (2012). The Political Economy of World Heavyweight Boxingduring the Great Depression. *Theoretical and Applied Economics, XIX 1*(566), 127–142.

Rotella, C. (2005). Reviewed Work: Cinderella Man by Ron Howard, Brian Grazer, Penny Marshall, Cliff Hollingsworth, Akiva Goldsman. *Journal of Sport History 32*(2), 289–291. January 17, 2021, from http://www.jstor.org/sta ble/43610422.

Rothbard, M. N. (1972). *America's Great Depression.* Fifth Edition, Mises Institute.

Runyon, D. (1935). The Cinderella Man – Damon Runyon –. *The New York American* – 6/14/1935, Deadline Artists, America's Greatest Newspaper Columns, November 29, 2012.

Schaap, J. (2005). *Cinderella Man: James J. Braddock, Max Baer, and the Greatest Upset in Boxing History.* New York: Houghton Mifflin Company.

Schlesinger, A. M. (2003). *The Coming of the New Deal: The Age of Roosevelt, 1933–1935.* USA: Houghton Mifflin Harcourt.

Shipton, P., Hollingsworth, C., Goldsman, A., & Cerasini, M. (2006). *Cinderella Man.* England: Pearson Education Limited.

Touchstone Pictures. (2005). Cinderella Man, Production Notes. *Touchstone Pictures,* http://static.thecia.com.au/reviews/c/cinderella-man-production-notes.rtf.

Tucker, J. A. (2018). Three Solid Movies on the 2008 Crisis. *American Institute for Economic Research.* September, 19. https://www.aier.org/article/three-solid-movies-on-the-2008-crisis/.

Wedding, D., & Conner, K. (2006). From Man to Myth: A Review of Cinderella Man. *PsycCRITIQUES, 51*, 13. American Psychological Association.

List of Figures and Graphs

List of Tables

www.ingramcontent.com/pod-product-compliance
Ingram Content Group UK Ltd.
Pitfield, Milton Keynes, MK11 3LW, UK
UKHW020153290926
15471UKWH00005B/847

9 783631 881132